A HISTORY OF CUBA

and its relations with THE UNITED STATES

Hatuey; Cuba's first national hero

A HISTORY OF CUBA

and its relations with THE UNITED STATES

by **PHILIP S. FONER**

Volume I   **1492-1845**

From the Conquest of Cuba to La Escalera

International Publishers · New York

This Printing 2020

Copyright © 1962 by International Publishers Co., Inc.
All rights reserved
Printed in the United States of America

ISBN 10: 0-7178-0860-2   ISBN 13: 978-0-7178-0860-1

PREFACE

Cuba is a long and narrow island, 780 miles in length from east to west, and some 25 to 125 miles in width, with an area about the same as that of Ohio. It is 50 miles west of Haiti, 85 miles north of Jamaica, and about 130 miles from Mexico across the Yucatan channel. Havana, which lies about one-third of the distance from the western end of the island on the north coast, is only 92 nautical miles from Key West.

Cuba can be described as a great plain, rimmed on the eastern end by high mountains, with only a few scattered chains and ridges in the central and western sections. The north coast is steep and rocky, gradually becoming more rugged toward the east. The central part of the island is a country of broad plains and shallow valleys. In the west, a range of small mountains sometimes reach a height of 2,000 feet. The east, on the other hand, is predominantly mountainous, with the sharpest and highest peaks on the southern coast having altitudes of over 8,000 feet. Pico Turquino on the southern coast rises from the sea to an altitude of some 8,400 feet.

Although Cuba is the largest island in the West Indies, with a total area of 44,218 square miles, it is still a small country. Yet its history has a significance out of proportion to its size. The story of Cuba's struggle for liberation from four hundred years of Spanish domination is one of the great epics in history. The story of its struggle for over a half century to change its status from a theoretically independent state, dominated by American imperialism, into a truly independent country is equally inspiring. Unfortunately, while the major outline of this story is available in English, there are no books in print today which present a full-length analysis of the history of Cuba and its relations with the United States.

In 1920, the five-volume work, *A History of Cuba,* by Willis Fletcher Johnson was published in the United States. Although this is a pioneer work for which all who write on the topic must be grateful, it is heavily weighted on the political and military side, and shows little awareness of the economic, social and cultural factors and of the role of the common people, Negro and white, in Cuban history. The history of Cuban-American relations, moreover, is extremely superficial in treatment and makes little use of the sources even then existent on the subject. While critical of certain phases of the United States' relations with Cuba, Johnson, in the main, viewed Cuba's links with her neighbor as completely beneficial to the island. He concluded his work with the prediction that Cuba's future prosperity was linked solely to the growth of "American enterprise in the Island Republic. . . ." Nowhere does he indicate the terrible price that the Cuban people had already had to pay by 1920 for the growth of "American enterprise in the Island Republic. . . ." As Professor Harold Underwood Faulkner pointed out in 1941, after describing the process of Cuba's economic domination by American big business interests: "From all this it is evident that Cuban wealth has fallen under American control and that Cuban political life from 1898 until 1934, and to some extent thereafter, has been largely directed from Washington. The result has been the impoverishment, degradation, and exploitation of the Cuban people. 'Cuba,' said one historian, 'is no more independent than Long Island,' and the history of her subjection presents a gloomy record." (*American Political and Social History,* p. 528.)

Much new information has been brought to light since Johnson's volumes were published. Numerous books and articles in periodicals and unpublished studies have appeared in and outside of Cuba, especially Herminio Portell Vilá's five volume *Historia de Cuba en sus relaciones con los Estados Unidos y España.* These works have filled conspicuous gaps in the history of Cuba and of Cuban-American relations, illuminating aspects of this story heretofore ignored. Despite these advances, the fact remains that since 1920, no American has undertaken to present in detail the history of Cuba and the history of the relations of the United States and Cuba.

For some years I have been engaged in a study of various aspects of the history of Cuba and Cuban-American relations. In my books, *Business and Slavery: The New York Merchants and the Irrepressible Conflict, History of the Labor Movement in the United States, The Life and Writings of Frederick Douglass,* and *Mark Twain: Social Critic,* I presented certain phases of this story. But my decision to write a series of volumes telling the overall story developed after the Cuban Revolution of 1959. Early in 1960, I interrupted work on the third volume of the history of the labor movement in the United States, with which I had been occupied for some years, to write the history of Cuba and Cuban-American relations. It was my belief that in doing this, I could make my best contribution to the true national interests of my country.

On April 21, 1960, Herbert Matthews, a member of the editorial board of the *New York Times,* told the American Society of Newspaper Editors: "In my thirty years on the *New York Times* I have never seen a big story so misunderstood, so badly handled and so misinterpreted as the Cuban Revolution." While much of this was due to deliberate distortion of what was happening in Cuba by the American press, radio and TV, it also stemmed from a total failure to see events in Cuba in the light of history. This theme was stressed again and again to me during several visits to Cuba in 1960 both by Cuban scholars and leaders of the revolutionary movement.

The truth is that it is impossible to understand the Cuban Revolution and the revolutionary regime which came to power on January 1, 1959, without understanding the historical development which long preceded it. The Revolution in Cuba today has its roots deep in the past. As Dr. Fidel Castro put it in a speech in Havana on July 26, 1961: "Revolutionary power is the product of a long series of struggles. It is the culmination of a dream of a people who began to fight in the last century."

"It is yet too early," wrote Russell H. Fitzgibbon in *The Annals of the American Academy of Political and Social Science* (March, 1961, p. 114), "to say with finality just why a revolution of the nature and extent of that in Cuba should have come to that country rather than to any of half a dozen others in Latin America." It may never be possible to say the final word on this subject, but it is certainly not too early for Americans to understand that the need of the hour is to lay aside name-calling and to concentrate instead on a study of the social, economic and political forces in the development of Cuba that made the present revolution inevitable. Does not the fact that Cuba had a one-crop economy, dependent upon and completely subordinated to, the economy of the United States, help to explain the revolution? Or that the political policy of the United States in Cuba for sixty years was to support any government, however tyrannical and reactionary, which gave normal protection to United States interests? Or that Cuba's average yearly per capita income for the period 1950–1957 was around $213, as compared with $829 for Mississippi, the poorest state in the United States? Or that before the Revolution, the Cuban unemployment rate *normally* stood at twenty-five percent? Or that Cuban land ownership was concentrated in so few hands that eight percent of Cuban farms accounted for seventy-one percent of the total arable land?

As a result of the Cuban Revolution, Socialism is being established in one of the smallest countries of the world. Efforts by the United States to destroy it—the unilateral ending of the Cuban sugar-quota system, the severing of diplomatic relations with the Cuban government, the sponsoring of the C.I.A.-organized invasion of Cuba, etc.—have failed. Moreover, as a result of the Cuban experience, millions of the Latin-American common people have been impelled to examine the basis of contemporary society. A growing number of them are beginning to find, as did the Cuban people, that their lives cannot yield them an adequate degree either of physical or mental satisfaction as long as their countries remain dependent upon and completely subordinated to the economy and politics of the United States.

There has appeared in the last three years in the United States an unprecedented volume of literature aiming at an interpretation of the Revolution in Cuba and its meaning for the United States. Regardless of shortcomings, this literature is symptomatic of the fact that the Cuban Revolution cannot be dismissed. It must be understood, and to understand it, the long historical background which preceded it must be known. It is this historical background I have attempted to provide in the present volume and in those to follow.

The *present* volume covers the first three and one-half centuries of Cuban history and the first half-century of Cuban-American relations. The *second* volume will picture the history of Cuba and its relations with the United States from 1845 to 1868: From the era of annexationism to the outbreak of the Ten Years' War for Independence. The *third* volume will cover the period from 1868 to 1895: From the beginning of the Ten Years' War to the outbreak of the Second War for Independence. The *fourth* volume will deal with events from 1895 to 1903: From the outbreak of the Second War for Independence to the birth of the Republic of Cuba. These will be followed by a group of volumes which will trace the history of Cuba and Cuban-American relations from the birth of the Cuban Republic to the Cuban Revolution of today.

As a whole these books will form a record of five hundred years of history, much of which touches American life intimately. In 1890, a writer in the *Overland Monthly* (vol. XV, October, 1890, p. 382) observed: "Our history has seldom been without a Cuban question. . . ." Events since 1890 have reinforced the truth of this statement.

A project like this would not be possible without the assistance of many institutions, scholars, colleagues and friends in Cuba and the United States. It would be difficult to mention all those to whom I am indebted, for the list would be too long. I must, however, acknowledge the generosity of the directors of the Archivo Nacional in Havana, who gave me unstinting co-operation while I was in Cuba in the use of manuscripts, documents, periodicals and books in the library, and sent me important documents and publications for use in the United States. Special thanks are also due to the directors of the National Archives in Washington, D.C., for permission to make extensive use of the records of the United States State Department.

I am happy also to acknowledge my indebtedness for facilities placed at my disposal by the Library of Congress, the New York Public Library, Duke University Library, Columbia University Library, Harvard University Library, University of Chicago Library, University of Colorado Library, Ohio State University Library, University of St. Louis Library, University of California, (Berkeley and Los Angeles) Library, New York University Library, and the Tamiment Institute Library. Mrs. Louise Heinze, librarian of the Tamiment Institute Library, and the staff of the Library, were especially helpful in assisting in obtaining material through interlibrary loans.

The writing of this and other volumes in this series was greatly facilitated by the generous assistance of a number of translators of sources in Spanish. I am particularly indebted to Dr. Guillermo Lorenzen, Dr. Javier de Varona and others of the staff of the Enciclopedia Popular de Cuba for assistance in translating published and unpublished sources in the Archivo Nacional. I have also received assistance in translations from Mrs. Nieves Posada, and my wife, Roslyn Held Foner, and I wish to take this opportunity to thank them for this valuable co-operation.

The translations from the Spanish are, generally speaking, rather free, especially in the case of poetry. But statements crucial to important issues are rendered as literally as possible. However, it is perhaps needless to remark that, despite the greatest care, some errors may have been committed in the course of noting, translating, condensing, copying and editing such a mass of material in a foreign language.

I also wish to thank Dr. Julio Girona for assistance in obtaining important documents, articles and books from libraries, public and private, in Cuba.

Above all, I am indebted to my wife, Roslyn Held Foner, who spent long hours translating sources in Spanish, preparing the manuscript for the printer, designing it for publication, and reading the proofs. Her assistance and encouragement have sustained me since the inception of the project.

PHILIP S. FONER

Croton-on-Hudson, New York
January, 1962

CONTENTS

*To the memory of the brave men and women
who fought for Cuba's freedom and independence
since the early nineteenth century
and to their descendants in Cuba today
who are building a country
in which freedom and independence,
for the first time,
have meaning for the Cuban people*

chapter 1

THE CONQUEST OF CUBA

Cuba became a Spanish colony early in the era of European invasion of the New World. While exploring among the Bahamas during his initial voyage, Columbus learned of a large island, called Cuba by the Indians. Convinced that this was Cipango, the land of gold and pearls, precious stones and spices, which Marco Polo had described in his journals, he sailed on and, on October 28, 1492, disembarked at Cuba, which he christened Juana in honor of the prince Don Juan, son of Isabella of Castille and of her husband, Ferdinand of Aragon.*

"When I reached Juana," Columbus wrote in the *Journal* of his voyage of discovery, "I followed its coast to the westward, and I found it to be so extensive that I thought that it must be the mainland, the province of Catayo [belonging to the Grand Khan]. And since there were neither towns nor villages on the seashore, but only small hamlets, with the people of which I could not have speech, because they all fled immediately, I went forward on the same course, thinking that I should not fail to find great cities."[1]

Still convinced that he was in Cipango, Columbus sent Luis de Torres, a Jew who had been forced, as an alternative to expulsion, to become a Christian,** and had been hired as an interpreter, knowing Arabic and Aramaic, along with Rodrigo de Jerez with two Indians, to search for the Great Khan. After three days, they returned with the information that they had "found an infinity of small hamlets and people without number, but nothing of im-

---

* After Prince Juan died, the island was rechristened Fernandina, but its Indian name, Cuba, gradually was adopted by the Spaniards.
** On March 31, 1492, the Jews of Spain were given four months, until July 31, to convert to Christianity or to get out of the country. Thousands of Jews chose exile, but others, like Luis de Torres, chose baptism.

portance."[2] Nowhere was there to be seen the capital of the Great Khan nor any of the marvels described by Marco Polo. However, among the "nothing of importance" was the discovery of tobacco on the island of Cuba. As Father Bartolomé de las Casas described this historic event in his *History of the Indies*, basing it on Columbus's diary:

> These two Spaniards met many people on the way going back and forth to their villages, men and women, and the men always carried a firebrand in their hand and certain plants to take their smokes, which are some dried, too, in the shape of a *mosquete* or squib made of paper, like those boys make on the day of the Holy Ghost, and they light it at one end and at the other they suck or chew or draw in with their breath that smoke with which their flesh is benumbed and, so to speak, it intoxicates them, and in this way they say they do not feel fatigue.[3]

This was not the first sight Europeans had had of tobacco. That had taken place in the island of San Salvador. But it was the first time that the use of the plant was discovered.[4]

Columbus called Cuba "the fairest island human eyes have yet beheld." He found purslane and wild amaranth and honey and "fruits of a thousand kinds." Its infinite variety of birds, unlike those of Spain, fascinated him, and he was amazed to find "the November air . . . soft and healthy, tempered like the month of May." He assured the monarch who, by such discoveries, hoped to replace the economic losses sustained by the expulsion of the Moors and Jews: "It is certain that where there is such marvellous scenery, there must be much from which profit can be made."[5]

Columbus's descriptions of luxuriant, semi-tropical beauty, green and fragrant woodlands, perfumed air and the singing of the birds in the thickets did not interest the Spanish monarchs. Gold, jewels, and spices were what they thirsted for. But of these Columbus saw none in the possession of the natives of Cuba. This lack caused Spain to lose interest in the island. No attempt was made to colonize it, and further exploration was desultory. Indeed it was not until 1509 that it was determined whether Cuba was an island or not. Sebastián de Ocampo settled the question by circumnavigating it.

In pre-Columbian times Cuba had been inhabited by three groups of aborigines, the Ciboneys, the Guanahacabibes, and the Taínos. The first two groups were nomads, hunters and fishermen. Their culture was that of the paleolithic or stone age, although they also used rough wood, sea shells and fish bones as implements as well as unpolished stone.[6] The culture of the Taínos had advanced to that of the neolithic age, the age of polished stone and carved wood. With the Taínos came agriculture, a sedentary as opposed to a nomadic existence.

The Ciboneys had migrated, under the pressure of more highly organized populations, down the coasts of Florida and across the narrow channel to the pleasant shores of western Cuba. Gradually they expanded eastward until in a sporadic way, they occupied most of the island. Later they pushed further southward in their unimpeded wanderings.

Pushed by the fierce Caribs, who from the Caribbean coasts were spreading over the Antilles, the Taínos had landed in Puerto Rico from whence they moved into Cuba, where they met the Ciboneys. They drove the latter to the hills and jungles, reducing those Ciboneys who remained, to serfs, *naborías*. On the eve of the arrival of the Spaniards, the Taínos had taken over the eastern half of Cuba, leaving only the extreme western end to a free, but fearful, remnant of Ciboneys and a small and unimportant group of Guanahacabibes.

Suddenly out of Europe came the Europeans, and in due time, they were to eliminate, through a process of genocide, all of the Cuban Indians, leaving only a memory of what had been the Indian society of Cuba.

Although the Taínos were further advanced in culture than the Ciboneys, they were still in a state of barbarism, and their culture could not compare with that which the Spaniards met in Mexico or Peru. The Taíno Indians and their predecessors, the Ciboneys, living in what can be called a "shell age," used the shells of large mollusks to make such utensils and tools as jars, awls, chisels, and scrapers, as well as trumpets or horns. Called *Lobo* by the Indians, the shell was important also in their mythology and religious practices.

The Taínos drew their subsistence not only from agriculture, but from hunting and fishing. Cultivation of the soil produced yucca (from which they made bread), maize, beans, peanuts, squashes, peppers, fruits and tobacco. They made canoes, hollowing them out of the boles of great trees, and used them in fishing at which they were expert, even employing nets, artificial fishponds and traps. Their handicrafts included wood carvings, basketry, pottery, cloth woven from the fibers of the *ceiba* or silk-cotton trees, and various stoneware implements. They constructed houses, which they called *bohios*, out of cane or bamboo, inside of which they slept on hammocks. These houses were grouped in villages, around a central square which served as a market place and dancing ground. "The diversion of the song and dance served as commemoration of great happenings and was used to transmit to the young people the traditions worthy to be preserved, the deeds of the ancestors, and the mystic vicissitudes of the race."[7]

They were ruled by *caciques* and *behiques* who exercised jointly the functions of chiefs, priests, doctors, and soothsayers. Polygamy was practiced, and the *caciques* especially had many wives. There was, however, considerable equality of the sexes, and women were anything but mere work horses. Many of the older women were doctors. They believed in supernatural Beings and in rituals to influence these Beings. The *behiques* used tobacco (cigar-smoking) in religion, magic, medicine, and tribal ceremonies.[8]

The Indians of Cuba were mainly a peaceful people. They had warmly welcomed the two Spaniards sent by Columbus into the interior, lodged them in their best houses, and feasted them with such food as they had to offer. "They signified their admiration and reverence of the stranger," notes a contemporary account, "by touching them, kissing their hands and feet, and making signs of wonder."[9]

The European strangers departed, and the aborigines returned to their peaceful ways. Although there was enslavement of the conquered, there is little evidence of the existence in this primitive Cuban society of a division into exploiting rich and exploited poor, of oppressors and oppressed. With the arrival of the Spaniards, this picture changed.

In 1510, following reports that Cuba might be rich in gold, King Ferdinand directed that an expedition be sent to explore and settle the island. "Because we have some suspicion that in the island of

Cuba there is gold, you should attempt to know it for certain," the King instructed Diego Columbus, son of the great discoverer, and governor-general of Hispaniola (the island now divided between Haiti and the Dominican Republic). The following year, Diego Columbus commissioned Diego Velásquez to conquer and settle the island of Cuba. One of many impoverished nobles of Spain who had come to the New World to improve his fortunes, Velásquez had become the richest planter of Hispaniola. With three hundred men, Spanish adventurers in the majority, Velásquez sailed to conquer and colonize Cuba.[10]

Velásquez anticipated little difficulty. "When Columbus visited this island on the second voyage, the Indians were hospitable," he told Captain Francisco de Morales, his second-in-command. "I do not expect that they will receive us with hostility." But Morales was not so confident. "If they have had communication with the Indians of Hispaniola," he replied, "I do not believe that they will receive us with music and flowers."[11]

These were indeed prophetic words. The Indians of Cuba had not only been in communication with the Indians of Hispaniola, but they had been alerted by refugees from that island to stand and fight for their very existence!

"What a troublesome thing it is to go and discover new lands," wrote Bernal Díaz del Castillo, the Spanish Conquistador. But he added swiftly that there was ample reward for the trouble. "The riches we took is hardly possible to exaggerate."[12] In Hispaniola, as elsewhere, the Conquistadores had at first been hospitably received by the Indians. But they had soon discovered to their dismay that their hospitality was rewarded with slavery and death. In *The Age of Gold*, José Martí, the Cuban liberator, vividly described the tragic fate that befell the Indians of Hispaniola:

> As friends they had received them, the white men with the beards; they had regaled them with their honey and their corn, and even King Behechio gave a handsome Spaniard his daughter Higuemota as a wife, she who was like a wild pigeon and a royal palm. They showed them their mountains of gold and their rivers of golden waters, and their adornments all of fine gold and they had put on these adornments on their armor. And these cruel men hung them

with chains; they took away their women and their sons; they put them in the depths of the mines to drag the weight of stone with their forehead, and divided them and marked them with a brand.[18]

Ruthlessly and systematically exploited, unprepared for the back-breaking labor in the mines, the Indians perished in great numbers. As the news of the wholesale slaughter of their people spread through the island, groups of Indians rose up to oust their tormentors. An uprising, led by the Indian Chief Caonabó, was temporarily successful, destroying the garrison which Columbus had left behind when he returned to Spain. But with their primitive weapons, the Indians were no match for the Spaniards, equipped with firearms, and the conquest of the island and the enslavement of its people continued apace.

The Spaniards finally came to the small island of Guahaba, today called Gonave, off the coast of Haiti. The leader of the Guahabas was the Indian chieftain Hatuey, who, despite his comparative youth, functioned more as a patriarch than as a military ruler, and had earned the respect and devotion of his people. Alone among the chiefs of Hispaniola, Hatuey had been alarmed by the news of the coming of the Spaniards, and had refused even to see Columbus when he learned that a rare type of man had landed in the island. When the merciless treatment of the Indians by the Spaniards became known, Hatuey, his fears confirmed, began to make plans to resist an invasion of his village. But before he could do much in this direction, the Spaniards had landed. After a bitter battle, Hatuey, realizing that his forces could not long hold out against the better-armed Conquistadores, ordered a retreat into the mountains.

Concluding that it was impossible to remain in Hispaniola, Hatuey decided to take refuge with the survivors of his people in the island of Cuba where there were as yet no Spaniards. The plan was approved by the remnants of the Guahabas, and preparations were begun for the migration. Canoes were built, and about 400 Indians—men, women, and children—set off, with Hatuey in command, for Cuba. "The irony of it," notes one historian. "While Columbus was searching for new lands, its inhabitants were fleeing, full of terror, from their own soil, in order not to be victims of the atrocities of the Conquistadores."[14]

The arrival of Hatuey and his followers in Cuba, near Maisí, so alarmed the native Indians, who mistook the emigrés for the marauding Caribs, that they fled to the mountains. Gradually Hatuey's emissaries convinced the Cuban Indians that they were peaceful brothers and sisters who had fled the white men to escape slavery and death. The Indians returned to their villages, and Hatuey tried to convince them to prepare for the inevitable invasion of the Spaniards. He invited the chiefs throughout Cuba to a celebration, and, after the singing and dancing, told them what had taken place in Hispaniola. He described how the Indians had greeted the Spaniards with gifts of gold, and how they had been repaid with slavery and death as the Conquistadores sought to extort more and more gold. According to Bartolomé de las Casas, who obtained a report of the speech, Hatuey told the assembled Indians:

> You know the report is spread abroad that the Spaniards are ready to invade this island, and you are not ignorant now of the ill-usage our friends and countrymen have met with at their hands and the cruelties they have committed at Hispaniola. They are now coming hither with a design to inflict the same outrages and persecutions upon us. We know not upon what account they come hither, but we know that they are a very wicked and cruel people. I tell you then that these Europeans worship a very covetous sort of God, so that it is difficult to satisfy him; to perform the worship they render to this idol, they will exact immense treasures of us, and will use their utmost endeavors to reduce us to a miserable state of slavery, or else put us to death.

Then placing before his audience a small basket of gold and jewels, he declared: "Here is the God which the Spaniards worship. For these they fight and kill; for these they persecute us and that is why we have to throw them into the sea, so that when they get here they won't find any stones like these and they will believe there are none." Then Hatuey pleaded with the Cuban Indians to mobilize to save their land and their people:

> Here they are, those whom we believed had come from the skies to liberate us from the Caribs and death. They are more cruel than the Caribs. Abusing our simplicity and prevailing with force, they believe they have the right to our land and to our liberty because a man whom they call Father has given the possession of all the land

to another powerful man whom they call their king and lord. They tell us, these tyrants, that they adore a God of peace and equality, and yet they usurp our land and make us their slaves. They speak to us of immortal soul and of their eternal rewards and punishments, and yet they rob our belongings, seduce our women, violate our daughters. Incapable of matching us in valor, these cowards cover themselves with iron armaments that our weapons cannot break. Doubtful even of their advantage, they use the ray which wounds us from a point our arrows cannot reach. . . . But they are few and we are many. They are fighting in this foreign land, and we on our own soil. They invoke a seditious God of blood and Gold, and we have, on our side, a just and wise God. . . .

Once again, let me remind you that the God that these tyrants adore is the Gold which is hidden in the entrails of our land. This is their Lord. This is what they serve. This is what they are after. Hence it is necessary that we tear out of the deep sleep of the river their God for which the Christians have caused us so much sorrow, for if we allow it to remain in our entrails, we will never be sure that these "Caribs" will not seek it out with our lives. Thus they will not know where it is and they will leave our land in peace.[15]

Hatuey's speech, one of the great documents in the history of man's struggle against oppression, made a deep impression on the Indians from the neighborhood of Maisí, Baracoa, and Bayamo. But many of the chiefs from the central and western part of the island simply could not comprehend the horrors related by Hatuey. Moreover, they were suspicious that Hatuey, a foreigner in Cuba, was using these stories to achieve leadership over all the tribes in the island. Their incredulity and suspicions sealed their own doom.

Although he could only rally his own people and the Indians of the surrounding area, Hatuey prepared to meet the dangers facing them. An around-the-clock vigil was set up on the beaches to watch for the coming of the Spaniards. When the ships of Diego Velásquez's expedition approached the island, the Indian sentries raised the cry: "The white men! The white men!" Immediately, at Hatuey's command, everything made of gold was thrown into the river; the women and children were sent into the mountains, and runners were dispatched to notify the chiefs throughout the island that the invaders had appeared, and to urge them to rally to the defense of the island.

Hatuey ordered his warriors to retire from the beach and take positions behind trees and rocks, with bows and arrows ready to attack the Spaniards. Velásquez followed by the Conquistador, Hernán Cortés, who was to outstrip him in fame, and Captain Francisco de Morales, led the Spaniards up the deserted beach. A reconnaissance group headed by Morales returned with the report that there were no Indians to be found. Velásquez then ordered Morales to lead a group of soldiers into the woods. Barely had the Spaniards reached the first line of trees when they were met by a cloud of arrows. The battle for Cuba had begun!

The Indians managed to wound several Spaniards, but as always in fighting the better-armed Conquistadores, they lost scores in dead and wounded for every Spaniard they managed to down. At the end of the first battle, the Indians were forced to retreat into the mountains, leaving many of their warriors dead on the battlefield.

Following this setback, Hatuey and his Indians received another blow. His emissaries returned to report that the other chiefs of the island refused to send warriors to aid in the defense. Hatuey was thus left with the fugitives from Hispaniola and the Indians of the region of Maisí, Baracoa, and Bayamo. To be sure, they far outnumbered the Spaniards, but the effectiveness of their military equipment was as nothing compared with the firearms and horses of the Spaniards. Hatuey decided, therefore, that it would be sheer suicide to fight the Spaniards in open battle. He instituted instead the tactic of "guerrilla warfare," which was to be followed in every liberation struggle in Cuban history.

Hatuey's strategy was to harry the forces of Velásquez by repeated surprise attacks, followed by speedy dispersals into the mountains. With superior numbers and knowledge of the terrain in which they were fighting, the Indians could terrify the Spaniards, force them to remain always on the alert, and perhaps eventually convince them that it was too dangerous to remain on the island. In any event, the Indians would gain time to persuade the rest of the Cuban chiefs to come to their assistance.

Hatuey's strategy brought some results. The Spaniards had easily conquered Hispaniola, drowning in blood the disorganized resistance of the Indians. But in Cuba they met a different type of foe.

Velásquez was unable to fulfill his mission of a speedy advance across the island, conquering it almost overnight. Instead, for almost three months his forces were locked up in the fort they built at Baracoa, compelled to remain on the defensive. Divided by Hatuey into small bands and instructed never to engage in open battle but to retreat the moment the Spaniards began a counteroffensive, the Indians kept the Conquistadores in a state of constant alarm. Even though they could inflict few casualties on the enemy with their primitive weapons, they made life for the Spaniards miserable, for the Europeans never know when the next attack would come. For the first time since they had arrived in the New World, the Spaniards knew the meaning of fear. Dissension broke out in their ranks, and it was only because he was a forceful commander and a man of indomitable will that Velásquez was able to prevent open mutiny. He kept assuring his followers that he knew the Indian mentality, and that all that was necessary to smash the opposition to the Spanish advance was to capture Hatuey. It would be only a matter of time before they discovered Hatuey's hide-out, and when he was captured, the Indian resistance would be over.

This proved to be an accurate prophecy. Although captured Indians refused, even under the most brutal torture, to lead the Spaniards to Hatuey's hiding place, the great chieftain was finally betrayed by an Indian who had once quarreled with him in Hispaniola and was seeking revenge. Guided by the traitor, the Spaniards surrounded the secret hiding place in the mountains of Oriente, and captured Hatuey. Velásquez promised Hatuey his life if he would tell him where the Indians stored their gold, but the chief refused.

On February 2, 1512, the jubilant Spaniards awoke to a celebration. This was the day Hatuey, their nemesis, was to be burned to death, a demonstration to all the Indians of Cuba of the fate that awaited them if they dared to resist the conquerors. A wooden post was erected and a pyre prepared. Four soldiers brought Hatuey to Velásquez.

"Your hour has arrived," Velásquez said coldly. "For the last time: where is the gold?"

"The gold, the cursed gold," Hatuey answered, "you will not

find in this land because we have made it disappear, and you will never discover where we have hidden it. The curse of the Gods will fall on whoever tells where it is hidden."

"To the stake!" Velásquez shouted. Hatuey was tied to the post. The padre, Juan de Tesín, approached the Indian and said to him: "Die in the grace of God, my son." At the same time, he presented Hatuey with a wooden crucifix, and asked if he would accept Christianity and be baptized before he died.

"Why should I?" Hatuey inquired.

"I want you to die in the grace of God so that you will be able to go to heaven, son, where all the good people go whom God pardons."

"And to heaven the Christians also go?" asked Hatuey.

"Yes, they go to heaven if they are good and die in the grace of God."

Scornfully Hatuey replied in words that impressed even the Spanish chroniclers: "If the Christians go to heaven, I do not want to go to heaven. I do not wish ever again to meet such cruel and wicked people as Christians who kill and make slaves of the Indians."[16]

Thus Hatuey met his death, refusing all consolations of the Church. The flames consumed the body of the first great fighter for liberty in Cuba and one of the truly heroic figures in the colonial history of the Americas.

With Hatuey's death, as Velásquez had predicted, the resistance of the Indians collapsed almost entirely. But it did not completely end the struggle. A fellow-countryman of Hatuey, named Caguax, assumed leadership of the Indians who were determined to continue to fight. But the better-equipped Spaniards pursued the Indians into the mountains, killed and captured them, and suppressed the revolt.

The final note to the tragedy was King Ferdinand's decree that all Indians taken in "Hatuey's rebellion" should be enslaved. They were branded on the forehead, like cattle, to remind the Indians that slavery awaited anyone foolish enough to resist the Spaniards.[17]

From Baracoa, where he had built a wooden fort and which now became the first permanent settlement in Cuba, Velásquez sent 150

men headed by Pánfilo de Narváez, to search the island for gold. Accompanying the expedition was the priest Bartolomé de las Casas, soon to be known as the "Apostle of the Indians." Las Casas had already become acquainted with the brutality of the Spaniards towards the Indians in Hispaniola, but it was during this expedition and other experiences in Cuba that he learned with sorrow the full measure of the unspeakable savagery of the Conquistadores. "No tongue," he wrote, "is capable of describing to the life all the horrid villainies perpetrated by these bloody-minded men. They seem to be declared enemies of mankind."[18]

Las Casas relates how, during Narváez's expedition, the Spaniards, suffering from lack of water and food, were given water, bread and fish by the Indians when they arrived at a large village called Caonao. Twenty-five hundred Indians, according to Las Casas, were peacefully watching the Spaniards finish the meal and admiring their horses when the attack on them began. The Spaniards slashed, disembowelled and slaughtered the Indians until the blood ran like a river. Las Casas tells how Captain Narváez watched the massacre from his horse without lifting a finger to stop it, and then remarked laughingly to the priest, "What does your reverence think of this that our Spaniards have done?" Las Casas replied angrily, "You and them and all I offer to the devil."

At the end of a week when the Spaniards departed, few of the inhabitants were left alive. "Of all which," Las Casas writes in closing his description of the week of terror, "I am a witness, for I was there and I saw it, and I omit many details for brevity's sake." As the Spaniards proceeded westward from Caonao, they found the country deserted. The Indians, having heard of the massacre, had sought safety on the little keys off the coast.

Las Casas was able to convince the Indians to return to their villages, and his description of their trek homeward—"men and women like sheep, each with his little bundle of poverty upon his back"—is deeply moving. But Las Casas lived to regret his advice to the Indians. He was to see them whipped, tortured, castrated, murdered, the women raped, the villages burned, the children left to starve. The land was expropriated, the native labor enslaved, the communal society extirpated, the population terrorized or liquidated, dragged off to labor for the Spaniards, working from dawn to dark in the mines, or standing for twelve hours at a stretch in rivers, washing the sands for gold.

Las Casas reported that in three or four months he had seen more than 7,000 children dead of famine, the parents having been driven off to the mines. Nor did the parents long survive their children, for he describes how the Spaniards "required of them tasks utterly beyond their strength, bending them to the earth with crushing burdens, harnessing them to loads which they could not drag, and with fiendish sport and mockery, hacking off their hands and feet, and mutilating their bodies in ways which will not bear description." But he could not refrain from describing the hideous practice that arose among his fellow countrymen of supplying meat for their bloodhounds by feeding them Indians. "It was a fairly common sight," wrote Las Casas, "to see armies accompanied by processions of slaves chained together to furnish food for the dogs. The more humane of the captains killed them first, but others turned the hungry dogs loose upon the terrified living naked victims." Of a piece with these Spaniards who were described as "much given to the sport of hunting Indians," were those who engaged in contests of beheading Indians just to test the keenness of their blades and their own mastery of the sword.[19]

The Indians, at least, were spared reading the pious declarations of the Spanish kings affirming that the Spaniards were in the New World to promote the welfare of the original inhabitants, and instructing the explorers and colonizers to convince the Indians of the wisdom of becoming Christians by humane and benevolent conduct toward them. When the king, on December 12, 1512, despite information that he must have received of the cruelties to the Indians, thanked Velásquez for his occupation of Cuba, and for his "humane treatment of the natives," he made clear just how much the Indians could rely on the benevolence and Christian spirit of the monarch.[20]

As soon as the Indians were conquered, they were organized into a labor force to work the mines, tend fields and flocks, carry burdens, and provide servants for the Spaniards. Indeed, for the first years after the conquest, the Indian was the prime labor force in the exploitation of Cuba.

Since the Indian worked not of his own volition, but only through force, institutional forms to organize and justify this forced labor developed. Foremost among these were the *encomienda* and *repartimiento*. The *encomienda* was, in theory, an arrangement whereby the Crown ceded to the individual Spaniard the tribute, which could be paid in labor, to which it considered itself entitled from its Indian vassals. The Spaniard, in turn, was obliged to protect and to indoctrinate these Indians in the Christian faith. The *repartimiento*, in its full development, was a means of implanting the *encomienda*. It consisted of farming out gangs of forced labor for particular tasks.[21]

The *encomienda* was thus the right to the labor of a specific number of Indians.* The pretext for exercising this right was that the Spaniard was held responsible for the spiritual life and economic welfare of the Indians temporarily "commended" to him. He was to teach them Christian dogma, instruct them in the new conditions of work, and attend to their necessities. In short, the Indians were to be fed and clothed, their health looked after—"to be civilized on earth and saved in heaven."

From the legal point of view, the Indians were not slaves but *encomendados* who could be taken away from the colonizers.** But in practice the system was slavery; and, indeed, the fact that the Indians might be taken away from the colonizer worsened the nature of this slavery. For the Spaniards were determined to get the utmost labor out of the Indians in their charge while they had them. They used them in farming, for care of cattle; but since their principal aim was to get their hands on gold, they mainly used them in mining it, and washing it out of the beds of rivers and small streams, clearing lands and making trenches. Such was the Spaniard's avidity for the yellow metal that he literally worked the Indians to death for it.[22]

---

* In 1522 the maximum number of *encomendados* allotted to each *encomendero* was set at 300.
** Legally, however, there was also a class of Indian slaves. These were Indians taken in battle against the Spaniards.

In the beginning, the grant of an *encomienda* did not carry with it the title to the lands within its limits, but as the institution developed, a *de facto* ownership emerged. Soon most of the *encomenderos* gained direct title to specific properties within the *encomiendas*, and they even began to sell land to outside parties. Land ownership was also derived from free grants from the Crown, purchase from the Indians, and, in many cases, usurpation of the village lands.[23]

The exclusive and individual notion of property brought by the Spaniard was something quite foreign to the indigenous Indian culture. Some Indian lands were communal in character, their product being assigned to the general needs of the villages, while others yielded their fruits to the particular families that worked them. But under such an arrangement, there had never developed the concept of a title which could be bought and sold, and which gave the holder exclusive right to dispose of the land as he pleased. This the Spaniard introduced. When the Indians who had enjoyed the use of certain lands were killed off and died, the *encomendero* simply assumed ownership of these plots before they could revert to the village common. He evolved ownership through continuous use. The Indians, of course, were helpless to defend their rights.[24]

In these ways, then, the original population and eventually the land of Cuba were divided among the conquerors.

The speedy abandonment of the supposed altruistic purpose of the *encomienda* system produced a demand for its abolition by a few humanitarian Spaniards, led by Father Bartolomé de Las Casas. The "Apostle of the Indians," who was better acquainted with the Cuban Indians and their customs than almost any other Spaniard, in a report to the King of Spain, described the injustices and cruelties which the Indians suffered under the *encomienda* system, and argued that the Indians were eminently rational beings, possessed of souls, and as much entitled to the good life as the whites.[25]

Las Casas was bitterly opposed by the Conquistadores, landgrant holders and clergy who had no scruples over reducing the Indians to a subhuman status so long as it brought them wealth. They charged Las Casas with jeopardizing the interests of Spain, and fostering an unrealistic view of the Indians who, they charged, were barbarians, "naturally lazy and vicious, melancholic, cowardly, and in general a lying, shiftless people." Their marriages were not a sacrament but a sacrilege; they were idolatrous, libidinous, committed sodomy, were given to phallic cults, erotic ceremonies, and aphrodisiacs, in all of which practices they used the devil's weed, tobacco. They were, in short, a soulless species intermediate between men and beasts, and to apply the laws and rules of ordinary Christian decency to a group without souls was to desecrate the meaning of Christian behavior. Essentially, the Indian should be confined to hewing wood and carrying water for his Christian Spanish master.[26]

The rationalization by which they sought to justify Indian enslavement was to misrepresent the culture of the Indians as a type of devil worship. As the noted Cuban historian, Dr. Fernando Ortiz, points out in his study of the Indo-Cuban culture: "The tenacious and heroic resistance of the Indians to their subjection demonstrates the virile quality of their spirit." He notes that the Indians were not opposed to work, but "as are all biological beings, were enemies of 'overwork' or total work or work partially unproductive or where the recompense is nil or disproportionately unequal to the greatness of effort used." To continue a practice of gaining wealth from the unpaid labor of the Indians, "certain commentators defamed them with the most nefarious imprecations."[27]

The din of this controversy even reached the ears of Pope Paul III who promulgated, in 1537, the famous bull *Sublimis Deus* which proclaimed that the natives were indeed human beings whose souls must be won for the church and whose property and lives could not rightfully be commandeered by the Spaniards. Under this pressure, Charles V planned to declare the Indians of Cuba free and abolish the *encomienda* system. He was warned, however, by the Spaniards in Cuba, that if his policy were adopted, the Indians would "rise, kill off all the Christians and return to their vices and idolatry." They therefore petitioned that the existing *encomiendas* be kept "because God would be served thereby and our [royal] revenues increased and the Spaniards benefited . . . and the said Indians would come the sooner into true knowledge of our holy

Catholic faith, being in communication with the said Christians."[28]

Charles V compromised by appointing Bishop Sebastián Ramírez of Hispaniola to study the *encomienda* problem in Cuba, investigate the charges of mistreatment of Indians, and punish any guilty masters. To facilitate his work, Bishop Ramírez was appointed protector of the Indians of Cuba. What trust could be put in his "protection" was shown when he accepted Indians under an *encomienda* for his own service, despite a ruling that prelates and protectors were not to hold Indians in service. When the Crown ordered Bishop Ramírez to give up his *encomienda*, he simply transferred it to a relative.[29]

Bishop Ramírez's case typified the attitude of Catholic church officials during the conquest of Cuba, which was expressed in the sentiment: "The Indians did not pay much for the salvation of their souls with the enslavement of their bodies."[30]

Later an order was issued by the Crown forbidding the use of Indians in mining. The local authorities in Cuba simply neglected to have it announced, and it was never enforced.[31]

Eventually, in 1550, the *encomienda* was officially abolished. But the measure was without force and effect. By then the Indians of Cuba were practically exterminated.[32]

The Indians did not submit to all this without a valiant struggle. Many groups fought against the Spanish exploiters, to the last man, and killed their women and children rather than permit their enslavement. When, as we shall see, the lure of gold in Mexico and silver in Peru drew many Spaniards from Cuba, the surviving Indians rose in arms, imitating the example of Hatuey. From refuges in islets along the coasts and in the mountains, companies of Indians, called *Cimarrones* from the chestnut color of their skins, raided the Spaniards' plantations, burning buildings and killing their conquerors. Such attacks were usually followed by speedy reprisals in which the Indians were killed, captured, enslaved and branded. But a more prolonged struggle, approaching the character of a civil war, was waged under the leadership of a chief named Guamá and his wife, Habaguanex, both born in Cuba. In 1529, Guamá organized a powerful resistance movement, and launched assaults upon the Spaniards from the mountains in eastern Cuba.

The rebellion was widespread, with thousands frequently engaged in open warfare. In December, 1532, the Spaniards finally dispatched so large a force into the mountains that Guamá and his followers were overwhelmed, and those who were not killed were enslaved.[33]

This appears to have been the last organized revolt of the Indians against the Spaniards, although small groups and individuals still maintained resistance "in the secret stockaded camps in the fastness of the mountains."[34] By this time, the number of Indians left alive in Cuba was too few to offer any real opposition to the conquerors.

Thousands had died through sheer cruelty. "The working of the mines," Fernando Ortiz writes, "was brutalized, and without satisfactions for the body or the spirit. It went on during the whole year, except forty days every five months, that the Indians had to 'dedicate to their farming,' and the pay, when it was made, was one peso for the year. Submitting to the mines, to the monotonous labor, unhealthy and hard, without religious rituals, was like tearing the Indian away from the reason for his life. It separated him from agriculture, from the games, in which institutions the Indian had the spiritual nucleus of his religion, his consciousness of time and cosmic solidarity, and of human brotherhood, the soul of his fatherland. No wonder so many perished."[35]

Thousands who were not murdered, starved, or literally worked to death, escaped these fates by committing suicide. Other thousands succumbed to new epidemic diseases loosed on the Indians by the Spaniards and to which they had acquired no natural immunity. In 1557, it was estimated that not more than two thousand Indians were left in all of Cuba.[36] In 1820 a resident in Cuba wrote: "Out of an indigenous population consisting of above 3,000,-000, who were spread over these islands, not one remains."[37]

In a little more than a single generation, the original inhabitants of Cuba, a whole people, had practically disappeared—killed off by overwork, malnutrition, and disease.[38]

chapter 2

ECONOMIC DEVELOPMENT OF CUBA, 1520–1790

The noted historian, statistician and geographer, Don Jacobo de la Pezuela y Lobo, wrote of the early economic development of Cuba: "The small importance of commerce to the island of Cuba during the two and a half centuries that followed its occupation by the Spaniards would not merit our sketching a picture of this long epoch of poverty. . . ."[1] The reasons for this slow economic development are not difficult to pin down. Once the island had been explored and subdued, and the fact ascertained that mining could be pursued profitably, there was an influx of Spanish colonists. Along with the gold-seekers came planters, artisans, and tradesmen, to provide their supplies. They settled in and around the seven cities founded in the course of Velásquez's conquests: Bayamo, Cienfuegos, Trinidad, Sancti Spíritus, Santiago de Cuba, Baracoa, and Havana.[2]

However, the Cuban gold deposits were soon exhausted; by 1535, the majority of the mines were beginning to fail. With the opening up of the immense wealth of Mexico, and especially of Peru, Cuba ceased to have much attraction for the Spaniards. The news so excited the settlers that even those who were firmly established had only one thought: *Dios me lleve al Perú!* (May God take me to Peru!)

From the year 1518 onward, the lure of riches in other Spanish colonies tended steadily to draw population out of Cuba: to Mexico and Central America, to the amazing kingdom of Peru, and to Florida about which little was known but much anticipated. With each new discovery of treasures, a new wave of emigration left Cuba. As López de Góonard noted, "in the Indies everyone wants to ascend in rank or win great wealth." This made it difficult to find men or capital for long-term investment in land or in sugar-producing enterprises. Indeed, by the middle of the sixteenth century, Cuba faced the danger of becoming an empty land.[3]

The Crown, anxious to prevent the utter abandonment of the island, made efforts to stimulate immigration and to assure permanent settlement. The death penalty, with confiscation of estates, was even prescribed for persons leaving the island without permission from the authorities. But these efforts were not successful. Indeed, the knowledge that, once there, they might not be able to leave, kept people from settling in Cuba. By 1602, Cuba's population was only 20,000, of which number 13,000 lived in and around Havana, the port city.[4]

Being a strategically situated port for navigation between Spain and her American colonies, its fine harbor protected from hurricanes and pirates, Havana's development was rapid. This was based, at first, largely on a floating population which entered the city to await the Spanish fleets coming from Cartagena (Colombia), Veracruz, and Santo Domingo to depart for the return trip to Seville. This provided a profitable business for taverns and inns which catered to the troops and crews. It also helped develop the growing of tobacco, for it was there that tobacco was bought to be smoked in Havana and during the voyage, and for future sale in Seville.[5]

Other Cuban economic activities of this period were stock-raising and the cultivation of yucca, to supply dried meat and cassava bread *(casabe)* for the Conquistadores' expeditions to the mainland. Cuba, during most of the first century of Spanish dominion, functioned chiefly as a base of operations for the conquest and settlement of the American continent, a transit station for the rich lands to the west and south, and not as a colony to be developed on its own.

Cuba's economic development was further retarded by the repercussions in America of the constant wars in Europe. The island was subject to repeated attacks by nations at war with Spain: France, England and Holland. Dutch, French, and English buccaneers terrorized the colony. In 1536 Havana was sacked by a Frenchman; the following year, Santiago de Cuba experienced the same fate. In 1554 the French attacked the latter city once more, and secured a booty of eighty thousand dollars. In 1555 another French pirate seized, pillaged, and burned Havana.[6]

These pirate raids made steady growth impossible. It was only after the Treaty of Ryswick in 1697, which outlawed buccaneering, that Cuba could begin to recover from the stagnation caused by these depredations.

Slowly thereafter the picture changed. At the beginning of the eighteenth century a considerable number of settlements were successfully planted in the interior of the island, which engaged in stock-raising and tobacco and sugar-planting. Other crops included indigo, coffee, cotton, and beeswax, the last exported to Mexican churches. However, beef, sugar, and tobacco remained the major products.

By this time the agricultural wealth of Cuba was already overshadowing the precious metals from the other Spanish-American colonies. To be sure, the modest scale of these agricultural activities did not compare with their development in the next century, but the colony was growing rapidly in importance, and it was recognized that Cuba's agricultural production, especially sugar, was a potential source of inestimable wealth.[7]

Among other factors that held back Cuba's economic development were the exactions of the clergy which, from the very beginning, heavily burdened the Cuban economy. All cultivated products fell under the tithe laws by which the tenth part of the value of the crop went into the ecclesiastical coffers. (The sugar-raisers could not even deduct anything from the tithe for the work of grinding the cane and processing the juice into sugar.) This burden was sometime mitigated by bribing the tithe-gatherers or cheating the Church in other ways, and the Church itself, anxious not to retard the economic productivity of the land from which it derived an income, joined the producers in opposing royal edicts restricting production. Nevertheless, when to the King's duties and taxes was added an ecclesiastical tax of ten percent of the gross production, or the heavy bribes when the tithes were evaded, the producers found it difficult to make ends meet.[8]

Then again, the Church put pressure upon landholders to bequeath their lands, upon death, to monastic orders and other ecclesiastical establishments in order to assure themselves eternal life in the hereafter. According to Pezuela, the ecclesiastical foundations in Cuba had accumulated, by the middle of the seventeenth century, a capital amounting to four million dollars. He goes on to add:

"They had drawn off one third of the public wealth. Don Gabriel de Villalobos, Marquis of Barinas, in a long report presented to Charles II, made this statement, which is perfectly exact: 'I hardly need to point out to your Majesty the grave disadvantage and burden from which the residents [of Havana] suffer, because of which, instead of prospering, the city will decline if this state of affairs is not remedied. Within fifty years all property will be in the hands of the clergy, and the laity will have only an insufferable burden to bear.' "[9]

This "insufferable burden" the people of Cuba continued to bear until the nineteenth century, and during this long period, the economic development of the island suffered severely from the greed of the clergy.

Even more crippling to Cuba's economic progress was Spain's obsolete mercantilist system of trade, particularly as exercised in her overseas possessions. To state it in a few words, Spain's commercial policy for her possessions was to make trade virtually a Spanish monopoly. The foreigner was to be barred both as a trader and as a settler. These policies were sanctioned by the Pope as a reward for Spanish exertions in spreading the faith.

Although she was by no means alone in applying the principle that the purpose of colonies was to provide wealth for the mother country, none of the other European colonizing powers enforced it as rigidly as did Spain* This was a reflection of her decline as a great power as a result of reactionary and imperialist policies and the corruption of her court and ruling class. To carry out her ex-

---

* Recent scholars, notably Professor James Hamilton, Professor Irving Leonard, and Salvador de Madariaga, have sought to modify the view that Spain clung to a strict policy of using the colonies solely for her advantage. They insist that there were really no Spanish "colonies" in the New World, but kingdoms with autonomous governments, and that the balance between the interests of the mother country and of the "kingdoms" worked at times one way and at times another. While there is some truth in this re-evaluation, the plain fact is that most of the time the balance worked in favor of the mother country.

pansionist policies, which produced one war after another, ever more crippling taxes were imposed upon the Spanish people. After the defeat of the Spanish Armada by Britain in 1587, "every device . . . of extorting more and more money at home or raising it abroad was invoked [by King Philip] until the people was pauperized. . . ." By 1596 the realm was bankrupt. As a contemporary report observed: "No one has either money or credit, and the country is completely desolated. Any money that is made is hidden away and the owner lives poorly upon it until it is gone. Trade is killed by taxation. In the principal cities most of the houses are closed and deserted."[10]

Under these circumstances, Spain looked to her overseas possessions to supply the means by which she could restore her deteriorating national economy. The Spanish government employed the strictest possible type of trade control, with the object, not of furthering the interests of the colonists but of replenishing the Spanish treasury, depleted by frequent wars. Thus the Crown made it illegal for the colonies to trade with any other country.

This policy was further complicated by restriction of legalized commerce with the home country to the port of Seville, under a monopoly which the government sold to private interests. To do business in the New World was a privilege conferred by the Spanish Crown only upon its subjects, and only to chosen ones among them, under whatever burdensome conditions the Crown might impose. Thus the trade of the Western Hemisphere was mercilessly exploited for the benefit of Seville's merchants. Spanish regulation required that merchandise purchased abroad by her colonies, including foodstuffs, be bought from Peninsular merchants and handled through Spanish ports. Thus profits, commissions, freight charges, and multiple taxes were added to the original cost.[11]

Cuba suffered, from the beginning of its history as a colony, substantially the same autocratic system applied to other Spanish colonies. But for many years it was less affected by Spanish commercial policies than other colonies for the simple reason that it then had little to export. Freedom to trade with other countries was rather an academic question to an island which had, as yet, no sugar and little tobacco, the products that were to become its chief exports. However, the high tariffs imposed upon merchandise entering the colony had always been a hardship, for they made such goods extremely expensive.

As Cuba's economy developed during the first half of the eighteenth century, it began to feel the full weight of colonial exploitation. The tobacco growers felt this most keenly.

Tobacco in Cuba was at first cured solely for domestic consumption. When, by the eighteenth century, smoking had become a firmly established custom in Europe, the export of tobacco from Cuba to Europe acquired importance. Tobacco growers in Cuba, however, had to combat the whole burdensome system of Spanish mercantilism with its many restrictions. Tobacco was heavily taxed, and its planting and sale were frequently restricted to sales to English, French, and Dutch smugglers. In 1614, a ten-year ban against the cultivation of tobacco in Cuba was lifted, but the entire crop had to be shipped to Seville. Disobedience was punishable by death![12]

As the consumption of Cuban tobacco increased, the Spanish government saw in it an excellent source of revenue and the system of monopolies and restriction became even more oppressive. A government monopoly was established by which Spain purchased tobacco cheaply in Cuba to sell at high prices in Europe. On April 17, 1717, a royal edict placed all Cuban tobacco production under government monopoly. A general purchasing agency *(Estanco de Tabaco)* was established in Havana with branch offices in Bayamo, Trinidad, and Santiago de Cuba. Tobacco-growers could only sell their crops to the monopoly which fixed prices according to quality, but did not guarantee to buy the *veguero's* (planter's) entire crop, only the quantity it wanted at the price it had itself established. The *veguero* was forbidden to sell his surplus to private merchants.[13]

The Cuban tobacco-growers were not the only ones to suffer from the monopoly system which favored private corporations at their expense. In 1740, the Royal Company of Commerce was established in Havana, capitalized at 900,000 pesos, of which 500,000 came from a few business men of Cádiz—the only port with which Cuba could then legally trade—and the remainder from a group of business men in Havana. Shares were issued, each valued at five hundred duros (dollars), and 200 shares were turned over immediately to the King and Queen to give them a special stake in the Company.

The Company was given a monopoly not only of the tobacco trade but of all the island's commerce—its entire export and import business!

During the twenty years of its existence, the Royal Company earned enormous profits for the directors and shareholders. Not only were the Cuban producers forced to sell their sugar, hides, tobacco, etc., to the monopoly at low prices, but the consuming population was mulcted by high prices of the necessities of life.* Moreover, the high cost of merchandise reduced the amount of goods imported into the island while the low prices for Cuban products cut exports. The commercial progress of the entire colony was thus seriously retarded.[14] Even the sugar-planters, who were especially favored by Royal concessions, receiving loans, grants of land, moratorium on debts, permission to import slaves, etc., were hurt by monopoly.

The first protest against the system of abusive privileges imposed on Cuba by Spain took the form of smuggling. The King's mandate that Cuba must not trade with any other foreign country was simply ignored. French, English and Dutch ships touched the coasts of Cuba, bringing linen, silks and other manufactured articles which were bartered for tobacco, hides, salted meat and indigo.[15] Smuggling became the principal occupation of the eastern city of Bayamo, even the clergy being involved. In 1602 the Governor of Cuba, Don Pedro de Valdés, notified Madrid that it was not only the laity that was engaged in smuggling but the clergy as well; that the priest of Baracoa ". . . was one of the greatest heretics and enemies to be found in all the Indies, and that all the friars and priests of the island imitated him openly, without any attempt at concealment."[16]

In 1603 the Spanish authorities, seeking to put an end to the activity of the Bayamo smugglers, decreed that the sale of tobacco to foreigners would be punished by death. But the practice was too widespread to be stamped out, and the smuggling not only con-

---

* A barrel of flour cost the Royal Company five or six pesos in Spain. It was sold in Cuba for 35 to 36 pesos.

tinued, but became a regular normal business. "Smuggling," Pezuela points out, "which was almost continuous from the end of the sixteenth century and throughout the seventeenth, laid the basis for even richer fortunes than the establishment of Havana as a center for the fleets; and these fortunes, assured of reproduction and increase by the same methods, were influential in gradually extending the cultivation of tobacco."[17]

The frank disrespect of the decrees of the Spanish government by the Bayamo smugglers, as early as the beginning of the seventeenth century, was evidence of the rising protest against the abusive restrictions imposed by Spain on the island.[18] In 1683 the Governor of Cuba complained to the King of the widespread opposition in Havana to his plan to levy a tax upon the sale of Havana tobacco: ". . . the people who live in the city are by nature so opposed to doing what they are ordered and so enamored of their liberty that everything involves a great deal of trouble."[19]

The first armed insurrections in Cuba against Spanish restrictions occurred three decades later, in opposition to the tobacco monopoly established in 1717.* Five hundred outraged *vegueros*, (tobacco-growers) took up arms against the Spaniards in the "*Sublevación de los Vegueros*" ("Insurrection of the *Vegueros*"), and captured Jesús del Monte Church in the environs of Havana. In the city itself there were demonstrations in sympathy with the *vegueros*, and the Abbess of the nuns of Havana sent a protest to the King, stating that "in all the lands where tobacco is grown" valuable taxes are paid to the convents for their upkeep, and that these would cease or diminish greatly under the proposed monopoly.[20]** So vigorous

* According to some historians, the traders or "speculators" in tobacco were the ones behind this insurrection and they duped the tobacco-growers into fighting for their interests. Undoubtedly, there were "speculators" in the uprising, but essentially it was a revolt of the tobacco-growers against monopoly. (*See* Willis Fletcher Johnson, *The History of Cuba*, New York, 1920, vol. I, p. 338, and Don Jacobo de la Pezuela y Lobo, *Diccionario geográfico, estadístico, histórico de la isla de Cuba*, Madrid, 1863–66, vol. II, pp. 58–59.)

** From the beginning of its cultivation, tobacco in Cuba came under the tithe laws, and the Church collected a tenth part of the value of the crop. Hence the clergy opposed all plans to reduce the value of the crop as would have occurred under the Royal edict of 1717. Bishop Fray Gerónimo Valdés openly aided with the revolting *vegueros* and even threatened the Governor with excommunication if he did not lift the siege of the Jesús del Monte Church. Father Salvador Suárez, a Dominican friar in Havana, so openly supported the rebels that the was the protest movement that the Governor General was forced to resign and return to Spain.

The tobacco monopoly, however, continued, and, in 1720, the *vegueros* again revolted. This time they obtained concessions which lightened some of the burdens. But when Governor Guazo refused to carry through the promised reforms, the *vegueros* revolted once again in 1723. Five hundred men in San Miguel, Guanabacoa, and Jesús del Monte met, pledged themselves not to sell to the monopoly, and to burn the crops of those *vegueros* who did.

The revolting *vegueros* proceeded at once to Santiago de las Vegas where they destroyed the tobacco fields of the cultivators who had sold their crops to the monopoly. The Spanish authorities ordered a detachment of soldiers to the scene, and the uprising was ruthlessly suppressed. Nine of the small farmers were killed; twelve were taken prisoners and executed on the same day, by order of Governor Guazo, without even the semblance of a trial. The twelve corpses were hung from the trees on the road that led from Havana to Jesús del Monte, a warning from the Spanish authorities to the tobacco producers that they had to submit to oppression or risk extermination.[21] The government monopoly of tobacco was not ended until the bloody and successful uprising of the *vegueros* in 1812.[22]

Although there were no further uprisings after 1723, this did not mean that dissatisfaction had ended. It found expression in scores of petitions from the municipal councils in the interior of Cuba to the King, praying that the restrictive policies should cease, and especially calling for the abolition of the Royal Company of Commerce.[23] The King paid no attention to the petitions, but an event of international significance was soon to give weight to the protests from Cuba.

On August 13, 1762, the British captured and occupied Havana.

King warned his superiors "to take special care that none of your subordinates disturb the peace of that Republic, nor upset or interfere with its proper administration and the fulfillment of my royal orders. . . ." In 1721, the King ordered Father Suárez sent into exile "to some remote place where he cannot stir up the spirits of the inhabitants." (María Virtudes Morán, "Church and State in Cuba," unpublished M.A. thesis, Columbia University, May, 1950, pp. 11–12; Fernando Ortiz Fernández, *Cuban Counterpoint: Tobacco and Sugar*, New York, 1947, pp. 217–18.)

The city was returned to Spain the following year in exchange for the Floridas. But the influence of this brief occupation was long-lasting. The British had opened the port to unrestricted commerce, sold merchandise and slaves at reduced prices, and given the Cubans their first taste of legal trade with all countries. During this single year of free trade, thousands of ships called at Havana with cargoes of merchandise from Europe and the British colonies in America, and with slaves from Africa.

This release from the commercial shackles of Spain rescued Cuba from the lethargy into which the monopolistic Spanish regime had plunged it. But it was not only in economic matters that Cuba gained. Significantly, it was during the British occupation that Freemasonry, which was, as we shall see, to play a leading role in the revolutionary impulse of the next decades, entered Cuba. For the first time, too, freedom of worship was tolerated in Cuba, possibly because the English Protestants hoped thereby to convert the Roman Catholics to their religion.[24]

Once the British had departed, the Spanish government found it practically impossible to reestablish the old restrictions. The Royal Company of Commerce failed, following the British occupation, to recover the monopolistic concession it had enjoyed for over twenty years.[25]

The year 1764 marked the beginning of a liberalization of Spanish colonial administration, and especial leniency with regard to Cuba.* The commercial decrees of Charles III, part of the era known as the "Enlightened Bourbon Despotism," consistently stimulated the agricultural and commercial development of the island. That of August, 1764, gave Cuba, among other things, the right to trade with Spain not only from Havana as before, but also from Santiago de Cuba, Trinidad, Batabanó, Nuevitas, Remedios,

---

* Actually, the first relaxation of the stringent commercial regulations occurred in 1748 when Charles II decreed the abolition of the convoy system, under which only two merchant fleets were allowed to sail each year, March and April, for trade with Havana. The fleets, convoyed to American waters by warships, discharged goods at Porto Bello (in Panama) and Veracruz (in Mexico) ; then, after visiting Havana, began the return trip to Spain. Under the new decree, individual ships were permitted to sail throughout the year to Cuba. (Clarence Harvey, *Trade and Navigation Between Spain and the Indies*, Cambridge, Mass., 1918, pp. 102–04.)

and Matanzas. It also broke the commercial monopoly of Cádiz, and opened other Spanish ports to Cuban trade, notably Barcelona. A year later, the Cádiz firm of Aguirre, Aróstegui and Company was licensed to introduce Negro slaves into Cuba, and to import flour, salt, meat, and clothing for them. A decree of May 3, 1774, permitted the free entry into Spain of sugar and other Cuban products. In these years, moreover, the trade between Cuba and the British North American colonies was legalized for the first time. The status of the island was further improved in 1777, when Cuba was given an independent colonial administration under a Captain General.[26]

The Cuban economy quickly reflected the relief from the former stringent regulations. In 1762 there were an estimated 70 sugar plantations, and while all together produced hardly as much as one of the great plantations a century later,[27*] this represented real economic progress. Moreover, the British occupation of 1762 led to a popularization of Havana cigars throughout Europe, and tobacco production increased.[28] In general, the growth of the economy is illustrated by the number of ships engaged in the trade between Cuba and Spain: from six in 1765 it had grown to 200 in 1778.[29]

The American Revolution, 1776–1783, further stimulated the Cuban economy. During this conflict American privateers moved boldly into Caribbean waters. Spain tolerated their presence since she welcomed any attacks upon her enemies, England and Portugal. A Royal order, November 5, 1776, allowed North American rebel vessels, under their own flag, to purchase needed supplies—provided they paid in cash, in bills of exchange, or in Negro slaves. American privateers were quick to take advantage of these concessions in their raids against British commerce, and their trade with Cuba boomed.[30]

The official entrance of Spain into the struggle against Great Britain in 1779, in support of Spain's French ally,** gave indirectly a further boost to this trade. The Spanish colonial supply trade having

---

* In 1763 the annual export of sugar was reported as only 13,000 boxes. (Alexander Von Humboldt, *The Island of Cuba*, New York, 1856, p. 252.)
** For a discussion of Spain's role in the American War for Independence, *see below*, pp. 56–57.)

been crippled by the British Navy, it was necessary for the Spanish government to grant temporary licenses permitting Cubans to import food from the United States.[31] This trade was hampered by many restrictions—high duties, and arbitrary detention of vessels—but it did flourish. The United States sent to Havana its first official agent in Latin America. He was Robert Smith of Baltimore, who was instructed by the Continental Congress to act in Havana as its agent, assist American traders, and, if necessary, intercede for them with the Spanish authorities.[32]*

All hopes in Cuba that Spain's modifications of her monopolistic colonial policy, begun in 1764, would be permanent, were quickly dispelled. As Cubans were to discover again and again, while there were times when the policy of favoring Spanish interests exclusively was relaxed, the concessions were usually temporary, and reforms were only half measures. The pressure for the return to the old policies was continuous. During the liberal interlude in the reign of Charles III, the favored Spanish merchants kept prodding the Crown to restore their monopolies and shut Cuba's doors against foreigners. One of their chief complaints was that foreigners were abusing the privilege of importing provisions by bringing in forbidden manufactured articles as well.[33]

Under this pressure, the Spanish authorities issued a series of decrees in January, 1784, ending the legal trade between Cuba and all countries other than Spain. They also expelled from the island all foreigners, including Oliver Pollock, who had succeeded Smith as American agent.[34] The United States, the country most seriously affected by these decrees, made an intensive effort in 1784 to persuade the Spanish authorities to exempt the new American nation from these restrictions and to enable it to trade with the Spanish possessions in America, especially Cuba, on the principle of reciprocity. The American proposal was summarily rejected. In relaying the proposal to the authorities in Madrid, Don Francisco Rendon, Spanish agent at Philadelphia, voiced strong objections to it. He asserted that Spanish commerce would be adversely affected

* Smith was refused official recognition by the Spanish authorities as was his successor, Oliver Pollock. (Roy F. Nichols, "Trade Relations and the Establishment of United States Consulates in Spanish America, 1779–1809," *Hispanic American Historical Review*, vol. XIII, August, 1939, p. 291.)

since the Spanish merchants could not compete with the American. What he actually meant was that, if these concessions were granted, Cuba would gradually become dependent economically on the United States, and this was a development Spain was determined to prevent.[35]

All the efforts of the United States proved futile. Spain would not open its colonial trade to foreign nations. The traditional monopoly was reimposed in Cuba. The flourishing trade with the United States declined. For almost a decade such trade as existed was clandestine.

The various concessions during the modified mercantilism of the Spanish Bourbons undoubtedly contributed greatly to Cuba's economic development. Yet compared with Haiti, for example, Cuban agricultural and commercial development was actually more potential than real. The Cuban economic scene on the eve of 1790 was that of a varied economy of many small and a few large holdings dedicated to the cultivation, on a modest scale, of sugar, tobacco, coffee, livestock and other products. The Census of 1792 listed 399 large stock ranches, 478 sugar plantations, and 7,814 smaller holdings devoted to tobacco, truck-farming and stock-raising on a minor scale.[36]

But this picture is that of the Cuban economy on the eve of revolutionary and momentous changes. Before turning to study these new developments, let us examine the nature of Cuban society and the conflicts within it during the era prior to 1790.

chapter 3

THE SOCIAL STRUCTURE OF CUBA, 1520-1790

During the several centuries of Cuba's economic development which we have traced—and in no sense did the preceding
discussion attempt to exhaust this subject—there gradually emerged
three groups in the island: white Cubans, Spaniards and Negroes.
At the same time there also emerged the beginnings of a threefold struggle: (1) the struggle between slaves and owners; (2) the
struggle of the white Cubans against Spain's system of feudal absolutism; and (3) the struggle within Cuba between Cubans and
Spaniards.

This, of course, applied to the whole Spanish empire, but it is
most clearly illustrated in Cuba whose history, more than that of
any other country of Hispanic America, was to be dominated by the
threefold struggle.

The Census of 1774 in Cuba showed a population of 172,620,
composed of 96,440 whites, 31,847 free Negroes and mulattoes, and
44,333 Negro and mulatto slaves.[1] The whites included *Peninsulares*, that is, Spaniards born in Spain; and Creoles, born and
reared in Cuba. Though the latter vastly outnumbered the former,
they were, regardless of wealth or culture, relegated to the second
rung of the social ladder. Beneath this top stratum of Cuban society
were the free Negroes and mulattoes, and at the base of the social
structure were the Negro and mulatto slaves whose labor produced
the wealth enjoyed by most of the Spaniards and many of the
Cubans.

"The impossibility of finding Indians . . . to do the work of break-
ing and cultivating the land demanded that this work . . . be delivered to more robust arms." So wrote King Ferdinand VII of
Spain in 1817, explaining the reason for introduction of Negro

slavery into Cuba.[2] That the reason for the "impossibility of finding Indians" was that none had survived the cruelty of the Spanish conquerors was apparently irrelevant. At any rate, the "more robust arms" were Negro slaves. They were brought to Cuba first from Spain itself, at that time full of slaves from Guinea and the Congo, and then directly from Africa—from the coastal regions along the Atlantic, Senegal, Guinea, the Congo delta, and Angola, and as far away as Mozambique on the opposite shore of that continent. There, as prisoners of chieftains of victorious tribes, they were sold to slave merchants—mainly British*—in exchange for trinkets or liquor, transported to Cuba in ships so overcrowded and so unsanitary, that between twenty-five and fifty percent died during the ocean voyage.** The survivors were sold in Cuba, netting a handsome profit for the slave merchants and the Spanish Crown which licensed the inhuman traffic. So profitable did this trade become early in Cuba's history and so large a revenue did it contribute to the Royal treasury, that the Spanish government insisted on its being conducted under a special charter from the Crown which was to receive a royalty on each Negro imported.

The first such royal permit was issued in 1513, but the first large-scale introduction of Negro slaves to Cuba occurred in the year

* Great as the slave traffic was as carried on by the Dutch, French, Spanish or Portuguese, it was nothing compared with the slave trade of Great Britain. "Nearly four times as many African slaves were transported in British bottoms as in all the ships of all other nations combined." (J. S. Redding, *They Came in Chains*, New York, 1950, p. 17.) Karl Marx drew special attention to the place played by the slave trade in the growth of British capitalism. "Liverpool waxed fat on the slave trade. This was its method of primitive accumulation." (*Capital*, London, 1954 edition, vol. I, p. 751.)

** This ratio continued throughout the history of the Cuban slave trade. In 1820 an observer in Cuba wrote: ". . . in the last thirty years more than 200,000 negroes have been brought from Africa to this island, and it is no vague supposition to presume that 50,000 more have perished in the transit. No comment is necessary." (*Letters from the Havana During the Year 1820, Containing an Account of the Present State of the Island of Cuba and Observations on the Slave Trade*, London, 1821, p. 36.) On the estimate that for every slave imported into the western hemisphere about five were killed in Africa or died on the high seas, Dr. W. E. B. DuBois asserts that slavery meant to Africa the frightful loss of some sixty million people! "Whole regions were depopulated, whole tribes disappeared. It was the rape of a continent seldom if ever paralleled in ancient or modern history." (W. E. B. DuBois, *Black Folk: Then and Now*, New York, 1939, p. 142.) Small wonder Karl Marx wrote that capitalism came into the world "dripping from head to foot, from every pore, with blood and dirt." (*Capital*, vol. I, p. 760.)

1524 when permission was granted to import 300 Africans to work the Jagua gold mines. Later, in 1550, "because of the laziness of the Cubans, who resisted all kinds of work," the Crown granted an exclusive privilege to a syndicate of merchants to import African slaves to Cuba.

The hoped-for development of the sugar industry did not materialize until years later, and while the importation of Negro slaves continued, it proceeded at a slow rate until the end of the sixteenth century. Among the slaveholders, the clergy formed a not unimportant group. Just as they had acquired Indian slaves so, from the first importation of Negroes into the island, the priests used them as domestic slaves and in business undertakings as well. The clergy operated several sugar refineries in Cuba as early as 1530, each with its complement of Negro slaves.[3]

Contrary to the view of certain historians,[4] the Negro did not accept his subjection passively. Among the very first Negro slaves, there were rebellious spirits who made common cause with the surviving Indians, particularly the Cimarrones. They joined forces against their common oppressors and fled to the hills to live free. The slave owners employed gunmen to hunt down runaways.[5]

The first recorded Negro slave revolt in Cuba occurred in 1533 at the Jobabo mines. Although only four slaves were involved, the Governor General dispatched a large force from Bayamo to quell the uprising. The four Negroes defended themselves to the death, and their heads were brought back to Bayamo to quiet the alarmed colonizers.[6] The grisly spectacle evidently was not enough to convince the slave owners that they were now safe, for they petitioned the Crown that Negroes be forbidden to carry knives longer than "a palm's length" or to travel in parties.[7]

The slave owners were justified in their alarm. In 1538, Negro slaves, taking advantage of the descent of French pirates on Havana, rose up in revolt and sacked the city.[8] Meanwhile, individual acts of protest continued, such as flight to the hills, and group action such as even the collective suicide of bands of slaves.* A slave up-

* The Mandingas were especially known for group suicide. These desperate slaves believed that they would be resurrected in body and soul in their native African villages. To discourage other slaves from following their example, the master mutilated the dead bodies to show the living that the suicides would be resurrected in Africa without head or limbs. (Ortiz, *op. cit.*, p. 86.)

rising occurred in 1727 at the sugar mill, Quiebra-Hacha, in the west of Havana. Three hundred slaves were involved, and only the dispatch of government troops prevented it from spreading further. In 1731 there was an uprising in the copper mines of Santiago del Prado. The unending series of slave revolts in Cuba was brought to a close only with the abolition of slavery in 1886!

While most of the slave uprisings of the eighteenth century were not as well organized and extensive as those of the following century, their increasing frequency made a deep impression on the Spanish authorities. In the hope of averting new slave uprisings, the Spanish monarch, Charles III, decreed a new slave code on May 31, 1789. A syndic was appointed protector of the slaves. Under the code, masters were to feed and clothe the slave according to prescribed standards, to instruct their slaves in the Catholic religion, to compel them to hear Mass, and to provide a priest for the purpose. Masters who abused their slaves, meted out excessive punishments, or failed to fulfill the requirements of the law were subject to fines, criminal prosecution, and the expropriation of the slave. The slave was then to be sold to another master, or on previous complaint to the syndic, he was to choose another master. Furthermore, there were to be only 270 working days a year.

The requirements upon the slaves were also defined. They were to obey and respect their masters; their work was to be adapted to their age and condition. Slaves younger than seventeen or older than sixty were to be exempted from a full day's work which lasted from dawn to sundown (except in the harvest season, when masters were allowed to work their slaves longer). A slave who failed to fulfill his duties, could be punished by being put in stocks or irons or by being flogged—but not more than 25 lashes.[10] The Spanish saying: *se obedece pero no se cumple* (submitted to but not complied with) aptly characterizes the effect of the new code in Cuba. Despite the effusive praise bestowed upon the code by some historians,[11] one of whom goes so far as to give the Spanish King "a niche in the gallery of human benefactors,"[12] the evidence is overwhelming that the obligations imposed on the masters were not enforced while those on the slaves were rigidly applied.[13] Officials were bribed to ignore the provisions of the code designed to protect the slaves. Some slaves in Havana did benefit, but those in the cane fields and mills not only continued to be wretchedly treated, but their oppression actually grew worse. Instead of being housed in *bohíos* (huts), as uprisings increased and more and more Negroes ran off to the hills, the slaves were housed in barracks that were virtual jails. In these barracks, with their single door and high, barred windows, men, women, and children were shut up when the day's work was done. On some sugar plantations there were watchtowers and block houses both in the cane fields and the mill yards, and private, hired troops, on twenty-hour alert, guarded against slave uprisings. Gunmen, called *ranchadores*, equipped with trained bloodhounds, were hired to hunt down the increasing number of Negroes who ran off to the hills.[14]

The free Negroes emerged originally from the practice under which slaves were rented out as day laborers by their masters. Everything extra they earned, after the day's required labor was over, they could use to buy their freedom.* Legally this system, whereby a slave could purchase his freedom, was first decreed in 1708. It permitted a slave to buy his freedom on the installment plan, providing he made an initial payment of 25 to 50 pesos to his master. He could then pay off the balance in installments, gaining a percentage of his freedom with each payment.[15] Often, the slave was quite old by the time he could make the final payment, and the master was quite willing to use the payment to purchase a young slave who would give him a better return. The slaves who had purchased their freedom were known as *coartados*.[16]

Some slaves became free by escaping to parts of the island where they were not known. More frequently, a group of slaves would flee to the mountains, and sow crops in order to survive; they defended themselves vigorously if they were tracked down. These free Negroes were called Cimarrones, a name originally applied, it will be recalled, to the Indians who had pursued a similar path to freedom from forced labor.

---

* There was also, for a brief period, a group of Negro slaves who were owners of taverns and inns in Havana and who used the money derived from the sale of tobacco and wine to buy their freedom. But the City Council, in an order of May 14, 1557, barred Negro slaves from owning taverns and inns, and specifically from selling tobacco and wine, on penalty of fifty lashes. The ordinance ended this opportunity of purchasing freedom.

The mulattoes were the children begotten by white masters on Negro slave women, frequently by rape. While many of these children remained in slavery, taking the status of their mothers, some were granted freedom by their fathers. They, in turn, produced other free mulattoes.

The situation of the free Negroes and mulattoes in Cuban society, though not as undesirable as that of the slave, was bitter enough. "They are subject to most of the restrictions imposed on the slave," wrote a contemporary observer. They were considered inferior by the white groups, and their freedom was often more nominal than actual. Whenever they found an occupation that promised a fair livelihood, the whites, to reserve such forms of livelihood for themselves, put pressure on the authorities to forbid the Negroes to continue in that pursuit. Thus the Negro was forbidden to sell or cultivate tobacco, except for his own use, nor could he operate an inn or bar.[17] Frequently, government edicts lumped slaves and free Negroes together in meting out punishment for their violation. Thus a Royal decree of September, 1586, regulating the sale of tobacco, stated: ". . . and if the person [who violated the edict] should be a Negro or Negress, free or slave, any of these penalties [imposed upon a white violator of the edict] shall be doubled, and in addition they shall receive two hundred lashes in the public streets."[18] So much incidentally, for the so-called racial tolerance toward the Negro in Cuba as compared with other countries!

In the slave code of 1789, the free Negro was, for the first time, accorded certain rights, but when he sought to exercise them, he often discovered that in practice they did not exist. Moreover, with the increasing demand for slave labor to produce sugar, free Negroes and mulattoes were always in danger of being seized and enslaved. While a handful became landowners, merchants and professionals, the vast majority of the free Negroes were day laborers, and found the road to further advancement closed.

Without political rights, and suffering social and economic ostracism in a slave society, it is not surprising that the free Negroes and mulattoes came to hate slavery as much as the slaves themselves. They understood that every road to improvement in their status was closed as long as slavery existed. Time and again, the free Negro was active in slave insurrections.

There were whites in Cuba, too, who protested against the system of oppression. In the first literary work in the island, *Espejo de Paciencia* (A Mirror of Patience), 1608, the poet Silvestre Balboa pays tribute to the Cuban Negro soldier, Salvador Golomón, who he calls a "Creole," and announces that even his pen could not reveal:

> In what I wrote, how much affection I have
> For a Negro enslaved and captive without cause.[19]

There were other white Cubans who shared this sympathy. Especially was this true of the small middle class whose members were condemned to poverty in a society which relegated to Negroes, slave and free, all manual labor, in the pernicious doctrine that such labor was beneath the dignity of a white man. These white Cubans gradually came to realize that they could not improve their status as long as slavery existed, and they, too, as we shall see, were to join in the struggle against slavery.[20]

But the upper level of Cuban white society, Spanish and Creole alike, was fully determined to maintain slavery unimpaired. On other issues these two groups became more and more antagonistic, but they were united on the maintenance of slavery. Both groups, as in all slave societies, lived in constant dread of insurrection, and believed that only intensified repression could forestall it.[21]

In other respects, the interests of these two groups were in sharp conflict.

The *Peninsulares* (Spanish born) were either in the governmental class or merchants, many acting as middlemen in commercial transactions, for they had the necessary connections with the Spanish businessmen of Seville and Cádiz. As a rule, the *Peninsulares* were classified as merchants or bureaucrats. Governmental offices from the central administration of the island down through the provinces and towns were virtually their monopolies.[22]

Inordinately proud of their Spanish birth, the *Peninsulares* looked down upon other social groups, and regarded the native-born Cubans as their inferiors. Since they monopolized the colonial offices and governmental functions, they convinced themselves and the authorities in Madrid that the Cubans were incapable of governing themselves and indeed, that Cubans in general could not be entrusted with responsibilities of any kind. Spaniards returning from Cuba spread reports of the low culture and inferior intelligence of the Creoles, the natural results, they charged, of a mixed and adulterated race in the Americas.[23]

As the wealth of the island increased in the eighteenth century, the positions in the governing circles became very desirable posts for Spaniards. The higher officials of the government had opportunities of enriching themselves; even a brief stay in Cuba guaranteed that they would come back to Spain with a fortune and social prestige. Naturally, Spaniards influential with the Crown or with merchants in Spain competed for the high posts in Cuba, but joined in putting them beyond the reach of the native-born Cubans.

The chief Spanish official in Cuba was the Captain General. Although he received instructions from the Spanish government as to over-all policy and might be recalled if he incurred royal displeasure, he held wide discretionary powers. While Cuba had several benevolent Captains General before 1790, the majority were despotic, their administrations marked by censorship, espionage, imprisonment, banishment, and execution.

The Captain General headed a host of lesser officials (all Spaniards) and commanded sizeable military and naval forces. He was the head of the sole government of the island, and even after municipal and provincial governments were instituted in the nineteenth century, he continued to dominate the local units. Captains General and their subordinates were changed frequently with a resulting lack of administrative stability.[24]

By the seventeenth century a new group of people had arisen in the island who had lost all contact with Spain and whose future was linked only with Cuba. These were the Creoles (*Criollos*), descendants principally of Spaniards and, to a lesser degree, of the intermarriage of Spaniards and Indian and Negro women. Born in Cuba, inheriting land in the island, they became cattle-raisers and tobacco and sugar planters, and later, lawyers, journalists, educators, and other professionals. The Creole planter ranged from the wealthy sugar *hacienda* owners, who ran their plantations and mills with slave labor, to farmers who raised tobacco with their own labor and with perhaps an occasional Negro slave, to the *guajiro*, living on his tiny farm making a little sugar by squeezing the juice out of the cane with simple wooden presses.

Whatever their pursuits, the Creoles were not disposed to accept indefinitely a secondary role to the Spanish ruling and commercial class. They were ambitious to advance their own interests, but understood that the progress of the island and the advancement of their own interests were interrelated. They realized that it was necessary to obtain important reforms in the Spanish mercantilist system which would eliminate or, at least, reduce the backwardness of the island's economy. They were interested in raising the yield from the soil, developing the island industrially, and expanding trade by commerce with other countries besides Spain.

This inevitably brought them into conflict with Spanish authorities in the mother country and their spokesmen and agents in Cuba, the *Peninsulares*. Clearly, the Spanish mercantilist policy, under which the colony was to serve Spanish rather than Cuban interests, kept Cuba backward. But it was just this from which the *Peninsulares* profited. Maintenance of the old monopolistic practices guaranteed them a comfortable and riskless exploitation of the island. In addition to loaning the Creole planters money at usurious rates to realize their harvests, the Spanish merchants in Cuba served as middlemen in the sale of the planters' products and the purchase of their necessities. Naturally, they opposed direct trade with foreign merchants who were prepared to exchange necessities for the planters' products. Small wonder they had looked askance on the progressive changes in Cuba's trade relations during the "Enlightened Despotism," and had put increasing pressure on the Madrid government to restore the former monopolistic system.[25]

Although the sugar planters, unlike the tobacco growers, received various types of support from the Spanish government throughout this period, they had not gained what they most desired: the opening of the island's ports to free trade and the free introduction of slaves. Furthermore, like the tobacco growers, they suffered from the taxation levied on consumer goods. Materials were taxed at every stage from the raw state to the finished product. Another burden on the economy was the general corruption of the officials. In some instances taxes were threatened solely to extort bribes. While the government in Madrid expected Cubans to identify themselves completely with Spain, the *Peninsulares*, its agents in the island, acted in such an arbitrary and selfish manner as inevitably to antagonize the people born and reared there.

Considering themselves the producers of the wealth upon which the *Peninsulares* existed and which they exported to Spain, the Creoles came to regard them as parasites. Apart from fewer restrictions on commerce and other restraints on the island's economic progress, they wanted a voice in the government of the island commensurate with their social and economic status. It was not until the last ten years of the eighteenth century that Cuban national consciousness showed itself in a clearly recognized pattern. But already the literature of the centuries we have been studying reflects an emerging pride in being a Creole, and a conflict of interests between Cubans and *Peninsulares*.*

One sees this in the poem of 1608, referred to above, *Espejo de Paciencia*, by Silvestre Balboa. It is a colorful portrayal of a society forced into smuggling by Spanish monopolistic practices. In praising Balboa's concern with the needs of Cuba as opposed to those of Spain, another poet, Captain Pedro de la Torre Sifontes, who lived in the neighborhood of Puerto Príncipe, wrote:

> Receive from my hand, good Balboa
> This sonnet native to the land
> As token of my homage.[26]

In 1733 there appeared the first theatrical work by a Cuban author of which there is a record, *El Principe Jardinero y Fingido Cloridano* (The Gardener Prince and the False Cloridano), by the Havana Captain, don Santiago de Pita. Despite its defects, compared with the work of European contemporaries, it was evidence of the emergence of a native culture.[27] In *Key of the New World*,

---

* Regardless of the literary quality of these works, one must, contrary to some authorities, view them as the beginnings of a Cuban literature. For the view that Cuban literature "dates only from the nineteenth century," see Willis Fletcher Johnson, *The History of Cuba*, New York, 1920, vol. II, p. 255.

Havana Described: News of its Foundations, Growth and Condition, written by a native of Havana, José Martín Félix, and published in 1761, pride is expressed in the author's identity as a Creole, and bitterness over the absence from the administrative posts of the government of those born in the island. The repeated use of the term Creole to distinguish the native-born of the island from the Spaniards is evidence of a dawning Cuban national consciousness.[28]

There undoubtedly would have been more concrete literary reflections of the basic discontent of many Cubans, had there been a free press. But only that which was approved by the Captain General could be published.[29] Defiance of the strict Spanish censorship meant a summary trial and a dungeon in Morro Castle. Still, even Spanish restrictions on freedom of expression could not entirely prevent the smuggling into Cuba of what was considered "subversive" literature. Translations of the American Declaration of Independence, the French Declaration of the Rights of Man, and of the writings of Voltaire, Rousseau, and particularly those of Thomas Paine, were circulated in Cuba, and found their way, surreptitiously or legitimately, into the libraries of the better-educated Creoles. [30] Some Cubans corresponded with North American political leaders, and were thus aware that certain grievances of the thirteen colonies against British policies were identical with those against which Cubans were beginning to protest.[31] Did not the complaint of the North American colonists "Taxation without representation," apply to Cuba as well? Moreover, did not the American colonials declare, on July 4, 1776, that their defiant Declaration of Independence was not for themselves alone, but for all the peoples of the world?

When the American colonials, in their Declaration of Independence, pronounced the doctrine of the equality of all men, asserted the right of each nation to determine its own destiny, and proclaimed that governments derived their powers from the consent of the governed, the Cuban Creoles began to think: in what way does Cuba differ from the rest of mankind? Of course, they quickly dismissed the thought that these doctrines applied to Negroes in Cuba as well as white—a conclusion made easier by the knowledge that, while the North American Declaration of Independence advocated liberty and equality, the colonists held 600,000 Negro slaves. Nor were the lessons of the War for Independence lost on the discontented colonials of Cuba. At first the people of Cuba received their information in haphazard and tardy fashion via privateers from the newly-formed United States; but after the Royal order of November 5, 1776, allowing North American vessels to trade with Cuba, and especially after the entrance of Spain into the war, in 1779, and the departure of expeditions from Havana to help the rebels, regular news of the course of the war in the United States reached Cuban ports.

The Spanish colonial administration, correctly apprehensive of the influence of the new republic on their own American possessions, sought in every way, even after it was involved in the war against England, to depict the struggle of the American people for independence as a struggle of a few greedy men for economic and political advantages for themselves. But this propaganda could not hide from the Cuban people that thirteen colonies, not possessed of great wealth and resources, had successfully defied the most powerful nation in the world. At the close of the year 1783, despite the Spanish news censorship, the people of Cuba knew that the new nation to the north had achieved independence. The control of Great Britain over her thirteen American colonies was ended. It was possible for a colonial people to become a free nation.[32]

Six years later came the startling news of the French Revolution. The doctrines of the "Declaration of the Rights of Man and of Citizens" adopted by the National Assembly of France in 1789, proclaiming, like the American Declaration of Independence in 1776, that all men are created equal, that all have equal rights, that the sovereignty of a country must reside in its people, and that the people have the right to revolt when they are oppressed, had a profound influence in Cuba as in all of Latin America.[33]

Some Cubans made their first acquaintance with the "Declaration of the Rights of Man and of Citizens" in Thomas Paine's pamphlet, *Rights of Man*. This brilliant defense of the French Revolution carried the full text of the Declaration, the authorship of which has sometimes been attributed to Paine. It was translated into Spanish and circulated surreptitiously in Cuba.[34] Its presentation of the case for a democratic republic as against monarchical-feudal despotism had a profound influence on the more enlightened Creoles. But of special interest to many Cubans was Paine's reference to the "enslaved Spaniard," and his advocacy of "the independence of South America from Spain, and the opening of those countries, of immense extent and wealth, to the general commerce of the world, as North America now is."[35]

For years the Cubans had been restive under Spanish domination. Occasionally, as in the case of the Bayamese smugglers, the uprising of the *vegueros*, and petitions against the Royal Company of Commerce, the discontent had taken concrete forms of action. But these, important though they were in sowing the seeds of future revolts, had been limited to protests against economic restrictions. By 1790, increasing experience and the stimulus of revolutionary events abroad had added new dimensions to the earlier protest movements; to demands for freedom from economic restraints were added demands for political and human rights—for whites only, to be sure. The next decades saw some of these concepts put into practice.

chapter 4

THE ERA OF THE GREAT AWAKENING, 1790–1808

In the year 1790, four distinguished figures appeared on the Cuban scene: Francisco de Arango y Parreño, economist and statesman; Dr. Tomás Romay, physician and scientist; José Agustín Caballero, Cuba's first notable philosopher; and Manuel de Zequeira, lyric poet—the first truly significant names to stand out in Cuban history. With their appearance began the great Cuban awakening at the close of the eighteenth century and the opening years of the nineteenth. It was characterized by an intense interest in economic, social and political reforms, scientific innovation, the introduction in the island of modern currents of philosophical thought, the expansion of education and the inclusion of scientific subjects in Cuban education such as experimental physics, botany and agricultural studies. And all these were directed towards the development of Cuba, for the benefit of Cuba and not of Spain. It was the interests of Cuba, the future of Cuba, the beauties of Cuba,* the thought of Cuba that preoccupied these men.

Under the influence of Arango and his colleagues, and with the

---

* In Manuel de Zequeira's poetry, the beauties of Cuba are repeatedly extolled. In a poem to the pineapple, he wrote:

> "In the honied nectar of the pineapple
> All the gifts, all the delights
> Which nature in her worship forms
> Are gathered into one.
> . . . .
> Keep your splendor so that you may be
> The grandeur of my country."

Another poet, Manuel Justo de Rubalcava, writing in Santiago de Cuba, praised the fruits of Cuba as exceeding in beauty and succulence the best of Europe. (José Antonio Portuondo, *Bosquejo Histórico de las Letras Cubanas*, La Habana, 1960, pp. 14–15.)

cooperation of Governor Luis de las Casas, appointed Captain General of the island in 1790, a man who was aware that the wind of change was blowing and that the wisest policy was to adjust to it, a number of important organizations were founded in Havana by Royal decree in the early 1790's. They were *La Sociedad Económica de Amigos del País* (The Economic Society of Friends of the Country), *Real* (Royal) *Sociedad Patriótica o Económica*, which later changed its name to *Junta de Fomento* (Society of Progress), and the *Real Consulado de Agricultura, Industria y Comercio* (Royal Consulate of Agriculture, Industry and Commerce). They immediately undertook programs for the advancement of economic and cultural life in the island. These societies were semi-political associations, serving the government in a consultative capacity, and in the case of the *Junta de Fomento*, sometimes even in an administrative capacity.[1]

The *Sociedad Económica*, founded in 1793, devoted its first attention to filling one of the greatest voids in Cuban life—the almost complete lack of public instruction. After three centuries, the island had only a handful of schools open to children of Cubans and these had been founded by private individuals.* In order to promote education, the *Sociedad Económica* encouraged the founding of schools, arranged for their inspection, collected statistics, and established a newspaper. This publication devoted its profits to the educational program.

Later the society was able to obtain a small appropriation from the government for popular instruction, and was authorized to negotiate with the bishop of Havana concerning the best means of raising funds for educational purposes. However, the society soon discovered that neither the government nor the Church was really favorable to such projects, nor would they sanction popular education. The society was thus forced to establish its own free schools: two were set up, one for each sex. In addition, it encouraged the

* The first public school in Cuba was founded in 1788 by Fernando de Ayerbe, a mestizo priest. That this was 277 years after the beginning of colonization is, itself, significant of the narrow viewpoint of Spanish colonial policy. Actually, Spain established a university in Cuba—the University of Havana, founded in 1728 by Royal decree—before she set up a primary public school. But it was a monastic institution, which was not secularized until 1841.

founding of liberal schools by private individuals. To no small extent, then, whatever education was provided for Cuban children was due to the continuous work of the *Sociedad Económica*.[2]

Cuba had its first newspaper in 1790, the *Papel Periódico*, a weekly which, when taken over by the *Sociedad Económica* in 1793, became a semi-weekly and by 1810 a daily, devoting its earnings to the founding of a library. When one considers that in 1774 Spain had opposed the establishment of printing presses in its colonies, and that, until 1790, only the press of the Captain General existed in Cuba[3], this development was of extreme importance. To be sure, continuance of the strict censorship on everything published in the paper limited its effectiveness as the expression of Cuban aspirations.

In addition to publishing the *Papel Periódico*, one of whose five editors was Arango y Parreño, the *Sociedad Económica* encouraged research by its members in Cuban history. This later resulted in the publication by the society of a series of "Memorias."[4] The public library founded by the *Sociedad Económica*—the first and the only public library in Cuba for many years—gave an impetus to studies, literary and scientific, for the advancement of the island.[5]

A strong pillar in the growing intellectual structure of Cuba was the *Real Colegio Seminario de San Carlos y San Ambrosio*. Established in Havana in 1773, it was by 1790 not only an important ecclesiastical center, but its influence extended throughout the entire island. Teachers like Bernardo de O'Gavan and José A. Caballero, who occupied the chairs of philosophy and theology, influenced the thought of their own time and trained a group of Cuban leaders who were to emerge in the next generation.[6]

The great awakening of the early 1790's had barely gotten under way when the attention of Cubans was riveted on events in the half-French, half-Spanish island of Haiti, a few hundred miles off the coast of Cuba. The insurrection of the slaves in August, 1791, in the French portion of the island, was followed by more than a decade of bloody conflict in the entire island. In June, 1793, the white population in the French portion fled with the French fleet, when the insurgent slaves took over the chief city. This was followed by the invasion and occupation of the entire island by the Spanish from the Spanish sector and by the British in Jamaica who were frightened by Negro rule so close to their possessions. Late in 1794, led by the ex-slave, Toussaint L'Ouverture, the Negroes drove out the Spanish. Four years later, weakened by fever, the British forces withdrew. Toussaint L'Ouverture had the entire island under his direction. On July 1, 1801, L'Ouverture promulgated a constitution officially abolishing slavery and, while acknowledging the sovereignty of France, declared the island independent of all foreign interference.

The recovery of the French portion of Haiti and the restoration of white supremacy there held first place in Napoleon's colonial scheme. In 1801, he dispatched an army of French veterans under his brother-in-law, Victor E. Leclerc, to restore French domination. L'Ouverture, tricked into sailing for France to negotiate a settlement, was treacherously seized and imprisoned. Although he died in prison, his spirit remained strong in the rebellious island, and when Napoleon attempted to restore slavery in 1802, a general insurrection broke out. The Negroes inflicted terrible losses upon the European troops, already decimated by yellow fever. On November 29, 1803, the eight thousand survivors of the forty-three thousand men whom Napoleon had sent overseas, surrendered. Two years later, the Negro Republic of Haiti was proclaimed, the first in history.

These events had a profound and lasting influence on Cuba in a number of ways:

1. Before the rebellion of 1791, Haiti had been more valuable to France than all its other colonies combined. It was a leading producer of coffee, cotton, tobacco, indigo, and, above all, sugar. By 1742, the sugar production of the French portion of the island alone exceeded that of all the British West Indies combined,[7] and soon Haiti became the chief source of the world's sugar. The insurrection of the slaves and the bloody wars that followed destroyed the sugar and coffee plantations and brought about a collapse of the Haitian sugar and coffee industry. Cuba, which was already raising these products in appreciable quantities, now started to

supply the world market with the sugar no longer available in Haiti. From this period forward, sugar production in Cuba expanded enormously. The annual production increased from 14,000 tons in 1790 to 34,000 tons in 1805.[8]

2. From 1795 to 1805, white Haitian planters, many with their slaves, swarmed into Cuba. This influx amounted to fully 30,000 by the end of this period. They settled mainly in the eastern districts of the island, and introduced there the culture of the coffee plant, which rapidly grew to an important industry and constituted a significant element of colonial commerce.[9] They and their slaves gave French names to many parts of this section of the island, and the French language and customs became common.

3. The white Haitian immigrants brought to Cuba tales of the horrors of a Negro revolution and intensified the ever-present fear in the minds of white Cubans of a similar occurrence in Cuba.[10] This fear was not a mere conjecture. The developments in Haiti raised a ferment of excitement within the Negro population of Cuba, although one historian incorrectly notes that, during this period, "the Negroes in Cuba seem to have been particularly docile. . . ."[11] Slave uprisings occurred in 1792 and 1793 on sugar plantations in the vicinity of Havana, Puerto Príncipe and Trinidad. They were suppressed, but in 1795, Nicolás Morales, a free Negro, led a conspiracy which started in Bayamo but spread rapidly through the entire eastern section of the island. Apart from its extent, what especially disturbed the slaveowners about this uprising was that whites and Negroes joined together in the revolt and demanded, as in the Haitian Revolution, equality between black and white. They also demanded the abolition of taxes, which bore down most heavily on the poor, and distribution of land to poor whites and Negroes.[12]

The uprising led by the Negro, Nicolás Morales, was suppressed by the Spanish army, led by Captain General las Casas. It was followed, a year later, by an uprising on the sugar plantation Boca Niguia, which was also suppressed. The King was informed that the Negroes engaged in the uprising had been executed. "The punishment imposed on these uprising Negroes," the report assured the Crown, "and the warning examples of these evil-doers will assure repose and tranquillity to to the public."[18]

But the slaveowners were not assured. In fear of rebellion, cruelty toward the slaves was intensified to keep them in terror. Still more stringent measures were adopted to deal with unruly slaves and runaways. It did not matter to the slaveowners that the combination of increased work loads, inadequate food and excessive punishment raised the slave death rate. As the production of sugar in Cuba doubled and then tripled, and the cultivation of coffee and cotton, scarcely known before, also boomed, the Cuban slave-holders, from their rising profits, could afford to replace the slaves who died under the worsening conditions.[14]

In the promotion of a prosperous agricultural economy in Cuba, as production declined in Haiti, a number of men associated with three organizations founded in the early 1790's, and especially the *Sociedad Económica,* took an aggressive part. They were wealthy Creoles, mainly from the *hacendado* (plantation owner) class, along with some professionals, and a small number of Spaniards, who sought to promote the island's prosperity, particularly as a center of sugar production. When the news arrived, in the summer of 1791, of the great slave rebellion in Haiti, these men saw it as Cuba's golden opportunity at Haiti's expense. But they believed that Cubans could not take advantage of this without freedom from arbitrary Spanish dictation.

More than any other man Francisco de Arango y Parreño saw the immediate necessity of Cuba's taking advantage of Haiti's decline. As delegate of the economic interests of the island, Arango sailed to Madrid in 1791 with the object of renewing the concession of 1789, opening the slave trade to the ships of all nations for a period of two years. The news of the rebellion in Haiti, which reached Arango while he was in Madrid, did not seem to him to threaten Cuba where slaves were still relatively few. To be sure, some 20,000 slaves had been admitted during the two years of free trade. But since only one out of 23 inhabitants of Cuba in 1791 were slaves, Arango felt that the island, in contrast to the French portion of Haiti (where, in 1790, the population included 32,000 resident whites, 24,000 freedmen, and 480,000 slaves) could maintain more slaves without danger.* Moreover, the immigration of white refugees from Haiti would still further reduce this danger.[15]

In a memorandum to the Crown, *Discurso sobre la Agricultura y los medios de Fomentarla* (A Discourse on Agriculture and the Means of Improving it), published in 1792, Arango projected the economic future of Cuba, analyzed the defects of the Spanish colonial system, and proposed a number of reforms. In the name of the aspiring economic interests of the island, Arango asked for a larger measure of free commerce, especially in slaves, and the free importation of refining machinery from the United States. He backed his appeal with the prediction that soaring prices of tropical products, due to the Haitian disaster, would make Cuba rich like Mexico or Peru and as important a source of Crown revenue. He also predicted that, under these reforms, Cuba would become a prosperous land of small white landholders who would greatly outnumber the Negro slaves. Hence there was no real danger that the importation of more Negro slaves would cause a repetition of the dreaded events in Haiti.[16]

Arango, who served forty years in the public administration of Cuba, lived to see these last two predictions fall to pieces. Instead of becoming a prosperous land of small white holders who outnumbered Negro slaves, Cuba became a land of great plantations where the fear of a new Haiti was a constant spectre haunting the slaveowners. However, in 1792, the King and his ministers saw in Arango's proposals only an unbounded horizon of unlimited revenue. Sugar would be the basis of this new prosperity, but the increase in sugar production, they knew, demanded an increase in slaves. The cycle of cutting, hauling, grinding, clarification, filtration, evaporation and crystalization required many hands in coordinated labor. Sugar meant cheap mass labor; it meant the hideous

---

* According to the census of 1791–92, the population of Cuba, totalling 172,620, included 96,440 whites, 31,847 free Negroes, and 44,333 slaves. Since the island contained about 44,000 square miles of land, there was but one slave to the square mile. This, Arango felt, was a very low concentration of slaves compared with Haiti, with its 452,000 slaves in an area of 11,000 square miles, or Barbados with its 62,115 slaves in an area of only 166 square miles. (Ramiro Guerra, *Azúcar y Población*, La Habana, 1928, p. 71).

slave trade and slavery. Sugar also meant vast profits for Spanish slave traders, for Spanish industrial towns which built some of the slaving ships and manufactured some of the guns and chains, cottons and trinkets used for the purchase of the black "bundles."

The opportunity offered by Haiti's troubles was thus obvious to Spaniards as well as to Cuban producers. Their pressure inclined the Spanish Crown toward Arango's ideas. But there were still the Peninsular merchants to be reckoned with who opposed every measure that might weaken their monopolistic control of trade with the Spanish colonies. The result was a compromise.

The Royal decree of November 24, 1791 renewed free commerce in slaves for six years, lowered duties on several Cuban imports, and allowed refining machinery to be imported free of duty from the United States, although only in Spanish vessels.[17] But Arango's call for commerce with all countries was rejected. Spain clung to her rigid system of monopoly, and the legal trade with her colonies, when allowed at all, was still at the mercy of decrees which, as we shall see, changed at the whim of the Madrid authorities.

The series of wars precipitated by the French Revolution, however, partially helped to achieve what Arango's arguments alone could not accomplish.[18] In 1793, Spain joined the monarchical allies against Republican France. This step immediately disrupted trade relations between Spain and her colonies. French privateers soon crippled Spanish maritime commerce and the overseas empire had to shift for itself. Especially pressing was the lack of foodstuffs. Even in normal peacetime the Spanish West Indies bought most of their flour outside the empire, and mainly from the United States. Now it was utterly impossible for Spain, in the face of French privateering, to meet the needs of the colonies.

The scarcity of supplies forced the governing authorities in Cuba to modify Spain's monopoly policy without even consulting the home government. On February 23, 1793, Captain General las Casas opened the island's port to American trade in clothing. Despite objections from Peninsular merchants, the Spanish government was forced, by the pressure of war, not only to approve this measure in June, 1793, but, at the same time, to extend the concession to include foodstuffs. This grant did not provide a free system of trade. Rather it established a system by which the Spanish diplomatic and consular agents in the United States were authorized to issue licenses or permits for the shipping of foodstuffs to Cuba.[19]

This concession, as always, was opposed by the Peninsular merchants, and as a result of their pressure, a partial suspension of the decree was ordered in 1794. But Spanish officials in Cuba simply refused to enforce it.[20]

Then, on July 22, 1795, Spain signed the Treaty of Basel with the victorious French Republic. One of the first acts of the Spanish government, after peace and normality were re-established, was to decree the Cuban ports closed to American trade. On June 12, 1796, the Spanish diplomatic agent in the United States issued a proclamation to the American press completely suspending commercial intercourse between the United States and Cuba, and declared the existing permits no longer valid.[21]

The period of legal trade between Cuba and the United States ended; but not for long, for Spain's enjoyment of peace was brief. On August, 1796, in a diplomatic maneuver after the Treaty of Basel, Spain became the ally of France. This meant war with Great Britain, which was declared by Spain on October 6, 1796. If the French privateers had presented a problem to Spain in the Caribbean earlier in the decade, the British navy proved an insurmountable obstacle. Communications between Spain and her overseas empire were cut off. Cuba, dependent upon imports for food and stores, swiftly suffered severe privations.[22] Spain tried to supply Cuba's needs through granting a trade monopoly to a concessionaire, but the lifeline between the mother country and her colony had already been cut and the effort failed.[23] The result was the Royal Decree of November 18, 1797, which opened to neutral trade, on a temporary and emergency basis, the Atlantic and Caribbean ports of the Spanish empire. It permitted neutral ships to enter these ports with foodstuffs, lumber, naval stores, manufactured goods, and slaves, and carry off the products of the colonies—sugar, coffee, tobacco, indigo, cocoa, and rice.

The United States, the leading maritime nation among the neutrals, was the chief beneficiary of the Royal Decree. American traders, geographically located to act swiftly, derived great and immediate advantages from the new system. Cuba was a major center of these commercial contacts since the continuous lack of foodstuffs in the island, due to wartime conditions, encouraged this exchange. Cuba bought flour and other provisions from the United States as well as wine, lumber, iron, shoes, hats, dry goods, and furniture, and, in exchange, sold sugar, molasses, rum, coffee, cocoa, indigo, tobacco and cigars. Spain was forced to permit American ships to carry these Cuban exports to Europe, and European and American cargoes to Cuba. The traffic was heavily taxed by Spain, but nonetheless flourished under the stimulus of wartime shortages and increasing Cuban production. Cuba's trade with the United States reached such proportions that, by 1798, its volume exceeded the island's commerce with Spain![24]

Naturally, Cuba's planters and native merchants, having profited greatly by the freedom of trade, wanted it to continue. A series of petitions was despatched to Spain by Cuban planters praying the mother country to let the trade go on after the end of the wartime emergency.[25] But their influence was ineffectual; the Peninsular merchants were closer to the Madrid ministry, and they were naturally opposed to the new commercial system which had deprived them of their lucrative monopoly. The Peninsular trading interests were also supported by the French government, Spain's ally, then engaged in a bitter undeclared war with the United States. Consequently, on April 18, 1799, a Royal Decree was issued from Madrid revoking the Decree of 1797 and closing the Atlantic ports of the Spanish empire in the Americas to neutral trade.[26]

The new decree reduced but did not end legal trade between the United States and Cuba. The Captain General of the island, faced with rising protests from the population, informed the Spanish government that he could not enforce the order of revocation. Despite objections from Peninsular merchants, the colonial authorities, using their emergency and discretionary powers, continued to admit United States vessels to Cuban ports. They informed the Spanish Ministry that the scarcity of foodstuffs and thus sheer necessity gave them no alternative.[27]

Nevertheless, with the coming of peace in Europe in 1801, the Peninsular merchants had their way and the authorities in Cuba were ordered to close the ports altogether to American vessels.* Thereafter, American ships were not even permitted to enter in ballast to carry away American property; the few captains who did put in were jailed. (Even Josiah Blakely who functioned in Santiago as an unrecognized American consul was imprisoned as a smuggler.) To all complaints, the Captain General merely replied that the "trade had never been opened but only suffered."[28] Between 1801 and 1803, the entries of vessels from Cuba into Philadelphia dropped from 98 to 20![29]

The slump was temporary. With the renewal of war between France and England in 1803, which Spain joined as France's ally a year later, the Spanish colonies were officially reopened to neutral trade.**[30] Since war with England cut off all commerce in Spanish vessels, Cuba was dependent upon American ships to bring supplies and market its produce. In January, 1805, a month after the new decree, ships from the United States were returning in large numbers to handle the commerce of the island. In a single day in October, 1805, as many as sixty American ships lay at anchor in Havana, and continued to arrive in increasing numbers during the next two years. According to Philadelphia Customs House Records, 138 vessels arrived from Cuba in 1807 and 115 were cleared from Cuba.[31]

This upward trend continued until 1808 when Napoleon invaded Spain. Spain then allied herself with England and opened Cuban ports to British merchants who were favored above the Americans. Consequently commerce between Cuba and the United States declined in 1808–09. Another factor in this decline was the

---

* Foreign flour, however, was allowed to enter Cuba to meet the island's desperate need, but the exclusive privilege of importing it from the United States was handed over to the Count de Mopox de Jaruco.

** In typical Spanish fashion, under the concession, the right to issue licenses for neutral trade with colonial ports was farmed out to court favorites and other individuals who, generally acting through subcontractors, sold the licenses to the highest bidder.

Jeffersonian Embargo Act, passed by the United States Congress to avoid American involvement in the war between Great Britain and France. The Act forbade foreign commerce altogether.*

Two conclusions can be drawn from the experience of Cuba during the European wars of the period 1792–1808. One is that the increasing demands for sugar and coffee at a time when Haiti's output had practically ceased, enormously extended production in Cuba. These were indeed prosperous years for the Creole landholders. In 1775, Cuba had produced about 4700 tons of sugar; by 1790 the crop had increased to 14,000 tons. This figure was more than doubled in the next decade, and between 1800 and 1805 the average annual production was 34,000 tons. This steady increase was accompanied by a rise in prices. Sugar which had been selling at 2 to 4 reales in 1790, according to quality, soared to 28 and 30 reales.[32] A powerful class of rich sugar planters emerged as a consequence, living sumptuously on the wealth created by a swelling number of slaves. More and more capital went into sugar production and more and more land was devoted to it.

Cuba could have raised corn and rice sufficient to feed its population, but the landowners preferred to grow the more profitable sugar and coffee. The concentration on these tropical staples necessitated the increasing importation of provisions; in turn, as European wars disrupted communications between Spain and her colonies, this linked Cuba economically more closely to the United States. During these years of on-and-off intercourse, the United States became the source of most of the supplies needed by Cuba

---

* Some historians believe that the embargo had only limited effect in the West Indies because it was generally violated throughout this entire period. However, the problem is not so simple. For one thing, the American prohibition of exports enabled the Spanish authorities in the island to lower duties on imports from other countries and to raise discriminatory rates on ships and cargoes from the United States. Britain, therefore, assumed leadership in trade with Cuba. Moreover, since over one hundred vessels, mostly American, had entered the port of Havana between January 1 and February 7, 1808, Cuba was well stocked with provisions from the United States when Jefferson's embargo went into effect. When news of the embargo reached Cuba, the Captain General forbade ships to leave in ballast, but compelled them to carry away full cargoes of Cuban produce. By the middle of the summer of 1808, it was clear that the embargo was not going to be severely felt in Cuba. (Anderson to Madison, Feb. 7, 1808; Gray to Madison, July 24, Nov. 18, 20, Dec. 15, 1808, Consular Letters, Havana, I, National Archives.)

as the island turned more and more to sugar and coffee production. The importation of foodstuffs and other provisions from the United States into Cuba, although theoretically a temporary necessity, became a permanent factor in the island's economy, which thus became dependent upon the United States.

The second conclusion is that the rising prosperity of the island occurred despite the obstacles placed in the path of its development by the home government. It is true, of course, that the government in Madrid made several important economic concessions to the Cuban sugar and coffee producers, especially the right to import slaves for an unlimited period. It is also true that Spain was forced to open the island to neutral shipping. But it did so as an unpleasant necessity and refused, during this period, to accord the trade a permanent status. The trade was carried on, moreover, under the handicaps of extortionate duties, repeated piracies, and even of occasional temporary imprisonment of those engaged in it. The Spanish government was still so monopolistically minded and so jealous of any weakening of its absolute control over the island that it was even unwilling to permit foreign consuls or commercial agents to reside there.

But in spite of piracy, high duties and official indignities, Cuba's trade with the United States flourished, and worked a great change in the life of the Cubans who profited from it. George C. Morton, a temporary agent of the United States in Havana, wrote in 1801: "The wealth and importance of this colony during the few years it has been open to American trade, has increased in a most astonishing degree, with regards to the habits of industry, knowledge of commerce, general civilization and comforts of life. . . ."[33]

One sign of the wealth of the colony, if not its "general civilization," was the flow of slaves from Africa whose labor enabled the planters to enjoy so many of the "comforts of life." From 1791 to 1805, 91,211 slaves entered the island through Havana alone. Compare this figure with the 33,409 who entered from 1764 to 1790![34]

The new class of powerful Cuban planters, though happy to enjoy the "comforts of life," were not fooled by the fact that the

Spanish government had been forced to permit free trade with neutral countries—mainly the United States—during the war emergency. They took this for what it was, a limited and temporary concession that would be withdrawn at the first opportunity. They saw, over the bright promise of the island's future expansion, the ever-looming shadow of the arbitrary Spanish court and its favorites whose selfish interests would always be put first. Enterprises initiated under a Captain General who understood the need of the island for free trade and dared to disobey orders from Madrid—a situation which had prevailed during the 1790's and the first years of the nineteenth century—could be ruined when these men were replaced by a different type of official. This made it well-nigh impossible to establish any long-range plans for expansion, particularly under the then prevailing methods of sugar production, with its large plantations requiring considerable capital and an abundant supply of cheap labor.

The Creoles were aware, furthermore, that Spain's opposition to free trade with the United States was motivated by political as well as economic considerations. Too close an association with the nearby North American Republic would, in Spain's eyes, only inflame the rising discontent of the Cuban landholders over their lack of any voice in governing themselves—a feeling which was intensified as the wealth and economic position of these men in the island grew. As Professor Roy Nichols points out: "Republican ideas were feared too strongly (by the Spanish government) to grant any permanent privileges."[35] Continued contacts with Americans would feed the flames of republicanism and independence and thus menace continued Spanish sovereignty.

Although the cleavage between Creoles and *Peninsulares,* based on economic and political factors, had grown during the period 1790–1808, it does not necessarily follow that all Cubans who resented Spanish domination were in favor of a change in the *status quo.* While they were influenced by their natural opposition to the oppressive Spanish tyranny, they were even more influenced by the growing importance of the institution of slavery as the keystone of the island's prosperity. As, under plantation conditions, the exploitation of slaves on sugar estates became harsher, the fear of a successful Negro uprising grew.

Moreover, the almost continual stream of slaves from Africa was threatening the numerical superiority of the whites. In 1804, the Council of the Indies, remembering Haiti, cautioned against the unlimited introduction of slaves. But while this advice was ignored by men greedy for more profits from the trade and labor of slaves, the warning to remember Haiti was not. Indeed, one lesson of the Haitian Revolution, emphasized by the white refugees from the French island, was an influential factor in keeping a section of the landowning Creoles from joining in any movement to change the prevailing state of affairs. The Haitian emigrés reiterated that it was dangerous even to discuss greater political freedom for the white population of the island. Their experience in Haiti had demonstrated that the Negroes would demand that freedom be extended to them as well—and, most important, would take concrete action toward that end. They pointed out that the white planters in the French portion of Haiti, long restive under royal control, had seized upon the opportunity provided by the French Revolution to demand freedom—*for whites only*. This immediately led to the demand by the Negro freeman for equality—*for freemen only*. And in August, 1791, the great masses of Negro slaves, hitherto seemingly inert, began to stir and demand freedom from slavery and a position in Haitian society commensurate with their proportion of the population.[36] The final result was the creation of a Negro Republic and the expulsion of the whites.

The Haitian immigrant posed the problem that was to constitute the dilemma of Cuban liberalism for years to come. Many Creoles, whether within or outside the planter group, were so frightened by the possibility of Negro revolts that they hardly dared to predicate political liberties for the whites. Where would the line be drawn? And to be a liberal on the slavery question was to risk being labelled a demagogue threatening the peace and economy of the country. "Remember Haiti," was the invariable reply of conservative Cubans to any change in the *status quo*, and for over sixty years after the Haitian revolution, not a single tract in defense of the *status quo* in Cuba overlooked this slogan.[37] During this half-century, as we shall see, Spain played upon these fears most effectively to ensure continued domination of the colony.

Aside from this Creole element which, out of fear that any change would hasten a repetition of Haiti, was willing to continue under oppressive Spanish domination, most Cubans were united in their desire for greater freedom. The principles of the great awakening, implanted by the liberal Cuban educators and writers who called for changes in the existing situation, were now too deeply rooted. Moreover, the war years had given these Cubans an awareness of their own abilities to forge ahead without Spain when communication between them was cut off, and a self-confidence which was to strengthen their determination to demand more freedom from arbitrary Spanish dictation.

But the Creoles were divided on the methods and the form in which a change should take place. One group favored working for reforms or autonomy; another called for annexation to the United States; a third advocated complete independence. These three ideological currents in Cuba ran side by side through the nineteenth century, in varying strength, but, eventually, the demand for complete independence, a minority in the early stage, became the majority current.[38] Despite the wide differences among these three trends, they had in common the fact that each was a Cuban protest against harsh reaction under Spain and each involved a political struggle. However, while reformism and independence stemmed solely from Cuban soil, annexationism was a hybrid product, given birth to and nurtured by forces in the United States as well as Cuba.

The reformers wanted to obtain from Spain administrative changes that would foster advancement in the economic, political and social spheres; they were not seeking to put an end to Spanish domination. They would be satisfied if Spain would grant the powerful Cuban landholders, who captained the reform movement, the opportunity for economic development and a voice in the governing of the island. The annexationists, on the contrary, did want to end the domination of Spain in Cuba, but not with the object of converting the island into an independent state. Rather their objective was that Cuba should form a part of the United States. Others favored joining Cuba to Colombia or Mexico, but this concept lasted only briefly, whereas the proposal that Cuba should become part of the United States was a more enduring concept. The advocates of independence, of course, represented the most radical current of thought. They wanted to cut the traditional bonds with Spain so that Cuba could set itself up as an independent republic and take its place alongside its sister republics in the Americas. While the reformers and the annexationists were terrified of the Negro slaves and sought, either through continued Spanish control or annexation to the United States, to maintain white domination of the island, the adherents of independence believed in union of black and white Cubans for common revolution against Spain. For years this advanced position brought down upon the independence movement the bitter hostility not only of the pro-Spanish party in Cuba but of the reformers and annexationists as well.

Of the three groups we have described, only one was appreciably in evidence before 1808: the reformists. Composed of the wealthy Creole sugar and coffee planters and headed by Francisco Arango y Parreño, their program was voiced through the three leading organizations of Cuba: the municipality of Havana, the Royal Consulate of Agriculture and Commerce, and, of course, the *Sociedad Económica de Amigos del País*. As wealthy absentee–landlords, the leaders of these organizations could afford to leave Havana to spend time in Spain, where they advanced the program of the reform movement.

This program had three main planks: economic, social and political. In the economic sphere, the reformers appealed to the government in Madrid to give Cuba complete freedom to trade with all countries, and, above all, the right to maintain uninterrupted commerce with the United States. This would guarantee the entrance of great quantities of sugar, and later coffee, into the growing consumer market of the United States.

In the social sphere, the reformers called for continuance of slavery and the slave trade. These two demands were linked together, for the continuance of slavery depended, to no small extent, on the ability of the Cuban planters to obtain new slaves from Africa, to replace those who died under the harsh conditions of plantation life. (Since relatively few female slaves were imported into Cuba, the increase in the slave population through birth was limited.) For the powerful Cuban sugar and coffee producers of the opening decade of the nineteenth century, these slavery planks of the reform platform were just as important as their free trade plank. One must remember, in this connection, that all the production of sugar and coffee in this period was based on the manual labor of slaves.

The principal political plank of the reform movement was the grant to Cuba of assimilation or autonomy or both. The demand for assimilation meant that the island should be treated by Spain not as a colony, but as a Spanish province, which should enjoy identical rights with those possessed by the provinces in the Peninsula. The plea for autonomy meant that the island should have an autonomous assembly, under the supervision of the Spanish Captain General, which would be elected by Cubans and would deal with problems relating to the life of the colony. Through this combined demand for assimilation and autonomy Spain was asked to consider Cuba as a province and not as a colony, with all the rights of the Spanish Provinces plus the right to an autonomous government, a governing body of its own in which Cubans would participate under the supervision of the Spanish governor.[39]

The first point to note about these three fundamental demands of reformism is that they embodied most of the ideas developed during the epoch of the great awakening. Their objective was to facilitate the island's economic expansion and to give the wealthy landowners a voice in planning its future. There was no place in the reform program, as there was none in the ideas of the great awakening, for that part of the population which was soon to become the majority—the Negroes, free and slave. There is not even a hint in the program of the possibility of finding some way to end the evil of slavery. On the contrary, the program envisaged the growth of slavery in the island, and asked for means by which this could be achieved. That this objective did not serve the "true interests" of the poorer Creole masses was beside the point. The wealthy Creole slaveowners took it upon themselves to speak for the island, and the Creole masses were as yet too inarticulate to challenge this claim.

It is important to note, however, that during the period before 1808, the wealthy Creole reformers were not yet paralyzed by fear that the Negroes would take advantage of their demand for self-government. In this respect, they were, during these years, far in advance of their fellow-Creoles who were afraid to do anything to alter the *status quo* lest it bring down the entire social structure. But soon enough, under the impact of revolutionary events in Latin America and in Cuba, this distinction was to disappear.

But this lay in the future. Meanwhile, the three fundamental demands of reformism—freedom of commerce, continuation of slavery and the slave trade, and assimilation and/or autonomy— were being discussed at meetings of the three leading associations in Cuba. It was agreed that they should be presented in Spain by Arango y Parreño in the name of the three organizations as soon as a propitious opportunity presented itself.

This opportunity arose during the tremendous political upheaval that swept Spain in 1808.

chapter 5

THE "EVER-FAITHFUL ISLE," 1808–1820

Despite the remoteness of her overseas possessions, the resentment of their oppressed populations, her unwieldy administrative systems and her antiquated mercantilist economy, and despite the attempts of England, France and Holland to break her hold, Spain managed to control her colonies down to the early years of the nineteenth century. During the previous century, several revolts against Spanish rule had broken out in the colonial world, some by Indian peons and Negro slaves and others by Creoles whose struggles began gradually to merge with those of the Indians and Negroes. Inspired by the American Revolution of 1776, the French Revolution of 1789, and the Haitian Revolution of 1796, these movements increased both in number and scope. However, not one of the several isolated insurrections developed into a full-blown liberation movement. Some of the uprisings, particularly those in Paraguay in 1721–35, in Caracas (Venezuela) in 1749 and 1797, in Quito (Equador) in 1765, in New Granada (Colombia and Panama) in 1781, in Chile in 1776 and 1781, and in Peru during the 1780's, were bloody and fierce. But they remained localized, and all were brutally suppressed by the Spanish armed forces.

It was not until 1806 that the efforts of the Venezuelan Creole leader, Sebastián Francisco de Miranda, launched an independence movement of serious proportions. A native of Caracas, Miranda fought with a detachment of Spanish royal troops against the English during the War for American Independence, and later, as an active participant in the French Revolution, served for a time as a general in the army of the French Republic. Miranda sought English support to achieve the independence of his native

Venezuela, but failed. In the United States, his pleas fell upon sympathetic ears, and in February, 1806, he embarked from New York on an expedition to free his native land.* It failed, and Miranda went to England to prepare a new expedition.

Two years later, the revolution in Hispanic America was finally touched off by dramatic developments in Spain. Napoleon, who was dethroning and enthroning monarchs throughout Europe had decided to set up a puppet in Spain. After his armies invaded and occupied a large part of Spain, the weak Charles IV abdicated in favor of his equally feeble son, Prince Ferdinand, who assumed the crown as Ferdinand VII. But Napoleon forced Charles to retract his abdication, and summoned the father and the son to Bayonne in France to discuss the succession. There, on May 6, 1808, both agreed, under Napoleon's pressure, to renounce their claims to the throne of Spain.

But Spain was not left without a king. Napoleon installed his brother Joseph on the Spanish throne in June, 1808.

The high-handed actions of the French emperor provoked a revolutionary outburst in the Peninsula. The Spanish people in cities and countryside threw themselves into a desperate fight for their independence against the "Intruder King" who had been imposed upon them. Though they had no great love for the corrupt and decadent Bourbon dynasty, the Spanish people would not recognize any other king but Ferdinand VII, and vowed to fight until the last Frenchman had been driven back across the Pyrenees. Local juntas, or committees, to organize resistance sprang up throughout the country, and as a first step swore allegiance to Ferdinand VII. The provincial juntas then set up a central junta to govern, in the name of Ferdinand, that part of Spain not occupied by French troops. This junta was later designated an Advisory of the Regency to function as the provisional government.

These events precipitated the struggle for independence in Hispanic America. On April 9, 1810, a provisional junta, organized

---

* Of the approximately two hundred men who embarked with Miranda from New York, a great number were Americans. (James Biggs, *The History of Don Francisco Miranda's attempt to Effect a Revolution in South America*, 2nd edition, Boston, 1810, pp. 55–57.)

in Caracas, deported the Spanish officials and adopted social and political reforms. The pattern was repeated in Buenos Aires where the Viceroy was deposed by a provisional junta in May, 1810. The following July a similar fate befell the Viceroy of New Granada (Colombia), at Santa Fé de Bogotá, the capital. Shortly thereafter, juntas were set up in Quito (Equador), Mexico City, and Santiago (Chile). Of Spain's mainland colonies only Peru failed to set up a junta that year. Formed ostensibly to conserve the authority of Ferdinand VII, these provisional juntas were a "revolution in disguise," and served to pave the way for independence.[1]

On July 5, 1811 came the declaration of the independent United Provinces of Venezuela. From Buenos Aires and Caracas the two great leaders of emancipation, José San Martín and Simón Bolívar, set out to achieve the expulsion of Spain from the New World. The Republic of Colombia was proclaimed on December 17, 1819. On July 28, 1821, Peru issued a declaration of independence from Spain, but its complete independence was not achieved until 1824. Ecuador was freed from Spanish domination in May 24, 1822. An independent Mexico was proclaimed in May, 1822, and a declaration was issued on September 15, 1821 at Guatemala City which established the United Provinces of Central America: Nicaragua, Honduras, Costa Rica, Guatemala, and El Salvador, a confedertion which subsequently split up into separate states.

It was not until 1824 that the complete overthrow of Spanish rule on the American mainland, north, central, or south, was achieved, never thereafter to be re-established. With the battle of Ayacucho in Peru, on December 9, 1824, the Spanish forces were decisively defeated by the patriots under Simón Bolívar.* Out of

* It was only fitting that Bolívar should have delivered the final blow to Spanish rule on the continent. His career was marked with reverses as well as victories, but he remained steadfast throughout in his resolve to free South America. Simón Bolívar, a Venezuelan Creole, was born at Caracas. Inherited wealth enabled him to travel and to get his education abroad. While in Europe, Bolívar spent considerable time in Paris and there absorbed the ideas of liberty and equality of the French Revolution. He was greatly influenced by the works of Montesquieu, Voltaire, and especially Rousseau in whose teachings he became an ardent believer. In 1807 he returned to his native Venezuela to live the life of a colonial landholder. In 1810, Bolívar associated himself with the independence movement, and devoted the rest of the next years—years of struggles, victories, reversals, exile in Jamaica and Haiti, and final triumph—to this cause.

the debacle, Spain saved only two islands in the West Indies: Cuba and Puerto Rico.

The news of the abdication of Charles IV, the enthronement of Joseph Bonaparte as King of Spain, the revolt of the Spanish people against the French, the organization of the provincial juntas and of the central Junta, was received in Cuba on July 14, 1808. The Marqués de Someruelos, Captain General of the island, immediately proclaimed his loyalty to Ferdinand VII, and announced that Cuba was in a state of war with France. The people of Cuba, aroused by the events in Spain, gave enthusiastic support to the declaration. A loan to provide necessities of war for Spain was quickly oversubscribed.[2] "The divisions and distinctions between the Cubans and the Spaniards, which had become more or less clear . . . were lost sight of at this time as the colonists strove by every means to aid their struggling countrymen in the Peninsula."[3]

Shortly thereafter, a *Junta Superior* was set up in Cuba. This brought Cuba into the junta movement springing up throughout the Spanish colonies to govern in the revolutionary situation. But whereas in nearly all the other Spanish colonies, this proved the first step toward independence, it was not to be the case in Cuba. In May, 1810, the *Junta Superior* received an invitation from the Caracas *Junta* inviting the Cubans to follow their revolutionary path and join in the revolt against Spain. Although this proposal was endorsed by a mass meeting in Havana, the *Junta Superior* rejected the invitation, and reaffirmed its loyalty to the exiled Spanish King, Ferdinand VII, and the Regency.[4] Although, as we shall see, there were frequent outbreaks and conspiracies in different parts of the island, demonstrating that there were Cubans who dared to link their country with the revolt in the continental Spanish colonies, the island remained faithful to the mother country during this revolutionary epoch. Thus the legend of the loyalty of Cuba arose—*la siempre leal isla de Cuba* (the ever-faithful isle of Cuba), as it came to be called in Spain.

The question naturally arises: why did not Cuba join the revolt of the Spanish colonies on the mainland? There is no single answer to this question. Let us examine the various reasons.

1. Circumstances were less advantageous for a successful revolu-

tion in Cuba than on the continent. Spanish authority was stronger in Cuba than in any other Spanish American colonies. Serving from the beginning as supply base and way station for her other New World colonies, Cuba had become Spain's major military stronghold there and was more securely garrisoned than the other colonies. Being an island, Cuba could easily be cut off by the Spanish navy from any support from the mainland.[5] And the United States, as we shall see, made it clear, as early as 1809, that while it was eager to annex the island, it feared the establishment of an independent Cuba which might be taken over by a European power. It preferred seeing Cuba in the hands of the weak Spanish kingdom to the risk of its transfer to a first-rate European naval power like Great Britain or France.

2. The Spanish authorities prosecuted anyone suspected of sympathy with the rebellious colonists on the mainland. Rigorous censorship forbade publication of journals other than official gazettes; foreign books were seized, and Cuban society was honeycombed with informers. The Masonic Order in Cuba was especially suspected on the grounds that its principles might instill in Cubans the ideals of the American, French, and South American revolutions.[6] On mere suspicion, men were jailed without even the semblance of a trial, and suffered imprisonment or perpetual banishment as revolutionary conspirators. A report by a commission of the *Junta Provincial* on the prisons of Havana, May 22, 1820, stated: "In the *Cabaña* they were horror-struck at finding dark dungeons, damp and unhealthy, which have been hitherto employed in afflicting humanity. They found prisoners who have been detained there for many years in rigorous confinement without condemnation solely on account of official intimation of their being suspected of want of fealty to the government of New Spain."[7]

3. Emigrés, to the number of 20,000, from the revolutions on the mainland settled in Cuba between 1810–26. These, together with the refugees from Haiti and the Spaniards from New Orleans who left after the purchase of Louisiana by the United States, considerably strengthened the fanatically pro-Spanish party, interested in conserving the old order. Indeed, in no other Spanish colony during the revolutionary era were there so many opponents

of revolution, men who gloried in being "unconditionally Spanish,"[8] who had fought against the independence movements before they arrived in the island and who spread accounts of confiscations and pillage of property by the revolutionaries.

4. In Latin America, generally, the majority of the revolutions against Spanish domination came into being supported by a large part of the lower clergy. This was true especially in Brazil, whose revolution of 1817 has been called a "revolution of the priests."[9] In Argentina, sixteen of the twenty-nine members forming the Congress of Tucumán in 1816, which proclaimed the independence of the country, were priests. In Mexico, where such names as Hidalgo and Morelos fill the pages of its revolutionary history, the priests were leaders in the independence movements.[10] In Cuba, on the other hand, the majority of the clergy were *Peninsulares* who sympathized overwhelmingly with the Spanish government. "It may be said that the Spanish priests as a general proposition, some with arms and others with words, all fought the Revolution," observes a Cuban historian of the Church in the island.[11]

Yet these four factors were only contributory causes of Cuba's failure to join the independence movement on the continent. Most important was the fact that the vast majority of the Creole land-owners, whose economic interests were so dependent on slavery, hesitated to support a movement that might lead to emancipation of the slaves. They were frightened of the consequences that separation and independence might bring in their wake. The Spanish Minister Calatrava hit the mark when he said: "The fear which the Cubans have of the Negroes is the most secure means which Spain has to guarantee her domination over this island."[12]

Since 1790, as we have seen, a strong movement for reform had arisen in Cuba. All the work of Arango y Parreño and of the leading societies had aimed at autonomy rather than independence, and the Creole landholders, for whom Arango and the societies spoke, thought only in terms of reform. Whereas the Creole land-owners in the other Spanish colonies saw an opportunity, in Spain's internal and external difficulties, of ridding themselves of Spanish domination, their Cuban counterparts saw a chance to realize their three basic demands: freedom of commerce, maintenance of slavery and the slave trade, and greater political rights.

Moreover, the Spanish authorities in Cuba, unlike those in the mainland colonies, were clever enough to exploit these aspirations of the Creole landowners while emphasizing that separatist aspirations, due to Cuba's insular location, were vain, and that those foolish enough to conspire to achieve them would incur certain death, imprisonment or exile. The Marqués de Someruelos, Captain General of Cuba, was well aware that the insurgent spirit of the continent was reaching the island, and he shrewdly combined a punitive policy towards anyone suspected of independence leanings, with a liberal one for the Creole landowners who sought only economic, social and political reforms. He assured them that the loyalty of Cuba would be rewarded in Madrid, and that when the French were driven out, special concessions would be made to the island.

The Creole landowners soon had the opportunity to test the validity of Someruelos's argument. The government of Spain in 1810 consisted of a Regency Council representing the executive power of the crown, and a single legislative body called the Cortes. The Cuban reformers failed to persuade the Regency Council to decree freedom of trade for Cuba, but Someruelos assured them that this would be granted. On receiving orders from Spain to limit Cuban trade to the Peninsula, Someruelos, anxious to retain the support of the powerful Cuban sugar and coffee planters, refused to obey the decree. He permitted free trade, especially between Cuba and the United States.[13]

The hopes of the reformers were buoyed when they learned that the Regency Council had given the Spanish colonies the right to send deputies to the Cortes, which was to meet in Cádiz. Through the two delegates representing Cuba, Bernardo de O'Gavan and don Andrés de Jáuregui, the Creole reformers had a new opportunity to press for the demands they had sought vainly from the Regency Council.

On December 16, 1810, soon after the opening of the Cortes, the Spanish American and Philippine delegates, with Cuba's delegates playing a leading role, issued a statement calling for reforms in the colonial regime. Among these petitions, number III specified: "The [Spanish] Americas will enjoy the widest liberty for exporting their natural and industrial produce to the Peninsula and allied and neutral nations, and there shall be permitted the importation of any article or produce they may need, either in national or foreign vessels. Therefore the ports of the Americas are hereby declared opened."[14] But, as in the past, the merchants in Spain and their agents in the colonies vigorously opposed the proposal, and it was shelved by the Cortes. Indeed, the reform demands were entirely ignored.

The news from Spain disturbed Someruelos. His assurance that a loyal Cuba would win for the reformers all they had been seeking since 1790 appeared to be only wishful thinking.[15] Then on March 26, 1811, during the debate in the Cortes on the proposed constitutions for the Spanish monarchy, a Mexican deputy, Miguel Gurich y Alcocer, had the honor of presenting the first formal abolitionist project in Spain's history. His eight propositions provided for the immediate abolition of the slave trade, agreed to already by Great Britain, the United States and other countries since 1807, the freedom of all children born to slave mothers, wages for slaves, the right of the slave to purchase his freedom, and better treatment for those remaining in slavery.[16] On April 2, 1811, the noted liberal Spanish politician, Don Agustín Argüelles, presented another proposal asking for the immediate abolition of the slave trade. He proposed, further, that Great Britain should be immediately informed so that the two powers, England and Spain, could work in harmony to abolish the hideous traffic in human flesh.[17]

Jáuregui, the deputy from Cuba, was able to persuade the conservative forces in the Cortes to postpone discussion of the two proposals. Then he persuaded them, using the argument of the dangerous effects public discussion would produce in the colonies with large slave holdings, to agree to argue the proposals in secret session. But later the Cortes backtracked and slated a public debate on the motions.[18]

The news of the two proposals and the agreement to hold public discussions concerning them in the Cortes caused great alarm in Cuba. The Creole slaveowners were aware that England, upon whom Spain was dependent in ousting Napoleon's forces, was applying pressure on the Cortes to adopt the proposal to abolish the slave trade, and they feared that even the conservative deputies would not be able to resist this influence. William Shaler, United States consul in Havana, informed the State Department that the news from the Cortes had "excited the highest degree of interest and anxiety" among the Creole planters, that they were furious because they had been promised special considerations on account of their loyalty to Spain, and that they were convinced that the abolition motions threatened the entire economy of the island.[19]

The Marqués de Someruelos knew that everything now was at stake. In a communication, read to the Cortes in secret session on July 7, 1811, he emphasized that the proposals were arousing widespread alarm in Cuba, and that there was great fear that the catastrophe of Haiti would be repeated. He implored the government to treat the matter with great caution *"in order not to lose this important island."*[20]

The municipality of Havana, the Patriotic Society, the Royal Consulate of Agriculture and Commerce, and the *Sociedad Económica* sent similar remonstrances to the Cortes, each underscoring the importance of doing nothing to destroy the economy of the island and disturb its loyalty to the mother country. In one memorandum, presented by the municipality of Havana jointly with the Royal Consulate and the *Sociedad Económica*, protesting against a public debate on the abolition question, the Cuban slaveholders were absolved of blame for the existence of slavery in the island. "The Negroes have come and are here to our misfortune; not by our fault, but that of those who first initiated and encouraged this course in the name of law and religion." To be sure, the proposals in the Cortes offered these highly moral men an opportunity to rid themselves of their "misfortune." But the memorandum ignored this logical point, and went on to argue that the fortunes of the island depended on slavery and therefore the slave trade must be allowed to continue for some time.[21]

But it was Francisco Arango y Parreño, the brilliant spokesman for the slave interests, who presented the shrewdest arguments against the abolitionist propositions, especially abolition of the slave trade. He conceded that the slave system was unjust, but he insisted that the Cortes of Cádiz was not legally empowered to deal with the problem until a constitution had been adopted. Nor could such a step be justly taken without hearing the colonial interests whose economic lives were at stake. Moreover, it had taken Britain and the United States twenty years before they had abolished the slave trade, and the Cortes should act just as gradually. He pointed out that the haciendas of Cuba lacked a sufficient number of slaves, especially female slaves for reproduction purposes, and that, before considering such a measure, the slaveowners should be given the opportunity to promote white immigration.[22]

The arguments of Someruelos and of the various Cuban societies, together with those advanced by Arango y Parreño, brought results. The Cortes abandoned further discussion of the two proposals.[23]

On the heels of this triumph for the Creole landowners came the news of the adoption of the Constitution of 1812 at Cádiz, a liberal document in the framing of which the Cuban delegates, along with other spokesmen from the New World, had played a leading part. In addition to establishing a limited monarchy with major powers in the hands of the Cortes, the constitution proclaimed, for the first time, equal rights for all Spaniards in both the Peninsula and the colonies. Moreover, half of the members of the Cortes would come from overseas, as would a minimum of twelve members of the Council of State which was to advise the King.[24]

In Cuba the inauguration of the new constitution was marked by festivities, and the joy was increased by the announcement that henceforth the civil power of the military executive was to be transferred to three intendants who were to be responsible to a civil governor residing in Havana.[25]

Someruelos could rejoice. To be sure, the pressure of the commercial interests in Spain had prevented the granting of relief from restrictive commercial measures. But he would see to it that such relief was obtained by continuing to ignore the orders of the junta in Spain. The mother country had given the Cubans a new constitution, and it had rewarded the Creole landowners for their loyalty with the gift most precious to them—the right to continue to reap huge profits from the enslavement of hundreds of thousands of human beings.

With this evaluation of the events in Spain the Creole land-owners fully agreed. Other Hispanic Americans were dissatisfied with the accomplishments of the Cortes, especially when it became evident that many of the concessions, due to the opposition of the powerful conservative commercial interests in Spain, were valid only on paper. But the Cuban Creoles had obtained much of what they had wanted, and would get freedom from commercial restrictions from the island authorities. The defeat of the proposals regarding slavery and the slave trade was triumph enough!

Certainly the Cuban sugar and coffee planters longed for political power as much as did the Creole landholders of the other Spanish colonies. Some of them were sympathetic with Bolívar's aspirations and with his dream of a Republican Hispanic-America. Since they were Creoles, born and bred on the island, they could not be "unconditionally Spanish." But their stake in slavery overcame all other considerations, and they feared independence more than domination by Spain.

Largely because the other colonies did not possess the flourishing slave economy characteristic of Cuba, the Creole landowners on the Continent, from Mexico to Argentina, welcomed the aid of Negro slaves in the revolutionary struggle against Spain, even though they made sure to maintain control of the independence movements and to play down the demands of the masses.[26] At least they did not hesitate to raise the question of liberties for the white man lest it lead to the dangerous question of liberties and the possible rebellion of the black man. This was definitely not true for most Creole landowners in Cuba. They were terrified lest a revolutionary struggle for independence arouse the slaves and undermine the system upon which their wealth was based. They knew that some of the independence movements on the Continent held that slavery was contrary to natural law and demanded its abolition.*[27] This argument was bound to be raised in Cuba, too, once the revolutionary impulse of independence was unleashed.

* Argentina abolished slavery in 1816; Colombia and Chile in 1821; Peru, Guatemala, and Uruguay, in 1828, and Mexico in 1829.

"Independence signified the abolition of slavery," notes the Cuban historian Ramiro Guerra y Sánchez, "and this was enough to align against it all the proprietors of slaves, the most numerous and influential class in Cuba during this epoch."[28] José de Ahumada, another Cuban historian, develops this theme further, pointing out:

> Every political movement, every system which would tend to divert the vigilance of the public authorities over the plantations, and the domination of the slaves by force by utilizing the armed might of the state to put down political conspiracies, would have to be considered as a powerful incentive to the weakening of slavery, for the slaves, inspired by the revolutionary propaganda of the era diffused by abolitionist instigators, would take advantage of any occasion which the divisions of the white population offered them to reproduce in Cuba the scenes of desolation and ruin which characterized the establishment of the Republic of Haiti.[29]

The Creole planters, of course, remembered Haiti. But they also saw early evidence in Cuba itself of how the revolutionary fervor of the independence movement threatened the system of slavery in the island.

The first independence conspiracy in Cuban history was organized in 1809 and was headed by Román de la Luz, a wealthy Mason in Havana, and by Joaquín Infante, a lawyer in Bayamo. Both tried to win the support of the Creole planters by assuring them that their movement would leave the institution of slavery untouched. In the constitution, drawn up by Infante, which was to go into effect the moment the conspiracy triumphed, every attempt was made to win over the Creole planters. The independent Republic of Cuba would be dominated by the wealthy landowners by a restrictive system of suffrage based upon property holdings; the preservation of slavery was guaranteed; Catholicism was made the official state religion; and the Republican army would be officered only by "Personas Pudientes" ("wealthy people").[30]

But not even these concessions attracted the support of the Cuban landholders, for, despite its conservative stand on slavery, the independence conspiracy of Román de la Luz gained the immediate support of free Negroes and slaves, who understood that, by participating in the revolutionary struggle against Spain, they could press for their own freedom. They could point out, as had the Negroes who had participated in the American War for Independence, the inconsistency between slavery and a revolutionary struggle for freedom from oppression by the mother country.* William Shaler, appointed consul in Havana by President James Madison, made very clear in his dispatches to the United States State Department why the Creole planters refused to support the conspiracy of Román de la Luz. On October 24, 1810 he wrote from Havana:

> I have been on a visit into the country. During my absence a revolutionary plot has been discovered and about fifteen persons arrested in consequence; several of them are of respectable standing and connections, but the majority are colored men, free Negroes and slaves, and vagabonds. The most odious coloring is given to their plan, the overthrow of slavery, robbery and murder are said to be the principal features in it, though it started out as a movement to separate from Spain. As the proceedings against them are secret, the public knows nothing more of it than what the government chooses to tell. In the meantime suspicion of slave revolts is wide awake. Strong patrols parade the streets every night.[31]

Is it any wonder that the Creole landholders, led by Arango y Parreño, rejected the proposal to join this first independence movement? Or that they rejoiced when, in 1810, the conspiracy was discovered and crushed by Someruelos? Román de la Luz was condemned to ten years' imprisonment at hard labor, and, on release, to permanent exile. Other conspirators suffered similar punishment. However, Joaquín Infante escaped to the United States; from there he went to Venezuela and then to Mexico.[32]

Even more alarming events for the Creole slave owners occurred in 1812. As they had feared, rumors of the proposals in the Cortes for immediate suppression of the slave trade and gradual abolition of slavery reached the Cuban Negro population, which awaited

* As a "Free Negro" correspondent in the United States noted during the War for Independence: "Do the rights of nature cease to be such when a Negro is to enjoy them? Or does patriotism in the heart of an African rankle with treason?" (Philip S. Foner, *The Life and Writings of Frederick Douglass*, New York, 1950, vol. I, p. 29.) For other evidences of this point and of the role of the Negro in the American Revolution, see Herbert Aptheker, *The Negro in the American Revolution*, New York, 1940.

with rising hopes the news from Spain. The Negroes of Cuba were also impressed by the preamble to the proposals of the Mexican deputy Alcocer which declared slavery contrary to Natural Law, to the liberal maxims of the present government of Spain, and destined shortly to be abolished by the civil laws of cultured nations.[33] On learning that all such proposals had been defeated in the Cortes, the Negroes of Cuba felt they would have to take by force the natural right to liberty which they could no longer hope would become theirs by any other method.[34] A far-reaching conspiracy was organized by the young free Negro, José Antonio Aponte.

Aponte was a carpenter and wood-carver in Havana. A deeply religious man, he was strongly influenced by the example of Moses who had led his people out of bondage, and he saw himself in the same role for his enslaved brethren in nineteenth century Cuba. He was kept informed of the discussions over slavery and the slave trade in the Cortes by a Spanish priest who was his friend and confessor. Although his education was limited, Aponte was also aware of the revolutionary events of the era, and established connections with a Negro general in Haiti, Jean François.*[35] Promised Haitian support, Aponte broached the question of organizing a conspiracy to a number of free Negroes and slaves. He pointed to the debate over slavery in the Cortes, and insisted that the Cuban plantation owners and the authorities of the island were trying to suppress the news of the impending liberation of the slaves. This appeal, the Cuban authorities themselves admitted, produced results:

> They [the slaves] are seduced by false news and promises saying that the extraordinary Cortes had decreed their liberty and that the government of this island was hiding such an important thing from them. This was the principal way in which they could change the former submissiveness of the slaves; and they have effectively stirred up some of the mills without having any other precedent than in the

---

* There is some dispute over how deeply Aponte was influenced by the revolutionary ideas of the era. Some historians limit the influences upon him to the scriptures; others believe that he absorbed much of the revolutionary ideology of the period. (*Cf.* Elías Entralgo, *Los Problemas de la Esclavitud. Conspiración de Aponte,* La Habana, 1934, pp. 223–28.)

fatuous and heated brain of the mulatto José Antonio Aponte, and with several others who have joined with him. It is then necessary they should be disillusioned about the believed extinction of slavery showing that there is not and will not be such an order and showing them it would be impossible to hide such a supposed grace if it really existed.[36]

Aponte hoped not only to emancipate the slaves but to transform the economy of the island so that it would no longer require slavery. He planned to burn the sugar and coffee plantations. This would destroy the source of wealth used to buy slaves and, at the same time, would end the domination by the slaveowners of Cuba's economic life.[37] He was convinced that the time was ripe for a successful insurrection. Since the Spanish, confident of Cuba's loyalty, were transferring troops to combat the revolutions on the continent, Aponte felt that the rebel slaves could make considerable headway before troops could be brought back to Cuba; and then, with the help of the Haitians, they would be able to repel the reinforcements.[38]

Late in 1811, Aponte established a Central Revolutionary Junta in Havana whose emissaries set up subordinate juntas in other cities which, in turn, set up smaller organizations in the remoter districts. The conspiracy thus achieved national scope, with greatest strength in the present provinces of Camagüey and Oriente— Puerto Príncipe, Bayamo, Holguín, Baracoa—and leading mills of Guanabacoa and Jaruco in the present province of Havana.

Aponte, however, was not involved in the actual uprising itself. His conspiracy was discovered one night by Captain General Someruelos who overheard two Negroes in Havana discussing a coming insurrection, naming time and place. Under torture by the "cepo," an instrument which closes around the neck and limbs, they named Aponte as the leader of the planned uprising. In mid-February, 1812, Aponte and eight of his principal collaborators were seized and imprisoned.

Despite this setback, violent uprisings broke out in the areas organized by Aponte's juntas. The revolting slaves destroyed sugar and coffee plantations and other areas under cultivation. But before they could unify their struggle, the entire military might of the island, including militias organized by white planters, fell upon the slaves. A prize of 10 pesos was offered for each conspirator taken, dead or alive.

Aponte and eight of his companions, five free Negroes and three slaves, were sentenced to be hanged. Someruelos's proclamation of the sentence, posted on April 7, 1812, ended with this paragraph:

It remains only to announce to this respected public that on the morning of the next Thursday [April 9] I have designated the execution of the sentence referred to, and that the heads of Aponte, [Juan Bautista] Lisundia, [Clemente] Chacón, and [Juan] Barbrado will be hung in the most public and convenient places as a warning to those of their kind. With this is avenged, for now, the offended public and scandal which these culprits have brought to this tranquil people. . . .*39

On April 9, at 9:30 in the morning, the sentence was carried out, with added barbarities. "Justice was executed by superior order," said the *Diario* of Havana on the following day, "giving the inhabitants of this district a new proof of its instruction and religiosity."40 The head of Lisundia was exhibited in the district of Barbier in Trinidad, that of Chacón in the place where he lived in Puente Nuevo de Horcón. The head of Aponte was placed in an iron cage in front of the house where he resided at the beginning of the highway of San Luis Gonzaga, and his hand was nailed on another street. As a Cuban student of this period notes: "The same thing happened to Aponte that happened to many other South American heroes, among them Tupac Amaru,** who paid with their lives for their idea of independence. Their bodies, too, were cut to pieces and exhibited to serve as an example to those who might attempt to find happiness for their country."†41

The conspiracy of Aponte was now added to Haiti as another

---

* The names of the men sentenced to be executed indicates that some Haitians were involved in the leadership of the conspiracy. (*Cf.* Clemente Lanier, "Cuba et la Conspiration d'Aponte en 1812." *Revue de la Société Haitienne D'Histoire, De Géographie, et De Géologie,* vol. XXIII, No. 86, pp. 26–27.)

** Tupac Amaru II was the leader of the revolt of the Indians of Peru against Spanish rule in the early 1780's.

† "From 1812 on," writes Sergio Aguirre, "it was said to children to shame them. 'You're worse than Aponte.' Thus was manufactured a wicked legend for the benefit of the slaveholders." (*Lecciones de Historia de Cuba: Primer Cuaderno,* La Habana, 1960, p. 41.)

bogey to haunt the slaveholders of Cuba. The extent of the conspiracy, the degree to which it had been influenced by the revolutionary ideology stemming from Haiti and the Continental colonies of Spain, convinced the Creole planters that "the work crews of slaves were inflammable material which would take fire at the first attack on the colonial power of Spain in Cuba."[42] The Creole landowners identified their interests still more closely with the Spanish crown.[43]

For several years, the Creole landowners reaped rich rewards from their collaboration with Spain. To be sure, when the reactionary Ferdinand VII returned to his throne in 1814, ruthlessly suppressed the Constitution of 1812, and imprisoned every advocate of constitutionalism, there was concern in Cuba lest the gains of the past be wiped out. But this fear proved groundless. In Cuba the repression was more form than reality, and many of the measures put into effect under the Constitution remained practically in force after its abrogation.[44]

The reason for this is simple. While Ferdinand was instituting a reign of terror in Spain, he was also making plans for an expedition against the rebellious Spanish American colonists. For this he needed Cuba as a base of operations. This required good relations with the Creole sugar and coffee planters who clung to the privileges gained by the reforms. With Cuba enjoying prosperity, he expected to obtain from her the money and supplies for his military campaigns against the colonies on the mainland.

Ferdinand got what he wanted from the Creole landowners—money, arms, gunpowder, foodstuffs and other supplies.*[45] In return, while governing in Spain with an iron hand, Ferdinand permitted the Cuban landowners to retain many of the gains of the annulled constitution. Then, between 1816 and 1819, the King granted a series of concessions to Cuba as a token of his gratitude to the people of the island for not joining the rebellion then raging

---

* In all of Spain's efforts to combat the revolutionary movement in her mainland colonies, Cuba and Puerto Rico were the arsenals and bases of operations of the Spanish navy and armies: Cuba as far as Mexico and New Granada (Colombia and Panama) were concerned, and Puerto Rico in regard to Venezuela. (Cf. José L. Franco, *Política continental americana de España en Cuba, 1812–1830*, La Habana, 1947, p. 329.)

on the Continent and for the help it had given him. "This," notes the Cuban historian Sergio Aguirre, "was the pay for the fifth-columnism of the island."[46]

In 1816, Francisco Arango y Parreño, who had succeeded in gaining the confidence of Ferdinand, was designated Counsellor of the Indies (*Consejero de Indias*), a position of ministerial rank, in which he could play an important role in protecting the slave interests of Cuba. A year later, Ferdinand ended the Estanco de Tabaco which for one hundred years had made the tobacco trade a royal monopoly at the expense of the Cuban tobacco farmers.[47] That same year 1817, in accordance with a persistent demand of the Cuban reformers, the crown issued the decree of October 21, 1817, to promote Catholic immigrant labor in the island as a means of reducing the Negro majority in the island's population, revealed in the Census of 1817.* A Royal Decree of February 10, 1818, finally granted the long-hoped-for economic demand of the reformers: permanent admission of foreign vessels and freedom to trade with foreign nations. Though this trade was still subject to heavy duties, the decree of 1818 definitely opened Cuban ports to foreign vessels.[48] In 1819 a Royal Decree granted the Cubans full legal rights to the lands they were occupying and using. Up to then, the land (called *las tierras mercedadas*) had legally remained Royal property; but now the Creole landowners could consider their land legitimately theirs—with the right to sell it, divide it, collect rent from it or do with it whatever they wished.[49]

There was one dark shadow over these optimistic developments so far as the wealthy Creoles were concerned: the decree of 1817 ending the slave trade to Cuba after 1820. But this was not an unexpected blow nor was it one which, by that time, could not be taken in stride.

At the Congress of Vienna, in 1814, the British ministry of Lord Liverpool, responding to the continued agitation of Wilberforce and other abolitionists, had attempted to secure a joint dec-

---

* According to the Census of 1817, the white population of Cuba was 291,021 (45.96%) and the Negro population 339,959 (54.04%). Of the Negroes, 115,691 (18.32%) were free, and 224,268 (33.55%) slaves. Thus, for the first time, the combined Negro population outnumbered the whites. (Ulpiano Vega Cobiellas, *Nuestra América y la evolución de Cuba*, La Habana, 1944, pp. 74–75.)

laration from the powers, abolishing the slave trade immediately. But Spain, now governed by Ferdinand VII, and Portugal opposed the proposal on the ground that it would seriously compromise the interests of their colonial subjects. Ferdinand had Cuba especially in mind. Concerned with conserving the loyalty and prosperity of her slaveowners, so necessary if he was to crush the revolutions in Spanish America, Ferdinand would only agree to accept a watered-down resolution. This, though condemning the African slave trade as "contrary to the principles of humanity and universal morality," allowed each nation to determine when it would be convenient to abolish it.[50]

But the British were not to be put off by the reservations made in the declaration of Vienna, and Lord Castlereagh immediately sought to induce the signatory powers to implement the declaration through treaties. Spain, however, would not be pinned down. After consulting the colonial interests involved, especially Cuba and Puerto Rico, Ferdinand rejected England's request, and refused to fix a date for the abolition of the slave trade.[51] But British pressure did not lessen, and Castlereagh succeeded in convincing other powers, with the exception of Portugal, to apply similar pressure on Spain. It was only a matter of time before Spain must succumb.

The Cuban slaveowners, meanwhile, were not standing by idly. When, in February, 1816, the Council of the Indies submitted a report to Ferdinand urging that the slave trade be immediately abolished, Arango y Parreño, as spokesman for the Cuban slaveowners, drafted a minority report which decried haste in abolishing slavery, raised the prospect that precipitous action, as proposed by England, would weaken the loyalty of Cuba to Spain and might even lead to open resistance on the part of the colonists, which might mean the loss of the island.

These arguments had, of course, been raised before in the debate in the Cortes in 1811. But a new twist was added in this minority report. The charge was made that Great Britain's motive was to damage the prosperity of Cuba for the benefit of the British West Indian colonies. The British had taken good care to fill their colonies with slaves—there were ten Negroes to one white in Jamaica —before putting pressure on Spain to abolish the slave trade.

Cuba, with a ratio of one to one, was entitled to a more highly developed slave economy before halting the traffic. Above all, Cuba's loyalty to Spain justified that the mother country resist England's selfish plot to destroy the island's economic life. To yield was to deprive the slave interests of their reward as patriots.

But even the Cuban reformers knew that they could not ask weak Spain to stand against a coalition of the major powers. Hence they informed Ferdinand that they were willing to see the slave trade abolished north of the equator immediately, and south of the equator on April 22, 1821. Included in this proposal was the demand that Britain pay full indemnity for all losses incurred in the abolition of the traffic, and that the Spanish government adopt measures for promoting free immigrant labor.[52]

Thus assured that, in yielding to British pressure, he would not seriously weaken the loyalty of the Cuban planters who were aware that he had resisted as long as possible, Ferdinand signed the treaty of 1817. By it the Spanish King prohibited Spanish subjects from "engaging in the slave trade in the coasts of Africa," north of the equator after November 22, 1817, "upon any pretext or in any manner whatever," and that the slave trade should be entirely abolished throughout Spain's dominions on May 20, 1820. Thereafter, all Spanish subjects were forbidden to engage in the slave trade on the coast of Africa "South of the Equator." Foreign ships introducing slaves in Spanish dominions were subject to the same laws. It was also provided that the British government pay an indemnity of 400,000 pounds (10,000,000 *pesetas*) to the Spaniards for losses suffered in "legitimate trade" as a result of these treaties, to be paid in London on February 22, 1818.

The warships of both nations were authorized to inspect the merchant ships of either nations whenever there was a well-founded suspicion of illicit cargo. If contraband cargo were found aboard, the ships and their crews were to be detained and taken before the tribunal established for the purpose. These Mixed Courts were composed of an equal number of judges named by both nations. One was to be established at Sierra Leone in Africa and another in Havana. There was no appeal from their rulings. Thus the treaty provided for a mutual right of search and for confiscation of vessels on which slaves should be found.[53]

Enlightened people in Cuba saw a new bright future opening for the island as a result of the historic treaty, though their vision was somewhat blinded by their white supremacy point of view. Thus a resident in the island wrote from Havana:

> I am inclined to think the island will be considerably benefitted by the abolition of the slave trade. The island of Cuba is entitled to rank higher than a mere sugar colony. The variety and richness of its soil render it fully capable of other field products within the ability of *white* cultivators. The vast tracts of country yet untouched or unoccupied, if divided into small farms or *estancias* amongst white settlers, either native or foreign, would increase the wealth and population of the island in a higher degree than if its surface was covered with sugar and coffee.[54]

But the wealthy Creole planters had other visions. Though they did not openly protest the legal termination of the slave trade, they were never reconciled to it. Stimulated by the Royal decree of 1818 which permitted Cuba to trade more freely with all nations, they were planning to increase sugar production; consequently the demand for slave labor was growing greater precisely at the hour of the Anglo-Spanish treaty against the slave trade. The Creole planters were confident that the demand would be met, treaty or no treaty.* They had had too long an experience with smuggling and other clandestine methods of getting around restrictions on trade to believe that the treaty actually doomed the slave trade. Nor did they anticipate receiving anything but cooperation—for a fee, of course—from greedy Spanish authorities, from the highest to the lowest. As we shall see, their confidence was to be amply justified.

As the year 1820 approached, relations between the Spanish authorities in Madrid and in Cuba and the wealthy sugar and coffee producers were more cordial than ever. The Cuban reformers, made up of these landowners, had gained many of their demands in return for their loyalty to Spain—especially the opening of Cuba's

---

* Naturally, the slaveowners took advantage of the three year respite to import slaves at a feverish rate: 25,976 in 1817, about 17,000 in 1818, and 14,668 in 1819. On April 29, 1820, *Niles' Weekly Register* of Philadelphia reported that 1276 slaves were landed at Havana from April 3rd to the 8th.

ports to unrestricted foreign commerce, which fulfilled one of their most cherished goals and satisfied one of their long-standing demands. The persistent efforts of the Captains General to win the Creoles to the side of Spain had proved successful.

The wealth of the Cuban landowners, based on slave labor, had grown enormously. With the expansion of markets due to wartime conditions and commercial reforms, exports of sugar had risen steadily, reaching an annual average, during these years, of 200,000 boxes. The Census of 1817 had revealed that the population of the island had increased 358,680 since the Census of 1791. The population had more than doubled in less than thirty years! And there were now 625 sugar plantations, 779 coffee plantations, 1601 *vegas* (tobacco plantations) and 2,127 cattle ranches.[55] The value of Cuban exports during the five years from 1815 to 1819 rose to 56,224,041 pesos and that of imports to 26,039,030 pesos. The revenue derived by Spain from tariffs on this commerce reached millions of pesos, enough for the first time in Cuba's history to cover the island's public expenses without the help of Mexico, and with enough left over to cover the salaries of the legations and Spanish consulates in the United States.[56]

Thus, while nearly all the other Spanish colonies were engaged in bitter warfare for independence, Cuba prospered, and her prosperity enabled Spain to intensify her efforts to crush the liberation movements. Small wonder the Spanish government boasted in 1819 that "nothing is further from the thoughts of the heroic people of this island than division from the interest of the Peninsula, notwithstanding the efforts made by a few ignorant individuals to persuade them that they lie separate."[57]

In the decade opening in 1820 the number of such "ignorant people"—the truly "heroic people" of the island—was to increase, and their efforts to establish an independent Cuba were to assume significant proportions.

chapter 6

THE INDEPENDENCE MOVEMENT, 1820–1830

On April 15, 1820, a merchant vessel brought to Cuba a copy of the Madrid *Gazette* of the 7th of March. It contained an account of the uprisings in Spain against Ferdinand's despotic rule and of the King's agreement, under pressure, to restore the Constitution of 1812. "Let us walk frankly, and I the first, along the Constitutional path," ran his manifesto in the official *Gazette* which was publicly displayed in Havana for all to see.

When Captain General Juan Manuel Cajigal refused to acknowledge the restoration of the Constitution, which elevated Cuba from a colony to a province of Spain, the people of Havana took energetic steps to make him change his mind. Crowded into the Plaza de Armas where the government buildings were situated, they demanded that the Captain General immediately proclaim the Constitution and take an oath of allegiance to abide by it. He took an oath and was followed by other public officials. The Constitution of 1812 was re-established in Cuba on April 16, 1820.

Then began a round of joyful celebrations. A dispatch from Havana in *Niles' Weekly Register,* captioned "Rapture in Cuba," went:

All the bells were set to ringing in Havana—the people filled the streets shouting "Viva la Constitution," and the soldiers joined them. . . . Pipes of wine, and other good things were freely distributed to the soldiers and to the people and a general jubilee was observed. . . . "Live the Constitution," "Live the Nation," "Down with superstition and hypocrisy" was the almost unanimous cry of the people as well as the military. The Franciscan monks who, on the return of Ferdinand [in 1814], caused the Constitution to be religiously burned, had to perform a most unpleasant task—they were compelled to ring all the bells of the convent the whole night through for joy.[1]

The following day the people liberated all political prisoners in the dreaded Cabaña fortress; renamed the streets to celebrate the new constitutional regime—Plaza de Fernando Séptimo became the Plaza de la Constitución and the Real Lotería became the La Lotería Constitucional. They ousted all municipal officials who had been appointed after the suppression of the Constitution, reinstating those who had held offices under the rule of the Cortes. The civil organization, as it had stood under the Constitution, was reestablished throughout the colony.[2]

The new atmosphere of freedom was reflected in the press. Within a few weeks, fourteen periodicals made their appearance along with scores of sheets, all carrying odes, sonnets, essays, on the restored Constitution, "all filled with politics and details of the abuses that existed under the late form of government."[3]

Although the Creole masses had been the most active elements in the successful struggle to restore constitutional government in Cuba, the slave-holding planter group continued to speak for Cuba. The Cortes of 1820 again included the deputies from the colonies. In the elections of Cuban deputies, property-holding qualifications for voting disfranchised most of the Creole masses and the three deputies thus voted in were pledged to the wealthy landowners.[4]

These landowners gave the three elected deputies explicit instructions to advance a program in the interest of the sugar and coffee planters: to reduce the tariffs on trade between the United States and Cuba, and to revoke the Treaty of 1817 (ending the importation of slaves), or, at least, to secure a delay of six years in its application. The instructions pointed out that no other province of the Spanish empire had as much at stake in the slave trade as Cuba. "Therefore the damages caused by the sudden cessation . . . are incalculable. The quantity received for compensation is most inadequate. . . . And if no delay is obtained . . . an enormous weight of debts and obligations will weigh upon the subjects of the nation."[5]

In behalf of the slaveholders, Juan Bernardo de O'Gavan, one of

Cuba's three deputies, published in Madrid his *Observaciones sobre la condición de los esclavos Africanos* (*Observations on the Condition of African Slaves*) which urged the Cortes to protect the slave trade of Cuba against British designs to ruin the colony. Speaking as an ecclesiastic, O'Gavan declared that he was not a defender of slavery, yet "work was ordained of God," and since "the Africans were the laziest people known," slavery was a means of making them live up to God's precept. Since the slave trade was also a means of civilizing the Africans, wise legislation, "if humanitarianism were truly understood," would not only compel the Negroes to work but would foster and protect their transportation to Cuba. Finally, O'Gavan repeated the now familiar theme that Cuba's slaveowners deserved special consideration because of their loyalty to Spain and the assistance they were rendering the mother country in combating treason on the mainland.[6]

But the Cuban slaveowners discovered to their dismay that their influence in Spain was not what it had been before the liberals gained control in 1820. For one thing, Ferdinand had been forced to dismiss the ministers with whom the Cuban reformers, especially Arango y Parreño, had had such good relations. For another, the newly-assembled liberal Cortes was determined to wipe out the slave trade. It rejected all appeals to delay putting the Treaty of 1817 into effect, and, in order to stop violations of the treaty, decreed that provisions for its enforcement be included in the new criminal code.[7]

The Cuban slaveowners were in for still further disappointments. Three new deputies to the Cortes were elected in Cuba to serve in 1822–23. They were given the same instructions to work for the repeal of the Treaty of 1817 or for a delay in its operation. But Father Félix Varela, one of the deputies, had reached the conclusion that slavery was an evil force in Cuban society and that the island could never really progress until it was abolished. Not only did this distinguished leader of Cuban liberalism ignore the instructions to press for the repeal of the Treaty of 1817, but he proposed the gradual abolition of slavery in Hispanic America. Varela argued that, until slavery was abolished, the Antilles would always face the danger of slave insurrections. It would be foolish to imagine that the slaves would remain tranquil and content while the whites rejoiced in the new-found liberties embodied in the restored Constitution of 1812 and in the new atmosphere of freedom that had swept through Cuba with the restoration.* "The barbarian is the best soldier when he finds someone to lead him," he declared, and Haiti had demonstrated that there would be no lack of leaders.

He urged the Cortes not to confuse the interests of the slaveowners with the "true interests" of the islands, insisting that "the general wish of the people of Cuba is that there were no slaves, they only want to find some other way to supply their necessities." Varela proposed the emancipation of all slaves who had served fifteen years with the same master, free status to all those born after the publication of this decree, establishment of a lottery whereby the slaves selected would be enabled to purchase their freedom, and the formation of philanthropic groups charged with gathering funds, protecting the rights of slaves and directing abolition. Father Varela had planned, down to the most minute detail, the abolition of slavery in Cuba.[8]

Varela, of course, was roundly condemned by the Cuban slave interests who informed him that "the deputy from Cuba who would ask for abolition of slavery ought to have his tongue cut out."[9] The Cortes, however, was impressed by his proposal, and plans were drawn up for the gradual abolition of slavery and for promoting production by small landowners.

But a change in the European situation, particularly as it affected Spain, put the Cuban slaveowners at ease. In April, 1823, the King of France, commissioned by the "Holy Alliance,"** sent 100,000 soldiers into the Peninsula. Behind their bayonets, the despot Ferdinand VII dissolved the Cortes, revoked the Constitution of 1812, and sent hundreds of liberals to the gallows, while thousands fled into exile. The proposals to abolish slavery in the

* It is interesting, in this connection, to read this report from Havana just after the restoration of the Constitution of 1812: "It is curious to see how suddenly this city of statutes started into life. The very slaves, as if refreshed by the air of freedom that blew around them, seem elated with the change." (*Letters from the Havana, op. cit.,* p. 50.)

** The "Holy Alliance" was a league of reactionary monarchies—Russia, Prussia, Austria, and France—formed in 1822 to halt the advance of all liberal ideas and restore absolute monarchies wherever they had been overthrown.

Antilles were abandoned, as was strict enforcement of the Treaty of 1817.[10]

The slaveowners rejoiced, but for the island as a whole the overthrow of the liberal regime by the "Holy Alliance" was a tragedy. Cuba felt the full force of the renewed despotism. In May, 1823, Captain General Francisco Dionisio Vives initiated a drastic program to suppress Cuban liberalism. At the same time, the financial burden imposed on Cuba was increased. The loss of revenue from Mexico and Peru was to be made up by heavier taxes on the Antilles.*

Taxes were imposed on all documents, property and activities, from Papal Bulls and crucifixes to cockfighting and entertaining friends in the home, and on all crops except sugar. According to one contemporary observer, the taxes now imposed exceed "in variety and extent that of any taxation imposed by any Government in any country on earth."[11] In a Royal Order of May 29, 1825, a military tribunal, called the Permanent Executive Military Commission, was set up and empowered to seize anyone suspected of conspiracy. In the infamous decree of May 28, 1825, the Captain General was given almost absolute authority. Called "facultades omnímodas" ("all-embracing"), the authorization invested him with "full and unlimited authority to detach from the island, and to send to this Peninsula all officials and persons employed in whatsoever capacity, and of whatsoever rank and class or condition, whose presence may appear prejudicial, or whose public or private conduct may inspire you with suspicion. . . ."[12] Thus the Captain General could detain, punish, banish from the land, and confiscate the goods of whomever he wanted. Under the "facultades omnímodas," which lasted from 1825 to 1878, all residents of Cuba lost the protection of law. In effect, they lived under martial law, for the Captain General had been invested *"with the whole extent of power granted to the governors of besieged towns."* This was, in fact, the island's only constitution.[13]

From 1825 onward, Spain kept an iron heel on Cuba. The government of the island was once more a military oligarchy. The

---

* During much of the time before 1800, Cuba had hardly been self-supporting and had not been expected to contribute to the revenues of Spain.

Captain General, at its head, was now both a civil and military ruler, whose authority was the sheerest despotism.

Thus, within a few years, the influence of Cuban reformism vanished.* Ferdinand, who attributed the loss of Spanish America to the reforms of 1812, had tolerated their existence in Cuba only to retain the island's loyalty while he used it as a base of military operations against the rebellious colonies. But, as the Spanish authorities gave up their hope of ever reconquering their mainland colonies, one of the two reasons for continuing the concessions to Cuba disappeared. And events after 1820 eliminated the other, for they proved that Cuba was not as "loyal" as the reformers pictured her.

In no period of Cuban history before the outbreak of the Ten Years' War in 1868, was the independence movement as strong as during the decade opening in 1820. Before examining the forces behind the movement, it is worth noting that the wealthy Cuban planters were not among them.

The Creole *hacendados* were still dominated by the fear that a revolutionary movement would doom slavery. "If the Cubans had supported such an idea," wrote Ramón de Palma, a Cuban slaveowner in 1849, "Cuba would have been independent a long time ago. . . . But we were opposed to such a step then and we are opposed to it now."[14]

In 1822, a private expedition, fitted out in New York City and Philadelphia, set out from the United States with the avowed purpose of conquering Puerto Rico, ending Spanish domination, and establishing the "Republic of Boriqua," a name derived from Boriquén, the pre-Columbian name of the island.** Although the

---

* In 1825 Arango y Parreño was removed from the post of superintendent of the Hacienda of Cuba. He was replaced by an ex-reformer: Claudio Martínez de Pinillos who was rewarded with the title of the Count of Villanueva.
** The expedition was initiated by a group of Puerto Ricans who approached one of Bolívar's officers, Ducoudray Holstein, in Curaçao, where he was then teaching, and offered him funds to outfit an expedition from the United States to invade the island and establish an independent republic there. Ducoudray Holstein was joined by Baptis Irvine, an American journalist and advocate of Latin American independence. The expedition, assisted by some American merchants and composed of several Americans and many more Europeans then resident in the United States, left on August 13, 1822, in two schooners from New York and a brig from Philadelphia. After mishaps at sea, the expedition was

attempt failed, the episode aroused considerable excitement in Cuba, especially the fact that the Negroes of Puerto Rico were actively involved in the conspiracy, one of the chief objectives of which was to abolish slavery in the island and to give people of color equal rights with those enjoyed by the whites. On November 19, 1822, the *Diario Noticioso* of Havana reprinted the following proclamation of the Puerto Rican conspirators:

> May all people in our Republic from this moment onward be only one and the same family; may the two walk together toward the welfare of their new fatherland; may the rivalry between them for the attainment of military and civil positions in the government be only in respect their talents, probity, and good conduct. The one with the greatest merit will occupy the position *without taking into consideration, his religion, nationality, or color.*

The Cuban paper then commented:

> It is clear from this that the main feature of the conspiracy in Puerto Rico was to promote a rebellion of the blacks against the whites and to transform the island into a new Santo Domingo. This is not surprising, for this is the objective of all the incendiaries who seek to promote separatism from the mother country. We know that this is their goal in our own fair island, and that they think nothing of provoking the most dreadful disorders which will destroy the country. Fortunately, the loyal members of our community have too much at stake to countenance such subversive activities.

The "loyal" Cubans were, of course, the wealthy planters for whom the news from Puerto Rico strengthened the conviction that separatism and abolition, with all its consequences, were inter-related. Nor, as the *Diario Noticioso* emphasized, did they have to look far for further proof. The Cuban independence movements of the 1820's sought and welcomed the participation of the free

---

forced into Curaçao where Holstein and Irvine were arrested by the Dutch authorities.

In Puerto Rico, plans had been made for an uprising to coincide with the arrival of the expedition. One of the leaders of the conspiracy was Pedro Duboy, a mulatto, who secretly organized free Negroes and slaves. With the failure of the expedition in Curaçao, the conspiracy in Puerto Rico collapsed. The Negro leaders of the conspiracy were arrested and shot. Ducoudray Holstein and Baptis Irvine were deported from Curaçao, after first having been tried and sentenced as disturbers of the peace.

Negro and slave in the struggle against Spain, and promised the latter that he would soon be redeemed from bondage in the Republic that their united forces would create.[15] As Manuel Villanova puts it: "The revolutionary cycle in Cuba during the decade 1820–1830 is characterized . . . by the complete preoccupation that the revolutionaries had for gaining the adherence of the people of color."[16]

This was enough, of course, to alienate the wealthy planters from the independence struggle, a position they maintained despite the mounting evils of the political system after the overthrow of Spanish liberalism. But there were other reasons. There were many advantages for the planters even during the despotism. Sugar and coffee production rose steadily, and tobacco, now freed of government monopoly, enjoyed great prosperity.* The increasing demand for slave labor in the production of these crops was met despite the Treaty of 1817.

The Captains General, so prompt and forceful in their measures to suppress the liberties of the Cuban people, proved feeble and dilatory when it came to enforcing the laws against the slave trade. While the Spanish government, to appease England, regularly sent instructions to the insular authorities to enforce these laws, it was understood that these instructions were not to be taken seriously. After all, taxes on Cuban wealth, especially the revenue from the sugar trade, were now the life blood of the chronically anemic Spanish treasury, and this revenue was derived from a slave economy. Moreover, the Captains General built up fortunes from the bribes of the slave-traders and, like the home government, they were not disposed to kill the goose that laid the golden egg.

At the same time, the continued flow of slave labor into the island served to keep the powerful merchant and slave-holding class loyal to Spain. The Spanish merchants also had an important stake in slavery, for they had furnished the capital to expand sugar and (to a lesser extent) coffee production, through the importation of ma-

---

* By 1825 the annual export of sugar had reached an average of 200,000 boxes; the annual export of coffee was 499,000 quintales, and in the period 1825 to 1830, 128,644 quintales of leaf tobacco and 245,097 million cigars were exported. A quintal equals a hundred-weight. (Alexander Humboldt, *The Island of Cuba*, New York, 1856, pp. 282, 289.)

chinery, the cultivation of new land, and the increase in the laboring force. Loans were made in anticipation of sugar or coffee crops and interest rates ran as high as twelve to sixteen percent. The cutting off of slave labor would have threatened the collection of these loans. Thus the Creole planters and the Spanish merchants had a mutual economic interest in the maintenance of slavery. This united the two groups, hostile to each other in other ways, in a common front against independence.[17]

In short, the Cuban slave trade thrived even after 1820, the date on which it was to cease. "The Treaty of 1817 was always a dead letter," Ramiro Guerra observes.[18] During the period 1821–1831, an estimated 300 slaver fleets landed 600,000 slaves in Cuba![19]

Thus the *hacendados* enjoyed phenomenal prosperity even under the despotism. It is understandable, therefore, that the wealthy Cuban planters would cling to an anti-independence "reform" position in an era when ideas of independence were taking root among other Cuban Creoles.

The phenomenal prosperity of the wealthy planters and commercial interests was not shared by other classes in Cuba. In the eastern end of the island (Provincia de Oriente), remote from the merchant capitalists of Havana, the smaller planters found it difficult to keep abreast of the rising cost of sugar production. A distinct rift of interests between the two classes of planters emerged during this period, and the dissatisfaction of the planters in the Oriental provinces helped to make this part of Cuba an important section of the independence movement.[20]

Another significant development of this era was the emergence of a larger middle class in Cuba, the effect of measures taken between 1816 and 1819 to encourage white colonization, end the tobacco monopoly, and promote free trade. Unlike the favored wealthy planters, this middle class received few compensations for the evils of the political system. Consequently, they felt closer to the lower classes in Cuban society than to the wealthy planters. Nor were they terrified by fear of the Negro masses raising the cry of independence, for their stake in the slave system was small.[21]

An important role in the independence movement was played by intellectuals and students. Among the former was the first great

Cuban poet, José María Heredia. Born in Santiago de Cuba on December 31, 1803, Heredia identified himself early in his life with the cause of Cuban independence. His first important poem, "The Star of Cuba," written in his teens, expressed a readiness to die, if need be, for Cuba, leaving his head upon the scaffold as a token of the brutality of Spain. The following lines expressed Cuban aspirations for freedom:

> Cuba! in the end you will be
>   free and pure
>   as the air, full of light, that you breathe. . . .
>
> The cruelty of the tyrant is futile,
>   In spite of the traitors who
>   serve them.
>
> It is not in vain that the sea
>   stretches immensely between
>   Cuba and Spain.[22]

Heredia's yearning for the independence of Cuba was shared by groups of students, sons of wealthy Cubans, especially those at the Seminary of San Carlos, where they came under the influence of the liberal Father José Agustín Caballero, director of the Seminary, and Father Félix Varela, one of its outstanding teachers.

Although Varela had shown little interest in politics when he assumed the chair of philosophy in 1811, he began to move in that direction when he took charge of the chair of constitutionalism nine years later. Then, in staunch defense of the Constitution of 1812, he fostered in his students admiration for liberalism in government and hatred of the reactionary absolutism of Ferdinand VII. While Varela himself did not abandon his advocacy of reformism until several years later, he was deeply impressed by a pamphlet published in Spain by the priest, José Mariano Méndez, advocating the independence of Cuba and Puerto Rico.[23] Varela discussed the manifesto openly in his classes, giving his students insight into the illusions of reformism. Moreover, Varela's conviction that the abolition of slavery was essential for the well-being of Cuba, a position he was to set forth so brilliantly before the

Spanish Cortes, made a deep impression not only upon his students but on other Cubans ouside of the slave interests.[24]

One other feature of the independence movements is worth noting before we examine them specifically, and that is the degree to which they were inspired and encouraged by the United States and by the recently-born republics that had broken from Spain, especially Mexico and Colombia. Naturally, the Spanish authorities charged that the Cuban independence conspiracies were hatched either in the United States, Haiti, or Colombia, and that North American, Haitian and Bolivarian agents had entered the island to incite slave revolts and overthrow the government. This charge, of course, was intended to obscure the conditions within Cuba itself and the fact that the independence movements were organized by the Cubans. Nevertheless, there is no doubt that many Cubans were "infected" by the revolutionary "plague" introduced from the United States and the South American Republics. But it is necessary to emphasize that the Cubans themselves were more often the carriers than foreign agents.

Sons of wealthy Cubans sent to the United States for their education, returned with stories of the liberties enjoyed in the neighbor nation and contrasted them with the oppression under which the Cubans lived.[25] Similarly, Cuban volunteers, some of whom rose to high rank in the insurgent army in Venezuela, returned to Cuba with inspiring accounts of the heroic struggles of the white Creoles and Negroes, fighting side by side, and pointed out how a similar unity could bring liberty to the island.[26] The ideas of a number of these Cubans were even in advance of those of the revolutionary leaders in the South American Republics. The latter feared the Negro and Indian masses, and based themselves primarily upon the big landowners and merchants.* In contrast, many Cuban revolutionary leaders, aware that the wealthy landowners and merchants bitterly opposed independence, put their hopes in the unity of small white farmers, free Negroes and slaves.[27]

Certainly revolutionary propaganda, filtering into Cuba from the mainland, influenced the islanders. Certainly the Cuban in-

---

* A notable exception, however, was Miguel Hidalgo, the pioneer revolutionary in Mexico, who spoke for the Indians and Mestizo (mixed-blood) peons.

dependence movements were encouraged by forces outside of the island. But the government of the United States was not among them. As we shall see, Washington preferred that if it did not, itself, annex the island, Cuba should remain a Spanish possession. The chief encouragement to Cuban independence came from Colombia and Mexico. Apart from the fact that they felt indebted to the Cuban patriots who fought in their armies, and hoped to repay them by helping to liberate Cuba from Spain, the revolutionary leaders knew that as long as the island remained in Spanish hands, it remained a danger to the liberation cause. For Cuba was the base in America from which Ferdinand planned to reconquer the newly-independent states. Hence it is not surprising that, during this period, Colombia and Mexico should have tried to foment rebellion in Cuba against Spain.

The activity of Cuban revolutionists was reflected in the rapid organization of secret societies after the triumph of the Spanish liberals in 1820. Although many were ostensibly fraternal orders, it was openly acknowledged that their real objective was "to overthrow the present government and establish the independence of Cuba."[28] The Cuban Masonic lodges, with their ties to Masons in the United States, Mexico and Colombia, were especially active in the independence movements.*[29] (Spain actually accused Philadelphia Masons of promoting revolution in Cuba through their related lodges in the island.[30]) By 1821 so many of these revolutionary organizations were functioning underground in Cuba, forming what came to be known as the "Cadena Eléctrica" (Electrical Chain) that Vincent Gray, an American merchant long resident in the island and several times consul of the United States, wrote to

---

* According to one student of the Cuban independence movement of the 1820's, "the social and political aspects of the Masonic establishments in Cuba and their role in the conspiracies for the independence of Cuba cannot be exaggerated." (Roque E. Garrigó, *Historia Documentada de La Conspiración de Los Soles y Rayos de Bolívar*, La Habana, 1939, vol. I, p. 153.) However, in dealing with the role played by Masonry in any revolutionary movement, one must distinguish between Masonry as an organization, and those of its members acting as individuals. This, unfortunately, many of the pro-Masonic scholars fail to do. Nevertheless, the spirit of Masonry appealed especially to the middle-class groups in Cuba who advocated political and economic liberalism, and the movement was important in the independence activities.

the State Department on October 31, 1821: "... it is clearly my opinion that if any Nation would come forward and offer them protection, with a competent Naval Force, the Island would be declared Independent in one month or less. This I communicate to you in confidence. Many wealthy men are selling off their property, for the purpose of leaving the country, fearing that it will be Independent in the present year."[31]

The most famous of the revolutionary organizations in this period of independence conspiracies in Cuba was the *Soles y Rayos de Bolívar* or Suns and Rays of Bolívar, organized in 1821. The society, as the name implies, took its inspiration from Colombia, the first Latin American state to achieve independence under the Presidency of the Liberator, Bolívar. Among the founders of the Cuban group were José Fernández Madrid, a Colombian revolutionary, and Sévère Courtois, a Haitian revolutionary who became a high official in the Colombian Navy. But it was directed by a native of Havana, José Francisco Lemus. A dedicated republican, Lemus had joined the Colombian army where he had risen to the rank of Colonel. Returning to Cuba in 1820, he found the people more concerned with restoring the Constitution of 1812 than in independence. He left for Spain on a commission for the Republic of Colombia, and here, in conferences with several confidential agents of Bolívar, arrived at the conclusion that the important task of the moment was to return to Cuba and work for its independence.[32]

Back again in Cuba, in 1821, Lemus organized the *Soles y Rayos de Bolívar*. This secret society was to set up cells throughout the island. Lemus made repeated trips all through Cuba, quietly organizing the cells, which included women, devoted to the independence cause.* He appealed to Cubans of all classes, but especially to students and the poorer white Cubans, urging them to unite with the Negroes for independence. Leaflets were printed and distributed secretly among free Negroes calling upon them to join the movement.[33] Lemus's emissaries carried the message into remote corners of the island, and made effective use of

---

* One of Lemus's close associates was Doña Socorro Mancebo, a Cuban woman who frequently corresponded with Simón Bolívar in behalf of Cuban independence.

intinerant peddlers. A report of the Spanish authorities noted that a "seller of clothes . . . goes around exciting and inciting various individuals with the object of revolutionizing against the present government."[34]

The effectiveness of the organizing work was evident in the network of cells established in Cuba by October, 1822, in some of which leading figures of the community—judges, chiefs of militia, even mayors—were members. In others, students of Father Varela and intellectuals like the poet José María Heredia were the members. In quite a few of the cells in the rural areas, tobacco farmers, small sugar planters and free Negroes and slaves met together. As was to be expected, few of the wealthy Creole slaveowners, the rich sugar and coffee planters, joined the revolutionary society.[35]

The members of the *Soles y Rayos* had no uniforms, but each had a round badge (devised by Lemus) with folds imitating rays. Each member was required to equip himself with a knife, and a few had pistols, some of very original design, such as a pistol with a little machete at the end to serve as a small bayonet. Some rifles were also stored away for use in the insurrection. In the main, however, the conspiracy depended on the militia, organized and equipped by the Spanish authorities, to furnish it with the arms necessary for success. The strategy worked out by Lemus called for chosen members to join the militia, and when the signal was given for the uprising, to bring their guns and ammunition to the revolutionary side.[36] Arms were also to be obtained from Mexico and Colombia to reinforce the independence fighters.[37]

The quick and large-scale organization of this conspiracy when Cuba was still operating under the restored Constitution, clearly indicates a wider support for independence than had ever been anticipated by the Spaniards. When Spanish liberalism was crushed by the "Holy Alliance" in April, 1823, the conspiracy gained even wider support. Precisely at this time, moreover, reports began reaching Cuba that the Spanish government was planning to sell the island to the British both as payment for outstanding debts and to buy British neutrality during the struggle in Spain. The conspirators seized upon the reports of the reactionary coalition against liberalism in Spain and the news of the impending cession of Cuba to England, and spread the information throughout the island. They warned the population that their liberties, like those of Spain, were in grave danger. The following unsigned notice was planted in a Havana newspaper by a group of members of the *Soles y Rayos:*

> Spaniards and citizens of Cuba. The war has burst into flames in Europe. The progress of the illustrious principles, the establishment of representative governments, the adoption of liberal constitutions, have alarmed the sovereigns of Europe who do not wish to recognize any power independent of the Crown. No right will be permitted other than those they themselves have abrogated to themselves and no prerogatives which they have not directed or adapted to their fancy. Influenced by these motives, they have just invaded Spain determined to destroy a Constitution which guarantees the rights of the people, to re-establish their power and authority and give character to the nation. Time alone will be able to show what will be the outcome of this combination of the despots of Europe. Perhaps they will be able to destroy the Constitution; give unlimited power to the King; and to rivet the chains that oppress the people. But never will they be able to subjugate its militant spirit. No. The descendents of Pelayo, of Cid and Padilla,* will never forget the glory and patriotism of their ancestors. But this war, citizens of Cuba, can expand, and the government of Spain, having to use all its resources and energies to preserve its own independence, will not be able to extend to its colonies, and particularly to us, that protection, care and attention to which you have been accustomed. The rumor is running and appears well-founded that in order to buy the neutrality of Great Britain in this war, and under the pretext of paying debts to that country incurred in former years for your utility, Spain has ceded to England, your rich and valiant island; and that there is already a squadron prepared with corresponding force to carry into effect the treaty and verify the cession.[88]

Although this notice did not indicate what the Cubans should do to preserve their liberties and integrity, it implied that serious

---

* Spain's outstanding epic hero, Ruy Díaz de Vivar, known to fame as the Cid, was a great liberating figure of the late eleventh century. The *Poema de mio Cid* (1150) is Spain's outstanding epic.

Pelayo was one of Spain's early heroic kings who, before he was elected as ruler, led a Spanish army to victory over the Muslims.

Padilla was a Spanish revolutionist of the 16th century.

action was needed. Meanwhile, in the discussions in the cells of *Soles y Rayos*, it was agreed that the news of the actual cession of Cuba to England would be the signal for the uprising. Posters were designed bearing the slogan, "Independencia o Muerte" ("Independence or Death").[39] Lemus prepared three proclamations which were to be issued, one after the other—the first, on the day of the uprising.* In these proclamations, Lemus set forth the reasons for the revolution and its objectives. In view of the significance of these documents, it is worth reprinting at some length the leading features of the first proclamation announcing the formation of the Republic of Cubanacán:

> Peoples of the World: You no longer see the political phenomenon which is presented to you in our apathetic and degrading quietude. We have started to march on the path of liberty and independence which alone can guide us to the temple of prosperity and glory. The Supreme Government will reside in the sovereign people of happy Cubanacán; and serene from today on, will be our sole masters and regulators of our employments, our industry and our friendship and commerce abroad. As the fortunate sons of the new Republics of Paraguay, Chile, Lima, Buenos Aires, Colombia and Mexico, full of honor, valor and justice, have shaken off the ancient and heavy yoke of servile dependence, so the valiant islanders of fertile Cubanacán, for the same causes, and to end the same scandalous abuse and suffering under Spanish rule, will make our country take the position that it merits among the nations of the world, augmenting the number of American Republics.
>
> Legitimate children of my beloved country: Through my accredited patriotism, and through my exalted love of independence, I have committed myself to the glorious task which happily I have begun to carry out . . . to free us all today of the heavy links of servitude. . . . Dedicate yourselves zealously to seek for our villages and fields those men, who by their honesty and patriotism, deserve to represent us in a legislative assembly which will constitute the Republic, making for our eternal happiness, laws adapted to our temperament, character and circumstances. . . . Beloved country: With what small cost we can concede to you such a great good, a happiness which envelops the future of each one of your children. . . . No, my country, none of

---

* The date on which Lemus planned to announce the uprising cannot be determined with accuracy, but the fact that he had prepared the three proclamations by the end of July, 1823, indicates that the revolution was to start some time in August. The proclamations were undated.

your children could *be* traitors or indifferent to your faith. To all of them you have given being—all wish your independence and liberty, and putting away only from your noble breasts the unworthy idea of vengeance, all will steep their swords in the blood of the tyrant who attempts to take away your prescribed rights.

Spaniards: . . . from today on, we consider you as the rest of the human species—*Friends in Peace, Enemies in War.* We do not wish to part from your friendship, nor to break the sweet ties of language, blood and religion. But never will we return to your dependence, nor to that of any other nation. Thus we have sworn before the great God of the Universe: *We will lose our lives or we will free our country from all foreign domination.*

Sons of Cubanacán: Keep on with the shining enterprise which we have begun. We have nothing to fear. For even if some nations deny us the abundant help and powerful protection which now with an open hand they offer us, we are strong in number and spirit. Everything abounds in our country. The Spaniards who live in it will not commit the folly of making themselves our enemies, risking their property and lives. They, like other immigrants, will seek to better their lot among us; since there is no man so stupid and ignorant who does not distinguish the difference between the equitable laws of a Republic and the oppressive and ferocious ones of an absolute empire. The tyrant Ferdinand returns to command despotically in unfortunate Spain where the cries of the victims of the Inquisition and of those in the royal dungeons are heard; and he will do away with anyone who has dared to love liberty. What recourse remains then to the Spaniards on this (Cuban) soil? Even if for love of Spain they do not welcome the independence of this island, they will gain our affection by rendering honorable obedience to the laws of our Republic. . . .

Cubanacán: Let us make known to the entire world our pledges to get rid of ridiculous ranks and hierarchies that foster arrogance and ignorance and are opposite to the virtuous character of free men. We do not recognize any other distinction than that owed to true merit. *Let us treat gently those unfortunate slaves, alleviating their horrifying destiny while the representatives of our country propose the means of happy redemption, without prejudice against individual interests. They are the children of our own God.*

Ministers of the Altar: You who of all inhabitants of my country merit the highest consideration. Preach to all the morality of the evangel, the love of our Republic, the horror of transgressions, and

obedience to the laws. Do not forget that the law of the good Jesus
is purely Republican. . . .

The hour has arrived. Fulfill your pledges, and speak the oath:
"Never expect pity from the Republican bayonets."

General Military Headquarters of Guadalupe, on the walls of
Havana, at . . . the . . . 1823. Press of the Republican Government of
Cubanacán.[40]

What is especially significant in this document is the fact that
Lemus dealt with the question of slavery in Cuba. Clearly, the new
Republic planned to abolish slavery, with compensation to the
owners of the slaves, and to allow the Negro a place in the government of Cuba. ("We do not recognize any other distinction than
that owed to true merit.") Thus Lemus brushed aside the pretexts
of the slaveowners that the slaves were "ignorant and debased,"
totally unprepared for liberty and a role in a Cuban Republic.
Indeed, in the messages to the slaves, Lemus had already appealed
to them to join in the fight for independence and liberty, prom-
ising them that the Republic would abolish slavery.[41] In this respect, at least, Lemus's program was in advance of nearly all of
the independence movements in the former Spanish colonies.[42]

In his second and third proclamations, Lemus dealt with the report that Spain had sold the island of Cuba to England; warned
the King of Spain that it would be useless to try to extirpate the
independence movement in Cuba;* and spelled out more specifically the aims of the Republic:

Cubanacanos: The whole world knows that our country has already reached the stage where its political transformation is inevitable. That is the only means of re-establishing among its sons moral
customs, of bettering the public administration, by appointing men
of capacity and virtue, and of guaranteeing a good income, well distributed, without the burdens which tyrannically oppress the day
laborer, the farm hand and the seaman. Public education must be
provided free from false notions, and propagating the true physical
and moral principles for each individual. . . .

Inhabitants of my country: Neither the army which follows me,

* "We are ready to live free and independent of all nations and neither the
absolute Government nor the Constitutional Government of Spain, can ever
hope again to make us the sad objects of their negotiations."

nor I, have been impelled by any kind of selfish ambition, nor any interest other than our common salvation and happiness. We long for a representative government under whose orders all the soldiers of this Republic and I will put ourselves; and we ask for our sacrifices no other recompense than the inward joy of a noble and virtuous conscience. . . . Thus they swear with me, before the God of the Armies, the valiant ones who stand with me in this glorious enterprise. . . .

"On the walls of Havana. . . . José Francisco Lemus . . . Press of the Government of the Republic of Cubanacán."[43]

While Lemus and his followers were preparing for the day when the proclamations would be issued, the Spanish authorities were preparing to smash the conspiracy. Spies of Captain General Vives had infiltrated the secret revolutionary society. In a letter to the government in Madrid, transmitting their information, Vives characterizes the conspiracy as the work of secret agents from abroad seeking to stir up a race war in Cuba. "They have been able to seduce with all their arts and mysteries, only many youths, men of the field, and a few Negroes on whom they count to raise the cry of independence ('el grito de independencia')." He had not discovered that any of the important planters, "from whom I have continually received the utmost proofs of loyalty to the nation, adherence to the government of His Majesty, and love of order," were implicated. "They know that the least intranquillity would put an end to the prosperity of the island and that the wealth of this soil is founded on the existing conditions, and, while the fallacious doctrines and democratic principles unveiled in the discussions of the different Republics which are constituted on the Continent have hallucinated many heedless men and stimulated the ambitions of young Cubans, they have not affected the loyalty of the substantial members of Cuban society."[44] It is clear from Vives' dispatch that the conspiracy was widespread; that it had the support of the intellectuals, the youth, the poorer classes and the Negro population, and that its only opposition came from the wealthy slaveholding class.

A few days before he believed the uprising was to take place, Vives closed in. Two dozen of the leaders, including Lemus and a free Negro, were seized; but many of the conspirators were able to flee the country.* Among them was José María Heredia who escaped to the United States, and then went to Mexica where he spent the remainder of his life.** With many of the leaders suffering capture or exile, the conspiracy collapsed.[45]

But Vives knew that the roots of the movement were imbedded in Cuban soil. He pointed out to the government in Spain that the situation in Cuba remained dangerous because of the presence of so many slaves and free people of color, and "where it is sure that after the outbreak of any revolution there cannot be any other ending than the extermination of one or the other of the two races as happened on the island of Santo Domingo." He had been fortunate in suppressing the conspiracy of the *Soles y Rayos* with the limited power he possessed, "but perhaps I will not be able to do it again without the necessary means to save the country if the government does not agree to the remedy I have indicated." Vives asked for extraordinary powers to govern the Cubans, particularly the "facultades omnímodas" granted to governors of a besieged fortress.[46]

Although Vives did not receive this unlimited dictatorial power until 1825, he clamped an iron hand on the island. The press was completely censored, and possession of liberal literature, political tracts of any nature, was forbidden. Hundreds of liberal Cubans fled to escape death or imprisonment. Father Félix Varela, condemned to death by Spain, found refuge in the United States, where he lived in exile until his death in 1853, without ever returning to Cuba. Now a decided adherent of independence, Varela began publishing in New York, in 1824, a newspaper favoring the independence cause. Called *El Habanero*, it was brought to Cuba and distributed secretly in the island.[47]

In 1824, a conspiracy led by Ensign Gasper A. Rodríguez was

---

* Several uprisings of slaves in sugar mills did take place, but they were quickly crushed. (Garrigó, *op. cit.*, vol. II, p. 140.)
** Though exiled, Heredia remained, through his revolutionary poems, a symbol of the struggle for Cuban independence. He died at Toluca, Mexico, on May 7, 1839. He is best known in the United States for his poem "Ode to Niagara," one of three of his poems translated into English by William Cullen Bryant.

discovered and suppressed. Vives once again appealed for unlimited powers, emphasizing that in the latest conspiracy, the slaves had once again been urged to rebel. This time the Spanish government heeded his plea. In 1825 Vives was given unlimited dictatorial powers, and the Permanent Executive Military Commission was established to supersede the courts. Now commerce, travel, social affairs, even the most personal activities, were placed under the scrutiny of the military. A strict censorship was exercised over all discussions in the press; public meetings were banned; mention of the "inciting word" independence, even a discussion of the evils of slavery, were forbidden, as was any public reference to political reform; and careful scrutiny limited the entry of foreigners. A special proclamation on April 8, 1826, prohibited the importation of "all books which oppose the Catholic religion, the royalty, rights and prerogatives of the sovereign, or which, in any other manner, defend the rebellion of vassals or nations."[48]

Forty thousand veteran Spanish troops terrorized the island. No Cuban officers were allowed in the army, no Cuban officials in the treasury, customs, and the judicial departments. Spies and informers penetrated all ranks of society and reported suspected persons; those who refused to pay blackmail were frequently condemned to solitary confinement in dungeons for life, without hearings or knowledge by their relatives of their whereabouts.

Many revolutionary leaders were imprisoned, including members of the distinguished and wealthy Creole families of Betancourt, Sánchez, and Agüero. Vives even sent an assassin to Philadelphia to kill Varela. The plot failed. But Varela, fearing that his appeals for independence might incite rash and futile revolts by the Cuban youth who revered him; and now convinced that the wealthy Cuban planters, determined to keep their slaves, would not join a revolutionary movement,—stopped publishing *El Habanero* in 1826, and gave up political activity.[49]

Others, however, took up the struggle where Varela and Lemus had left it. Although the Masonic lodges had been prohibited by a Royal Order of 1824, they continued clandestine activity in behalf of independence. They and others in the struggle were inspired to face the terror by such leaflets, smuggled into Cuba from Colombia:

Republic of Colombia
Habaneros.
Brothers of the Island of Cuba. Colombia has known your glorious efforts. She will soon help you with all her power. The reign of the tyrants is finished in America. Cuba is called to the independent position which she must occupy among the nations of the universe. The Liberator of Colombia and her soldiers salute you amicably and fraternally.[50]

On April 29, 1826, *Niles' Weekly Register* carried the terse announcement: "Two young men, natives of (Puerto) Príncipe, in the island of Cuba, who had just arrived from the republic of Colombia, were condemned to death and hung at (Puerto) Príncipe on the 16th ult. for attempting to revolutionize the country."[51] The two young men, nameless in the account, were the Camagüeyans, Manuel Andrés Sánchez, a free Negro, and Francisco de Agüero y Velazco. Their fervor for the independence of Cuba had led them to emigrate, first to the United States, and then to Colombia, with the purpose of preparing an invasion of Cuba. At meetings in Jamaica with two Colombian Colonels, and Sévère Courtois, the Haitian commander of the Colombian navy, a plan was worked out for the two Cubans to launch a revolutionary uprising in Cuba which would be backed by an expedition from Colombia.

Sánchez and Agüero landed February 19, 1826, equipped with arms supplied by Colombia, on the southern coast of Camagüey, near Santa Cruz del Sur. Hiding in a mill in the vicinity of Puerto Príncipe, they established contacts with secret revolutionary societies, and with free Negroes and slaves in the nearby plantations and mills. Their activity was discovered by Vives' spies, and they were captured.

Now Vives had a chance to show why he had wanted extraordinary powers. All previous conspirators had been tried by civil tribunals and thus their lives had been spared. But in 1825 the Permanent Executive Commission had superseded the courts. Agüero and Sánchez, the first conspirators tried under this new regime, were condemned to death, and shot in Puerto Príncipe on March 16, 1826. These two young Cubans, one white, the other Negro, became the first martyrs of Cuban independence.*[52]

The last conspiracy of the decade, 1820–1830, was that of *Gran Legión del Aguila Negra* (The Grand Legion of the Black Eagle). Formed as a secret society by Cuban exiles in Mexico and Colombia, the "Black Eagle" began plotting independence in Cuba in 1827. Within a year, it had branches in Havana, Guanajay, Remedios, and other parts of the island. Learning from the lessons of the past, the movement sought to prevent the penetration of its ranks by Vives' spies. Though the conspiracy was finally discovered and violently suppressed in 1830, the authorities never learned who were the real leaders. A prominent lawyer of Havana, Manuel Rojo, was suspected of being the head but it was never definitely proved. The Permanent Executive Commission sentenced six of the conspirators, and many others suspected of being connected with the movement, to prison. Possibly because he could not be certain of the exact role played by the condemned men, Vives commuted the death sentences to prison terms.[53]

Although little is known about the "Black Eagle" conspiracy, two things appear certain: one was that slaves were included in the movement, and the other that, though some wealthy Creoles were involved, the Cuban planter-slave interests did not support this independence movement.[54]

The Spanish authorities had succeeded in destroying every movement seeking independence. But this success was not won solely by their own might. In large part, the failure of the conspiracies was due to the opposition of the wealthy planter, slaveowning class. Independence was only possible through insurrection, but since any revolutionary uprising would endanger their hold over their slaves, these classes, both actively or passively collaborated

* There were, of course, others who died in prison. *Niles' Weekly Register* of June 17, 1820, carried the following report: "Gen. Renevales died in the Morro Castle on the 22nd ult. He had of late resided in New Orleans, but proceeded to Havana just after the news of the recent events in Spain [the liberal revolution]. He was arrested there with several other officers, on a charge of having attempted a conspiracy to overthrow the present government, and establish the independence of Cuba." (vol. XVII, June 17, 1820, p. 286.)

with the Spanish authorities, despite their despotic rule. The slave owners were not disposed, even if they chafed under the political despotism, even if they sympathized with some of the objectives of the Creole leaders in the newly-formed Hispanic-American Republics, to follow a revolutionary path that might curtail their profits or incur economic ruin. Not only did they withhold support from the independence movements of this period, but they urged the Spanish authorities to use violent means to crush the conspiracies.

The opposition of the slaveholding class practically sealed the fate of every independence movement of this decade. But, in no small measure, this outcome was also due to the reactionary role played by the government of the United States, a role too frequently obscured in myths perpetuated in American history textbooks, picturing the government of the first Republic in the New World as an ally of all of the early Latin American independence movements. Let us now analyze the role of the United States.

chapter 7

EMERGENCE OF UNITED STATES POLICY
TOWARD CUBA, 1800–1823

We have shown the growth of trade relations between Cuba and the United States, and how closely the two became interlinked commercially, despite Spanish efforts to prevent and severely limit this relationship. But this is only part of the story. From the time of Thomas Jefferson's first administration in 1801, influential elements in the United States regarded the "Pearl of the Antilles" with an interest that went beyond mere trade relations. They argued that Cuba, lying as it did across the opening of the Gulf of Mexico, and almost within sight of Florida, could serve, in American hands, as a bulwark of defense; while in other hands it constituted a danger. A strong power in possession of Cuba, they argued, would control the trade routes, cut off American trade with the West Indies, block the Mississippi and threaten the eastern coast of the United States. To stave off a future menace, the United States should take steps *now* to acquire Cuba.[1]

Thus, from the beginning of the nineteenth century, Cuba's geographical proximity to the United States was to be raised as the excuse for a policy of dominating the island in the interest of her more powerful neighbor.

Of all Americans who looked across to Cuba in this early period, it was Jefferson who looked most longingly. In that, as in some other respects, the story of Thomas Jefferson, who "more than any other American . . . impressed himself on the nation's future,"[2] and stands as a vital and enduring symbol of democracy, shows some blemishes. Although his words in the Declaration of Independence inspired oppressed people the world over, and especially in Latin America, he was no friend of Cuban independence. On

124

the contrary, as the National Congress of Cuban historians put it in 1947: "The precursor of the annexation of our island to the United States was President Thomas Jefferson . . . (who was) a constant spokesman for incorporation of Cuba into the Union."[3]

As far back as 1793, Jefferson had expressed his annoyance over Spain's restrictions on American trade with her colonies, and his irritation increased with the passing years.[4] Soon after the Louisiana Purchase of 1803, convinced that Spain would never allow free and unlimited trade between the United States and Cuba, Jefferson began to think of ways of acquiring the island. At his suggestion, American agents in Cuba were told to watch the events of political significance for any signs of interest in union with the United States.[5] In November, 1805, Jefferson told the British Minister in Washington that the United States would not be deterred from seizing Florida by the risk of war with Spain. In that case "East and West Florida and successively the Island of Cuba . . . would be an easy conquest."[6] Jefferson even welcomed the idea of war with Spain, since then, as he informed Madison, Cuba could be seized without much difficulty.[7]

Although Jefferson continued corresponding and scheming about acquiring Cuba,[8] no step was taken towards annexing the island before 1808. In the spring of that year, while the Spanish people were at war with France to prevent the imposition of Joseph Bonaparte as their king, Jefferson sent General James Wilkinson to Cuba to sound out its Captain General Someruelos. To him Wilkinson expressed the sympathy of the United States for Spain but commented that there was an unabridgeable abyss between the mother country and her colonies, and hinted Someruelos's interests would best be advanced if he facilitated the transfer of Cuba to the United States.

Someruelos was not seduced, and Wilkinson's mission was a failure.[9] But Spain realized that this was not to be the end of American designs on the Spanish colonies. In a report to Havana, sent by the Spanish chargé d'affaires in the United States to the Minister of State in Madrid, the opinion was expressed that the Wilkinson mission was part of a grand scheme to achieve "a reunion of the kingdom of Mexico and the Islands of Cuba and Puerto Rico under these United States."[10]

Jefferson left the presidency in 1809, but he continued to give advice as to how the United States might acquire Cuba. He counselled President Madison, his successor, to prepare for a deal with Napoleon whereby he would give Cuba to the United States in return for being given a free hand in his plans for empire in Spanish America.* "That would be a price," he wrote in April, 1809, "and I would immediately erect a column on the southernmost limit of Cuba, and inscribe on it a *ne plus ultra* as to us in that direction."[11] Cuba, in other words, would be the limit of American acquisitions to the South—a vain hope as we shall see.

Madison did not share Jefferson's confidence in such an arrangement with Napoleon. (Even Jefferson conceded that Napoleon's policy was "so crooked that it eludes conjectures.") He believed Napoleon might offer the Floridas for such a concession, but had designs on Cuba for himself, and was planning to use the French emigrés from Haiti toward that end.**[12] Moreover, while Jefferson, strangely enough, was certain that "Cuba can be defended by us without a navy,"[13] Madison was more realistic. He knew that if the United States occupied the island, our naval power was then too weak to hold it against England which, desiring it for herself, would never consent to the United States acquiring it.[14] The best that could be accomplished, under the circumstances, was to uphold the sovereignty of a weak country like Spain over Cuba, to permit no strong country to occupy it,† and to maintain the doctrine of

* The cession of the Floridas would also be part of the deal, but Jefferson did not consider this as really part of the "price" Napoleon should pay "because they are ours in the first moment of the first war." (Andrew A. Lipscomb and Albert Ellery Bergh, editors, *The Writings of Thomas Jefferson*, Washington, 1904, vol. XII, p. 274).

** In March, 1809, a minor disturbance, fomented in Cuba by French residents, was promptly put down. Later, a Bonapartist agent, Alemán de Peña, was seized in Havana with some thirty letters, signed by Joseph Bonaparte, in his possession. He was executed for treason. (Justo Zaragoza, *Las insurrecciones en Cuba*, Madrid, 1872, vol. I, pp. 190–91.)

† This was part of the general policy of the United States toward the West Indies and Caribbean regions which, according to Professor J. Fred Rippy, had begun to take shape in 1810, and "accords with a maxim almost as unchanging as a law of mathematics or physics. That maxim is the domination of the area at least to the extent deemed necessary to prevent its domination by any other first rate power." (Foreword to Ludwell Lee Montague, *Haiti and the United States, 1714–1938*, Durham, N. Car., 1940, p. v.)

the United States' paramount interest in the island while waiting for conditions more advantageous for its acquisition. In 1810 Madison instructed William Pinckney in London to make it known that:

> The position of Cuba gives the United States so deep an interest in the destiny even of that Island, that although they might be an inactive, they could not be a satisfied spectator at its falling under any European Government, which might make a fulcrum of that position against the commerce and security of the United States.[15]

Commenting on Madison's instructions, the National Congress of Cuban historians declared in 1947: "From then on, and continually, Yankee policy in respect to Cuba was support for the continuation of Spanish sovereignty while it could not be convenient for the island to be part of the North American Union."[16]

Although Madison was more cautious than Jefferson, he did not abandon the idea of annexing Cuba. William Shaler, appointed in 1810 as consul in Havana, was instructed to make it known that his government would not permit any Spanish territory to come under the sway of any other foreign power. But at the same time Shaler was instructed to sound out the disposition of Cubans toward becoming part of the United States.[17] It is clear from the instructions that Shaler was sent to Cuba to foment annexation.[18]

Shaler, a pronounced expansionist, lost no time in contacting annexationist elements in Cuba, with a view to organizing a conspiracy in favor of annexation. At first he reported some success. The planters "seem to regard a close connection with us as necessary for their happiness and prosperity."[19] Frightened by the abolitionist proposals in the Cortes at Cádiz, a section of the wealthy Creole planters authorized José de Arango and Núñez del Castillo to confer with Shaler on the possibilities of Cuban annexation by the United States. They told Shaler that the wealthy planters preferred annexation to the United States where slavery would be protected, to the risk of losing their property through the threatened legislation. The United States would also gain if Cuba were to "become one of the states in the Union. Our situation guarantees the navigation of the Mississippi; and our harbors, our soil, our climate, offer incredible resources to commerce and agriculture, and when these advantageous qualities of our island come to be developed by such a government as yours, they would besides making us rich and happy, add incalculably to your national wealth and political importance."[20]

But nothing came of the conspiracy. The Cortes, for one thing, turned down the abolitionist proposals. For another, Arango informed Shaler that the planters were frightened that Britain would use a Cuban revolt for annexation to the United States as an excuse to occupy the island. This would create a situation of "anarchy," since the British occupation would certainly arouse the slaves to revolt. To prevent disorder, it was essential that the revolting planters "have the aid of a powerful friend to act in concert with them and give force and dignity to their measures." Before acting, therefore, the planters asked for a guarantee from the United States that she would support their revolt with military forces sufficient to break a British blockade of the island.[21]

Shaler offered such a guarantee. "I observed," he wrote to Secretary of State James Monroe from Havana on December 6, 1811, "that in case of the event he [Arango] dreaded, it would be the policy of the United States to give them the necessary aid, and I added, 'Your friends should rely with confidence on the American people. We are able to support and protect you in all cases, if you are true to yourselves.' "[22] But the Madison administration, facing difficulties with England on other fronts, was not prepared to underwrite Shaler's guarantee. Receiving no assurance from Washington, the timid Creole planters abandoned the annexation project.[23]

Shaler's activities had aroused suspicions, and he was arrested in November, 1811, and then asked to leave Cuba. Before departing, Shaler notified Someruelos that the United States was satisfied with a continuation of the existing status of Cuba, that is, as a possession of Spain, that it would never allow the island to pass into the hands of another power, and that the Spanish officials should appeal to the government of the United States for aid and protection whenever such a danger approached.[24]

Shaler's mission illustrated the basic policy of the United States toward Cuba during this period. Shaler, it will be recalled, also reported to Washington the existence of a revolutionary group in

Cuba advocating independence for the island and abolition of slavery, some of whose members were Negroes. This was the conspiracy led by Román de la Luz and Joaquín Infante. But he established no contacts with this movement and did nothing to encourage it.[25] On the other hand, annexation to the United States was encouraged, and when this proved to be unpromising, possession of the island by Spain was virtually guaranteed.

Shortly after leaving Cuba, Shaler submitted to the State Department a plan for a confederation of the Latin American States. Part of the plan was to divide the Caribbean islands between England and the United States, the Floridas and Cuba falling to the latter.[26]

Shaler's was not the only plan for a confederation of Spanish colonies. Another was proposed by José Alvarez de Toledo, a native of Cuba who had been a deputy to the Spanish Cortes.* Facing arrest for plotting with revolutionary forces in Santo Domingo, Toledo fled to the United States. In November, 1811, he communicated his presence in Philadelphia to Secretary of State Monroe and asked for an interview. He was referred to Alexander Dallas, Secretary of the Treasury, who had several interviews with him, and then arranged for him to see Monroe in Washington.

Pointing to the growth of British commercial relations with the Spanish West Indies, Toledo proposed to go to Cuba with United States help, and begin a revolt to establish an independent Cuban government linked to the United States, commercially at first, and afterwards politically, through annexation. "I am ready to face any danger for the welfare of my native land and these United States," Toledo declared dramatically. He also planned to use his native island as a base for the formation of an Antillean confederation which would include Cuba, Puerto Rico, and Santo Domingo, all three eventually to be annexed to the United States. Puerto Rico, he was convinced, would quickly follow in the wake of Cuba once that island transferred its allegiance from Spain.

With the immediate aim of preventing British commercial su-

* Toledo, an officer in the Spanish navy, was in Cádiz when the Cortes met, and was chosen a deputy from the island of Santo Domingo, since there was not present in the city any citizen of that island.

premacy in the West Indies, and with the ultimate goal of annexing the islands, Monroe, with Madison's approval, encouraged Toledo. Toledo was set to leave "for the execution of the project," but the outbreak of hostilities between the United States and Great Britain in 1812 prevented Monroe from providing effective support. Toledo left, instead, to join Mexican revolutionists who were attempting to seize Texas from Spain. Later he turned royalist, became a spy in the service of the Spanish government, received a pardon, and returned to Spain in 1817.[27]

These plots and conspiracies in the United States did not escape the notice of the Spanish agents. On April 1, 1812, Don Luis Onís, Spanish Minister in the United States (though still not officially recognized as such by the American government) informed the Viceroy of New Spain that, with each passing day, "the ambitious ideas of this republic increase . . . and a map has already been prepared [in government circles] . . . which includes within these limits the island of Cuba, as a natural possession of this republic."[28]

During the War of 1812, the American commander on the Gulf Coast proposed an attack on Havana to prevent the British from using it as a base. A small naval force of 3,000 men, he felt, would suffice. But Madison rejected the proposal; the administration had enough problems on its hands without getting involved in a conflict with Spain.[29]

For several years after the War of 1812, American policy toward Cuba was strongly influenced by the fact that the island was enjoying considerable prosperity while trade declined in the rest of Spanish America, racked by the struggle for independence. Spain interdicted all commerce with the revolted Latin-American colonies, and though it lacked the sea power to enforce its blockade, it commissioned swarms of privateers, at Puerto Rico and Cuba, to prey on U.S. commerce with Spanish America.[30] U.S. trade with the newly-established republics was thus seriously reduced, and this made the increasing trade with Cuba (and to a lesser extent with Puerto Rico) doubly important. Under these circumstances, it is not surprising that the mercantile, shipping and other interests engaged in the Cuban trade should insist that nothing be done to anger Spain and risk the imposition of restrictions on trade with the island. Among the acts specifically warned against were: recognition of the independence of the new Spanish American republics, despite the public clamor for such a step; war with Spain over the Florida question; and encouraging annexationist and independence movements in Cuba.

Recognition for the new Spanish American nations was a moot issue. From the beginnings of the revolt of 1810, most of the people of the United States had called upon the government to aid the struggle for independence from Spain and recognize the newly-established republics. The 1810 Fourth of July celebration of the Tammany Society in New York, then a progressive organization, toasted: "The people of South America—Embarked in the cause of liberty, for the support of which, like the Congress of '76, they have pledged their lives, their fortunes, and their sacred honor—may we shortly hail them a republic free, sovereign and independent."[81] This was only one of hundreds of such toasts offered in cities and towns throughout the country year after year,* usually calling upon the United States government to recognize these republics. By March, 1812, *Niles' Weekly Register*, a leading advocate of recognition, reported that the popular sentiment in its favor was having effect on Washington: "From the present aspect of affairs, it is more than probable that the United States will soon acknowledge the republics of South America as free, sovereign and independent states."[82]

But this proved wishful thinking. Ten years were to elapse before the United States granted official recognition. In vain the friends of the South American republics called for a change in official

---

* Here are three other typical examples:
"South America. We view her struggles with a friendly and fraternal eye, soon may she also take her equal station among the nations of the earth."
"Spanish America. May the shade of Washington hover about her armies, inspiring them with a spirit of perseverance, and may all who oppose them in their struggle for liberty, fall beneath the thunder of their arms."
"The Republics of South America—may their rising spirit of liberty be accompanied by Franklins to direct, Washingtons to defend, and Thomas Paines to invigorate, all their energies."
(Philadelphia *National Intelligencer*, July 16, 1811; Louisiana (Missouri) *Gazette*, July 25, 1811; Philadelphia *Aurora*, October 5, 1813.)

policy from that of strict neutrality, which it had adopted at the outbreak of the revolt against Spain, to that of recognition.*

"Can we," asked the progressive editor, William Ritchie, "who see them following in our steps, with wrongs infinitely greater, can we see them struggling without wishing them success, and almost resolving to hand them an arm to assist them?—No; we cannot have forgotten our cause, our own struggles, our own success: we cannot be insensible to the fruits we reap. We should be the last people in the world to be indifferent to the cause of the natives of Venezuela and Pernambuco—and with all our souls wish them success."[33]

But there were, unfortunately, citizens who did not "wish them success." There were conservative Americans who maintained that the people of South America were "unfit to be free," were too steeped in ignorance, stupidity, superstition, and clericalism ever to be able to govern themselves.[34] Some charged that the revolutions in Latin America were directed by "Jesuits in British pay," on the presumption that the Jesuits, disgruntled by their expulsion from Spanish dominions in the eighteenth century, had entered the employ of Great Britain to foment revolt in Hispanic America.[35] The conservative press played up massacres of the Spanish by "the fierce monster Bolívar and his band of assassins and thieves."[36] Others said that the "people of colour" were spreading "plunder, bloodshed, devastation and terror, throughout the unhappy region," and warned that successful revolutions against Spain would spark Negro slave revolts in the United States.[37] Under no circumstances, therefore, should the government of the United States recognize the newly-established governments in South America. "We are very much afraid," the *Southern Patriot* argued, "that the people of these provinces [of South America] are not duly prepared for the enjoyment of that great boon and blessing—*well regulated freedom.*"[38]

These attacks on a people whose struggle "resembles that which secured the Independence of this nation" infuriated progressive Americans.[39] William Duane, liberal publisher of the Philadelphia

* This policy of strict neutrality was adhered to by the United States from 1810 until recognition finally came on March 8, 1822.

Aurora, condemned "the hostility against South American independence which is insinuated into so many of our public newspapers," pointing out that "every falsehood uttered against them [the republics of South America], should be considered as an offense premeditated against every republic; an hostility to the cause of all mankind."[40] Hezekiah Niles, whose *Weekly Register* was a consistent champion of the South American Republics,* accused the press in the United States of having "enlisted on behalf of the European Spaniards. . . . The success of their arms is called *glorious news.* . . . How then, is it, that a gloomy silence prevails regarding the American Spaniards, and that a short flippant paragraph is only occasionally found respecting them?"[41] The New York *Columbian,* in an article captioned "Enemies of South American Independence," explained this discrepancy. The people of the United States, it pointed out, favored South American independence, and wanted their government to take any step within reason to help this cause, especially through recognition of the new republics. Unfortunately, the wishes of the people were not reflected in the majority of the newspapers nor in the government whose policy of neutrality pleased the reactionary Spanish monarchy. This reflected the influence of American slaveowners, frightened by revolutionary struggles in which Negroes participated, so close to the United States; merchants engaged in the trade with Cuba and Puerto Rico who wanted to appease Ferdinand of Spain in the hope that he would allow this trade to increase; and the administration in Washington which was ready to sacrifice the cause of the South American republics in order to maintain an atmosphere favorable to negotiations for the American acquisition of Florida from Spain.[42]

Historical research has disclosed that there was considerable truth

---

* Volume X of the *Weekly Register,* March to September, 1816, bore the following on the reverse side of the title page:
"To the
Patriots of MEXICO AND SOUTH AMERICA
   Contending for
LIBERTY AND INDEPENDENCE
   and to all others struggling to obtain
CIVIL AND RELIGIOUS FREEDOM
THE EDITOR DEDICATES THIS VOLUME OF
   THE WEEKLY REGISTER. . . ."

to each of these charges.[43] Here we need concern ourselves only with one of the influences mentioned by the New York *Columbian*— the role played by the mercantile interests. What Simón Bolívar called the "conduct of business arithmetic,"[44] in describing the policy of neutrality adopted by the United States government toward the Spanish American revolutions, can be especially applied to this role.

In 1818, there was published in Philadelphia an anonymous pamphlet entitled, *Spanish America and the United States, A View on the Active Commerce of the United States with the Spanish Colonies by a Merchant of Philadelphia*. The pamphlet stated bluntly that the trade with Spain and with the loyal Spanish colonies, especially Cuba, should be decisive in determining the policy of the United States. The author, who was James Yard, noted that 80,000 to 100,000 bbls. of flour were annually exported to Cuba, and 45,759 hhds. of molasses, and 78,000 hhds. of sugar imported. Was it wise, he asked, to jeopardize this trade by antagonizing Spain, especially when the trade with the independent areas of Spanish America was of so little consequence, and when the economic depression, which had already started in the United States, made continuation of the trade with the Spanish West Indies so vital?[45]

Yard's thesis was endorsed by leading men of wealth. Nicholas Biddle, the conservative Philadelphia merchant-banker, wrote to President Monroe in March, 1818 that he had helped Yard in preparing the pamphlet, and that though he conceded that "the hearts of the country" were in favor of recognizing the rebellious Spanish colonies, he urged continuation of the policy of neutrality in the interest of our trade with the loyal Spanish colonies. Whatever "high moral and political reasons" there might be for recognition of the rebels, "the hopes of great commercial advantages from the emancipation [of South America] are completely illusory. . . ." The only hope of commercial advantage lay in a policy of strict neutrality.[46]

In the Congressional debate on neutrality legislation, the same viewpoint was advanced. On January 24, 1817, Congressman Smith of Maryland, a spokesman for the flour industry and shipping interests of Baltimore, declared that recognition would involve us in a war with Spain and thus "would deprive us of the best customers we have." He dwelt on American trade with the loyal Spanish provinces, particularly the flour trade with Cuba, which alone justified our observance of strict neutrality.[47]

On August 19, 1818, the Maryland *Censor*, published in Baltimore, openly charged that the reason President Monroe and Secretary of State John Quincy Adams still refused to recognize the independent republics of Spanish America* was fear in government circles

> that a war with Spain would be the consequence of these [United] States recognizing the independent provinces of South America; and that such a war would produce ruin to the commerce of these states, with Cuba, Manilla [*sic*], Porto Rico, a part of St. Domingo, and other places still in the possession of the Spanish Monarch.

The paper stated that the fears were preposterous since Spain, by herself, would never be able to make war on the United States; and, as for the other maritime powers of Western Europe, none of them would help Spain in a war that might result in a restoration of Spanish commercial monopolies in the Western hemisphere. It then accused the "timid and selfish speculators in politics" of underestimating the desire of the people of the loyal Spanish colonies for independence and freedom:

> Is it for a moment to be imagined, that the inhabitants of the above mentioned islands, still groaning under the same sort of tyranny which their brethren of the continent have experienced and certainly better able than they, from their locality, to estimate the blessings of liberty and free intercourse with the world, can be indifferent spectators of what is passing on the continent? No, they feel the same ardent aspirations after independence. . . . It is a fact

---

* The reference was to the defeat by the administration's forces in Congress of a resolution, introduced by Henry Clay, Senator from Kentucky, calling upon the President to take the initial step in recognizing the independence of La Plata. The motion was defeated by 115 to 45. (*Annals of Congress*, 15th Cong., 1st Sess., vol. II, pp. 1500, 1590–91.) At a banquet in Lexington, Kentucky, a toast was given to the "45"—the forty-five who voted in favor of Clay's motion, and the Kentucky legislature passed a resolution demanding recognition of the former Spanish colonies. ". . . the people of this state," the resolution said in part, "view with the most lively emotion, the patriotic struggles of their South American republican brethren, to throw off and break in pieces the yoke of Spanish despotism. . . ." (*Niles' Weekly Register*, vol. XIV, June 20, 1818, p. 371.)

well ascertained that the flame of insurrection has occasionally broken out in some of these very islands. . . .

The article concluded with a call for a new policy on the part of the government:

> Away then with the pretended "standard of sober statistics," on which certain cold-blooded and dogmatical oracles of the coffee-house may found their narrow calculation of loss and gain. It is evident that the commerce of the United States with the Spanish possessions can lose nothing by the success of the patriots, or by those measures which may favour and hasten it; but on the contrary, have much to gain by the more liberal system of government and trade, which all the colonies, free from the Spanish yoke and monopolies, will not fail to adopt.[48]

But the mercantile interests engaged in the Cuban trade were more disposed to value a bird in hand than one in the bush of future trade relations. As Professor Arthur P. Whitaker notes, the majority of the shipowners and merchants opposed recognition by the United States of the independence of the Spanish American republics, "on the ground that it would bring a war with Spain which would disrupt the valuable commerce of the United States with loyal Cuba and expose its whole merchant marine to the depredations of British and other privateers operating under commissions from Spain."[49] In short, in the interest of preserving this "valuable commerce," they favored a policy of appeasing Spain. And this, the friends of the South American republics insisted, was precisely the policy pursued by the government of the United States:

> "Can anyone suppose," asked William Duane in 1819, "that the *Machiavelian* policy of the cabinet in Washington, has not been acceptable to the court of Madrid; that the direct and indirect hostility of the American government against the South Americans, has not been duly appreciated and applauded by the perfidious councils of Ferdinand VII? . . . . There are men at Madrid who are perfectly aware that the independence of South America must have been determined in six months, if the independent republic of North America had only acted with as much generosity and respect for the liberties of mankind as the monarchy of France thirty years ago [during our War for Independence]."[50]

Monroe, it appears, was at one point ready to take a stand to promote the independence not only of South America, but of all other possessions of Spain in America. According to Secretary of State Adams, on July 23, 1818, the President "very abruptly asked me to see Mr. Bagot [the British Minister to the United States], and propose through him to the British government an immediate cooperation between the United States and Great Britain to promote the independence of South America." When Adams asked what part of South America, Monroe replied, "All South America and Mexico and the islands included." Adams advised the President that he thought Great Britain was not yet prepared for a direct proposition, and "entering into details I immediately found it was a crude idea, which he immediately abandoned."[51]

Since Adams was then involved in a favored project, the acquisition of Florida from Spain, it is hardly surprising that he should have thrown cold water on the President's proposal. The policy of appeasing Spain paid off when the Florida or Trans-Continental Treaty was signed on February 22, 1819, with the United States agreeing, in return for Florida, to pay the claims of its own citizens against Spain up to a maximum of five million dollars. Although Spain did not receive from the United States "a pledge not to precipitate measures concerning South America," Monroe and Adams had hinted that the conclusion of the treaty would lead the United States to take no action hostile to Spain.*[52]

The issue of Cuba emerged sharply during the Florida negotiations. The imminent pushing of the American boundaries almost within view of the Cuban coast brought a hue and cry from the British press. The British journalists demanded that England take immediate possession of Cuba in order to balance the newest

* Mateo de la Serna, the Spanish chargé d'affaires in Washington, was not reassured. On December 24, 1819, a few months after the signing of the Florida Treaty, he wrote to the Minister of State in Madrid, commenting on what he called the "bloody enmity" of the United States to Spain. "I venture to assure your excellency that this [enmity] will not diminish even after His Majesty agrees to the cession and sacrifices which have been negotiated, and that as long as Spain owns a square foot of land to the North of the Isthmus of Panama there will not be a diminution, neither in the unjust spirit of ambition nor in the hungry and dissatisfied greediness for gold which has taken exclusive possession of the inhabitants of this Union." (Jerónimo Becker, *Historia de las relaciones exteriores de España durante el siglo XIX*, Madrid, 1924, vol. I, p. 479.)

American acquisition; only in this way could the American drive toward dominance in the Caribbean be halted.*[53] Since Spain and Great Britain were then engaged in secret negotiations concerning Cuba and the Spanish West Indies, American newspapers took it for granted that the outcome would be the cession of Cuba to England.[54] (Actually, as we have seen, the Anglo-Spanish negotiations related not to the cession of Cuba, or any other Spanish West Indies island to England, but to the suppression of the slave trade.) A number of newspapers immediately raised the cry that the United States should anticipate British designs by seizing Cuba.[55]

This cry grew louder when Spain refused to ratify the Florida treaty. But the merchants interested in Cuban trade immediately voiced opposition to an aggressive policy toward Spain. Trade with Cuba, in their opinion, was worth more than Florida.[56]

During this period of tension over Florida and Cuba, the news arrived in the United States that a revolt had taken place in Spain. *Niles' Weekly Register* observed on March 4, 1820 that there was no longer any need to worry about war with Spain. "Florida will naturally fall into our hands without an effort; and Cuba, we trust, will assume independence—which, much as we are opposed to alliances, we should be almost willing at once to guarantee, so immensely interesting to us is it that this valuable island should remain in its present weakness or be possessed by a friend."[57] Two months later, it was even more positive: "By the late change in Spain, our fears of the transfer of this invaluable island are allayed. The Cortes will not surrender its sovereignty; and with the present disposition of its inhabitants, the nature of their climate and means of defence, it will not be an easy matter to take it by force."[58]

By the fall of 1820, the entire matter of war over Cuba was academic. The rumors that England was about to acquire the island

---

* An outstanding example of this type of alarmist literature is J. Freeman Rattenbury's article, "Remarks on the Cession of the Floridas to the United States and on the Necessity of Acquiring the Island of Cuba by Great Britain." Rattenbury held that the United States would soon threaten Britain's dominance on the ocean. British possession of Cuba would be the only security against the ambitions of the U.S. If England did not secure the island it would soon fall to the United States, which would then threaten the British West Indies. (*The Pamphleteer*, vol. XV, pp. 262–80.)

from Spain had proved to be without foundation. And in October, 1820, the Florida treaty was formally ratified by Spain.

During the Florida negotiations, certain groups in the United States had been restraining their annexationist hopes, for fear of upsetting the apple cart of profitable trade by antagonizing Spain.[59] Now with the treaty of cession ratified, they took steps to establish contacts with pro-annexationist elements in Cuba.

The slaveowners in the United States took the lead. They were aware of the rise of independence sentiment in Cuba, and the accompanying threat of ending slavery in the island. Furthermore, they feared that if either England or France acquired Cuba, they would immediately liberate the slaves.[60] And an end to slavery in Cuba would have a revolutionary impact on the slave system in the United States. One of the reasons the slaveowners had been so anxious to acquire Florida was that its possession by the United States "forever precludes foreign emissaries from stirring up . . . negroes to rebellion."[61] But this bulwark would be lost if slavery ended in Cuba. It is important, in this connection, to bear in mind that the period following 1819 was marked by the number and extent of slave revolts in the United States, climaxed by the insurrection in the spring of 1822 in South Carolina, led by Denmark Vesey.[62] Annexation of Cuba to the United States would stave off the imminent danger of abolition in the island which, as one Southerner wrote, "would be deeply injurious to the interests of the South."[63]

As we have seen, the sentiment for independence dominated the period from 1820 to 1830. Indeed, in no period before 1868 was the sentiment stronger. Nevertheless, and, especially in the early years of the decade, there were Cuban annexationists who sought affiliation with the United States.

Actually, there is a close relationship between these two developments. As the growth of the independence movement incurred the danger of the liberation of the slaves, the Creole planters looked about for a power to defend their interests. Spain, under the liberal regime established by the revolt of 1820, was not such a power; moreover, as we have seen, the Spanish officials in Cuba as yet lacked the all-embracing authority to deal with the danger facing the planter-slave interests. At first, some planters toyed with the idea of annexation by Great Britain or France, but were deterred by the anti-slavery strength in both countries which were pledged to abolition. Similarly, the progress of the antislavery cause in Mexico and Colombia caused abandonment of annexationist activity in that direction.

To the Cuban planters, therefore, the United States became the only logical choice. Slavery not only existed in the United States, but its influence in American economic and political life was growing stronger. The Cuban planters knew that the Southern slaveowners were just as anxious as they to prevent the liberation of the slaves in Cuba. Finally, the official closing of the slave trade to Cuba in 1820, though unenforced, made the Cuban slaveowners see a special advantage in affiliation with the United States where, unlike Cuba, a thriving internal slave trade existed, supplied by the slave breeding states of Virginia and Maryland.[64]

Early in 1822, precisely at the time the independence conspiracy, *Los Soles y Rayos de Bolivar*, with its appeal for unity with Negroes, was making headway in Cuba, the pro-annexationists became active. In February, 1822, Senator C. A. Rodney of Delaware received a communication from John Warner, the American commercial agent at Havana, which was highly encouraging to annexationists in the United States. Warner's business partner, Mr. Castillo, "who is one of the first politicians of the island," informed him that "the natives which amount to three-fourths or ⅔ of the white inhabitants of the Island, are decidedly in favor of being attached to the *U.S.*—as a *state* not as a *colony*." Warner considered the time ripe to establish contacts with the annexationist leaders in Cuba, for which purpose he thought it advisable to send a naval force and competent negotiators to the island. The presence of war vessels in Cuban waters could be explained by referring to the current piratical activities against American commerce.[65]

From Warner's letter, which was passed on to President Monroe, American officials received an exaggerated idea of the number of Cubans who desired annexation to the United States. They were encouraged to make contact with the Cuban annexationists, which was done in the summer of 1822 by Captain James Biddle of the

U.S. frigate *Macedonia*, stationed near Cuba. Biddle informed Monroe in August that a mission of "several respectable and influential Cubans" was proceeding to Washington to seek an interview with the President "to know the views of our government" with respect to the island.

Biddle explained that the Creole interests these men represented would "long since have followed the example of their countrymen on the continent" in leading a revolt against Spain except for the fact that "any revolutionary movement" by the Creoles would have been opposed by the European Spaniards in Cuba, and, more important, that a civil war between the two parties of whites would have brought the end of slavery and "the ascendancy of the blacks." Annexation to the United States was the logical alternative, for it alone could unite both parties of whites in Cuba. England's policy toward slavery ruled out affiliation with that country while the bitter feeling of the European Spaniards against the rebellious mainland colonies ruled out any tie with Mexico or Colombia. "It is unquestionable that a connection with our government would be greatly preferred by both parties." In conclusion, Biddle advised Monroe that the United States, under these circumstances, could afford to move slowly, and not jump at the first Cuban offer.[66]

In September, a Cuban agent arrived in Washington, using the pseudonym "Mr. Sánchez,"* whose trustworthiness had been vouched for by Biddle. Sánchez offered annexation of Cuba to the United States in the name of the Creole planters.[67] Monroe called a cabinet meeting to consider his plan. The tenor of the cabinet discussion is recorded in the diary of John Quincy Adams. All members were agreed that the transfer of the island to England would be a great disaster, but they were in a quandary over what course to follow:

> The question was discussed what was to be done. Mr. Calhoun has a most ardent desire that the island of Cuba should become part of the United States, and says that Mr. Jefferson has the same. There are two dangers to be averted by the event; one, that the island should fall into the hands of Great Britain; the other, that it should be revolutionized by the Negroes. Calhoun says Mr.

---

* "Sánchez's" real identity is still not known.

Jefferson told him two years ago that we ought, at the first possible opportunity to take Cuba, though at the cost of a war with England; but as we are now not prepared for this, and as our great object must be to gain time, he thought we should answer this overture by dissuading them from their present purpose, and urging them to adhere at present to their connection with Spain.

Adams was opposed to any action that might precipitate war with England. For the present he suggested that the Cubans be told that the President had no authority to promise Cuba admission to the Union as a state and that, if such were within his power, "the proposal is of a nature which our relations of amity with Spain would not permit us to countenance." The official response rejected the offer of annexation on the grounds advanced by Adams, but was accompanied by another, more secret answer. The man through whom the Cuban offer was made was asked for more concrete information, particularly the actual strength of the annexationist movement in Cuba, and its chances of success.[68]

From the cabinet discussion and decision, it is clear that the majority of the cabinet favored acquiring the island, but acknowledged obstacles almost impossible to overcome at this time.[69] There was a good deal of skepticism about the glowing reports from American agents in Cuba, and about Sánchez's own estimate of the extent and maturity of the annexationist movement in the island. Clearly, any step towards annexing the island at this time was likely to precipitate what the United States was anxious to prevent: the intervention of European powers with the avowed purpose of restoring and reaffirming the power of Spain there, an intervention which would, in the end, lead to control of the island by either Great Britain or France.

That Calhoun should have been the most ardent partisan of annexation is not surprising, since the South Carolinian was expressing the viewpoint of the Southern slaveowners whose chief spokesman he was. Southern fear of a revolutionary movement in Cuba which would end in liberation of the slaves was clearly voiced in Calhoun's argument for annexation. Yet even he agreed that the time was not ripe for such a move.

Annexation was not abandoned; it was merely posponed. The

alternative was to keep Cuba, for the time being, in the hands of Spain, now a minor European power; to use every device to prevent her from selling or ceding the island to a European maritime power —Great Britain or France. The policies of the United States toward Cuba converged on the goal of keeping Spain in power until conditions were ripe for acquiring the island.

It is significant, finally, that no attention was paid in the cabinet meeting to the increasing evidence of the growth of independence activity in Cuba, in reports to the State Department.[70] Encouragement of the independence of the island was then no part of the policy of the United States.

When, in 1823, the French armies marched into Spain, commissioned by the "Holy Alliance" to eradicate liberalism and constitutionalism, the United States was forced to review its policy toward Cuba. There were two dangers now: on the one hand, it was feared that Cuba would be the price France would exact for restoring Spanish absolutism; on the other hand, should the British assist Spanish liberalism against the French and the other European absolutists with loans and other support, it was likely that they would demand Cuba as a reward. The presence of a British flotilla in the Caribbean, ostensibly to suppress piracy, all but proved to the American press that such a deal between England and the Spanish liberals was on. Though the British, through their minister in Washington, officially denied any designs on the island, the Americans were only partially satisfied.[71]

In March and April, 1823, when English designs were most suspected, further cabinet meetings were held to discuss the Cuban question. Calhoun was especially agitated over the prospect of England's acquisition of Cuba, and the danger that this would be followed by British action abolishing slavery there. He had advanced to a stronger position since the last cabinet discussion, and now advocated "war with England, *if* she means to take Cuba." Thompson favored urging the Cubans "to declare themselves independent, if they can maintain their independence." Adams took it "for granted that they cannot maintain their independence, and that this nation will not, and could not, prevent by war the British from obtaining possession of Cuba if they attempt to take it." There was some talk of calling Congress into special session to discuss the situation, but Adams dismissed the idea as absurd. "Memorandum— to be cool on this subject," he jotted down in his diary.[72]

No action was decided on, but it was agreed to seek more information on the subject. For this purpose, Thomas Randall was sent to Cuba to obtain information on the political condition of the island. He was not to commit himself on any question beyond saying "that the first wish of the government [of the United States] was for the continuance of Cuba in its political connection with Spain; and that it would be altogether averse to the transfer of the island to any other power." He was not to identify himself with any proposal suggesting American co-operation in changing the political condition of the people, but was to report to Adams any such proposal.[73] The official pretext for Randall's visit was that he had to obtain certain papers relating to Florida as provided for in the treaty of 1819.

It is doubtful that Adams was expressing the administration's fixed opinion when he told the cabinet that the United States would not risk war to prevent the British from taking Cuba. A month later, in his instructions to Hugh Nelson, the new Minister to Spain, Adams wrote: "The transfer of Cuba to Great Britain would be an event unpropitious to the interests of this Union. . . . The question both of our right and our power to prevent it, if necessary, by force, already obtrudes itself upon our councils, and the Administration is called upon, in the performance of its duties to the Nation, at least to use all the means within its competency to guard against it and forfend it."[74]

Since Nelson would be arriving in Spain while French troops were marching to overthrow the Spanish constitutionalists, Adams carefully instructed him what stand to take during the coming conflict. He used this opportunity to spell out the motives for American interest in Cuba and its determination to leave the way open for future annexation. Since this historical dispatch contains the essence of United States policy toward Cuba for many years to come, it deserves quotation at length:

> It may be taken for granted that the dominion of Spain upon the American continents, north and south, is irrevocably gone. But the islands of Cuba and Porto Rico still remain nominally, and so

far really dependent upon her, that she yet possesses the power of transferring her own dominion over them, together with the possession of them, to others. These islands are natural appendages of the North American continent, and one of them [Cuba] almost within sight of our shores, from a multitude of considerations has become an object of transcendent importance to the commercial and political interests of our Union. Its commanding position with reference to the Gulf of Mexico and the West Indian seas, its situation midway betweeen our southern coast and the island of Santo Domingo, its safe and capacious harbor of Havana, fronting a long line of our shores destitute of the same advantages, the nature of its productions and its wants, furnishing the supplies and needing the returns of a commerce immensely profitable and mutually beneficial, give it an importance in the sum of our national interests with which that of no other foreign territory can be compared, and little inferior to that which binds the different members of the Union together.

Such indeed are, between the interests of that island and of this country, the geographical, commercial, moral and political relations formed that in looking forward to the probable course of events for the short period of half a century, it is scarcely possible to resist the conviction that the annexation of Cuba to our Federal Republic will be indispensable to the continuance and integrity of the Union itself. . . . *There are laws of political as well as physical gravitation. And if an apple, severed by the tempest from its native tree, cannot choose but to fall to the ground, Cuba, forcibly disjoined from its own unnatural connection with Spain, and incapable of self support, can gravitate only toward the North American Union, which by the same law of nature cannot cast her off from her bosom.* . . .

But Adams told Nelson to say in Madrid, "that the wishes of your government are, that Cuba and Porto Rico may continue in connection with independent and constitutional Spain. You will add, that no countenance has been given to any projected plan of separation from Spain, which may have been formed in the island." Adams ended this voluminous memorandum, consisting of some 10,000 words, with a request for the admission of American consuls into Cuba and Puerto Rico.[75]

This is the policy scornfully referred to by almost all Cubans as "la fruta madura" ("the ripe fruit")—a policy which, in the words of the Congress of Cuban historians of 1947, meant that the United States was "determined to annex the island, but was willing to wait patiently until Cuba would gravitate by necessity to the North American state, at which time it would be impossible not to take her to her bosom."[76]

Adams, however, was not the only leading American statesman of this period to advocate the "fruta madura" policy. In April, 1823, at a cabinet meeting when the Cuban question was under consideration, it was recommended that a proposal be made to England for a mutual renunciation of annexationist designs on Cuba. But both Calhoun and Adams objected to it as one that would bind the United States in the future, and their objections won out. Jefferson endorsed this decision. Having learned, through an interview with a Cuban named Miralla, that the Creoles would oppose any connection with England, Jefferson felt that the United States was under no obligation to give England, gratis, an interest she did not have, while tying the hands of this country. "It is better then," he wrote to Monroe in language reflecting the "fruta madura" policy, "to lie still in readiness to receive that interesting incorporation when solicited by herself. For, certainly, her addition to our confederacy is exactly what is wanting to round out our power as a nation to the point of its utmost interest."[77]

In his reply, Monroe was even more blunt:

> I have always concurr'd with you in the sentiment, that too much importance could not be attached to the Island, and that we ought if possible, to incorporate it into our union, availing ourselves of the most favorable moment for it, hoping also that one would arrive, when it might be done, without a rupture with Spain or any other power. [78]

Thus when the proposal of mutual renunciation was made, it came from England. In the summer of 1823, George Canning, the British Foreign Minister, made his famous proposal to the American Minister in London, Richard Rush, which eventually resulted in the enunciation of the Monroe Doctrine. Canning, in a confidential letter, suggested a joint Anglo-American declaration to the effect that the recovery of the South American colonies by Spain was hopeless, that neither England nor America aimed at the possession of any of them for herself; and they would not view the transfer of any portion of them to any other power with indifference. Although it was not mentioned specifically, it is well known that the future of Cuba loomed large in the minds of the statesmen of both countries.[79]

Jefferson, whose advice was sought by President Monroe, reluctantly advocated acceptance of Canning's proposal for joint action, since it was apparent to him that Cuba could not be gained except at the price of war. But he rather sadly added: "I candidly confess that I have ever looked on Cuba as the most interesting addition which could ever be made to our system of states." Madison also recommended acceptance of the proposal, but his question—"Does it exclude further views of acquiring Porto Rico, etc., as well as Cuba?"—indicates a hope that it was still possible to restrict the proposal to colonies which had already revolted.[80]

But Adams was certain that England would oppose European interference in Spanish America, and, in any case, believed that there was no more chance "that the Holy Allies will restore the Spanish dominion upon the American continent than that the Chimborazo [One of the highest peaks in the Americas] will sink beneath the ocean." He, therefore, refused to bargain away the future propects of annexation by joining in Canning's self-denying declaration. As he wrote in his diary, the inhabitants of either Cuba or Texas "may exercise their primitive rights, and solicit a union with us. They will certainly do no such thing to Great Britain. By joining with her, therefore, in her proposed declaration, we give her a substantial and perhaps inconvenient pledge against ourselves, and really obtain nothing in return. . . . We should at least keep ourselves free to act as emergencies arise, and not tie ourselves down to any principle which might immediately be brought against ourselves."[81] In plainer words: in order to leave the way open to future annexation, it was necessary for the Monroe administration to reject Canning's proposal.

With Adams carrying the day, Canning was informed that, since both countries understood the necessity of a declaration against the interference of the European powers with South America by force, it would be better for them to act separately.[82] Each country then enunciated its policy unilaterally. According to Professor William R. Manning, the action taken by the American government was due to the desire "to avoid doing anything that would make it impossible to accept Cuba in case the laws of political gravitation should cast that island in the bosom of the United States."[83]

In his message to Congress on December 2, 1823, Monroe enunciated the doctrine that now bears his name. It opened with the statement that the American continents "by the free and independent condition which they have assumed and maintain, are henceforth not to be considered as subjects for future colonization by any European powers"; it further stated that the United States would not meddle with European affairs; finally, dealing with the immediate crisis, it declared that any attempt by the European powers "to extend their system to any portion of this hemisphere" would be viewed by the United States "as dangerous to our peace and safety."

> With the existing colonies or dependencies of any European power we have not interfered and shall not interfere. But with the Governments who have declared their independence and maintained it, and whose independence we have . . . acknowledged, we could not view any interposition for the purpose of oppressing them, or controlling in any other manner their destiny, by any European power in any other light than as the manifestation of an unfriendly disposition toward the United States."[84]

Monroe's message did not enunciate the "no-transfer" principle— that the United States would not recognize or acquiesce in any transfer of American territory from one non-American power to another—but it was soon to become associated with the Monroe Doctrine.[85] It was to be asserted not only to prevent Britain or France from taking Cuba, but to prevent any change in the island's status.

Although it was announced unilaterally by the United States and was never incorporated into law, treaty or international agreement, the Monroe Doctrine helped maintain the independence of the Spanish colonies that had already liberated themselves. At the same time, it guaranteed that Cuba would remain in Spanish hands for the time being. ("With the existing colonies or dependencies of any European power we . . . shall not interfere.") The Doctrine thus closed the door to British or French ambitions to obtain the island while the United States was prepared to wait—confident that the "laws of political gravitation" would inevitably bring Cuba into the Union.

By 1823 the American government had resigned itself to the fact that there was little immediate prospect of annexing Cuba. But it had made it clear that it would not allow the island to pass from Spain to any country other than the United States. From these facts had emerged the clear policy of exerting every effort to maintain Spain in possession of Cuba while avoiding any commitment that might tie American hands on that day when Adams's law of "political gravitation" should begin to operate.

As we have seen, the chief beneficiary of United States policy, during this period, was Spain. The chief loser, as we shall now see, were the Cuban people fighting for the independence of their country.

chapter 8

THE UNITED STATES AND THE
INDEPENDENCE OF CUBA, 1823–1830

Revolutionary agents from Cuba had been operating in
the United States since 1810, seeking assistance for an independence
movement. Unlike the agents for the Cuban annexationists, they
were not invited to the White House nor were their plans discussed
at cabinet meetings. Their encouragement came from progressive
newspapers, Masonic lodges, and the steadily strengthening movement for recognition of the South American republics.[1] When on
May 4, 1822, recognition was finally accorded, "very timidly," as
one historian notes,[2] the Cuban revolutionaries took new hope. But
this was considerably diminished later, the same year, by the failure
of the ill-fated expedition to establish an independent republic in
Puerto Rico. Because the United States had been used by the Puerto
Rican backers of the expedition as its base, the press, which condemned the venture, warned Americans to shun the Cuban revolutionary agents who "are seeking to win support in this country for
a similar enterprise to liberate Cuba."[3] The New York *Evening Post*
sought to mobilize the press on that issue on the grounds that the
Puerto Rican expedition, by arousing Spain's indignation, would
have a serious effect on the "extensive commerce" with Cuba. "Is
it not the duty of every editor in the U[nited] States to discounten-
ance such criminal enterprises and prevent the unwary and in-
experienced youth of our country from becoming dupes of other
revolutionary agents from the Spanish West Indies and engaging in
them. . . ."[4] Southern newspapers expressed horror over the dis-
closure of the participation of Puerto Rican Negroes in the conspiracy and of the intentions of the leaders to emancipate the slaves;

150

and some warned that Cuban revolutionary agents in the United States had similar plans for their island. The Charleston (South Carolina) *Gazette* declared, on December 2, 1822, only a few months after the slave revolt in that state led by Denmark Vesey:

> To assist in any way the plans of these Cuban conspirators who are seeking to follow in the footsteps of the madmen of Porto Rico by promoting the rebellion of the blacks against the whites in Cuba is to commit a crime not only against that fair island, but against the interests of this state so recently endangered by similar madmen, and against the United States as a whole.[5]

The final blow to the hopes of the Cuban revolutionaries for American aid came with the Monroe Doctrine which pledged the United States not to interfere with the "existing colonies or dependencies of any European powers" in the Western hemisphere, thereby informing the Cuban revolutionists that they could expect no assistance here. The blow was aspecially severe, since it came during the restoration of absolutism in Spain and the despotic regime instituted by Captain General Vives to stamp out all revolutionary activity in Cuba. By 1825, it will be remembered, a total military dictatorship had been established in the island. No danger to American institutions was seen in such a regime by those in the United States who worried that an independent Cuba, ninety miles off the coast of Florida, posed a danger to the slave system in the South. On the contrary, they hailed Vives as "a constructive influence in the Spanish West Indies."[6] President John Quincy Adams, Monroe's successor in the White House, had the highest esteem for Vives, whom he had known as Spanish Minister, and thought his regime, one of the most despotic in the history of Cuba, worthy of commendation:

> He [Vives] was precisely the man to tranquilize and conciliate the submission of the people of the island to their old government, and he so effectually accomplished that purpose that the government of the United States heard nothing further of intended insurrection in Cuba during the remainder of Mr. Monroe's administration, and the whole of mine.[7]

Adams thus revealed that the adherents of the "fruta madura" policy were prepared to overlook any amount of terror imposed upon the Cuban people so long as it served to keep them under Spain's domination until the time would be ripe for annexation by the United States.* But in one respect, Adams's statement was incorrect. The Monroe and Adams administrations not only heard a great deal of "intended insurrection in Cuba," during Vives's regime, but they actually became associates of Spain in its suppression.

Recovering from the blow dealt their cause by the refusal of support from the United Staes, the Cuban revolutionists turned to Mexico and Colombia for aid.[8] Revolutionary agents from Cuba had been operating in both countries and, as we have seen, they had received encouragement; advice in organization, and supplies to be used in the struggle. But neither Mexico nor Colombia was yet in a position to do more, despite their own need to eliminate the island as a base of operations against them. Both countries were then too involved in their battles with Spanish armies to spare any patriot forces for an expedition against Cuba. Moreover, they were anxious to win recognition by the United States, and they were encountering enough difficulty in gaining this goal not to add to it by antagonizing an administration dedicated to keeping Cuba under Spain's domination.[9]

Even after American recognition had been won and Spanish sovereignty in continental America was practically ended, Mexico and Colombia were not yet able to render direct military assistance to the independence movement in Cuba. Spanish armies still held out in Peru in 1823, when a mission of Cuban revolutionaries arrived in Colombia, and interviewed General Santander and Colonel Gual of the Colombian Army. The Colombian leaders expressed great sympathy for the Cuban cause, but they made it clear that it was impossible for the government "to attend to anything else but the campaign in which General Bolívar is engaged to liberate

---

* Adams's Cuban policy was a blot on a career which was, in many ways, distinguished for progressive policies. Later, as a member of the House of Representatives, Adams became a leading foe of the Southern slaveowners and a champion of the civil liberties of the forces fighting slavery in the United States. (*Cf.* Russel B. Nye, *Fettered Freedom: Civil Liberties and the Slavery Controversy, 1830–1860*, East Lansing, Michigan, 1949, pp. 12, 35–39, 52, 119, 225, 229.)

Peru."[10] José Augustín Arango, a member of the Cuban mission, succeeded in interviewing Bolívar himself by marching with the Colombian troops departing for Peru.* Bolívar repeated what Santander and Gual had already told the Cuban mission. But he assured Arango that he had long ago decided to assist the Cubans, partly because he wished to repay Colombia's debt to revolutionary Cuba for the heroic services of Rafael Heras, a native of Havana, who had enlisted in the Colombian army and died in battle against Spain. The time, however, was not yet ripe for an expedition to liberate Cuba.[11]

Even after Peru was liberated in the decisive battle of Ayacucho, December, 1824, "the Liberator" was not yet ready to assist the Cuban cause with direct military aid. Instead, he proposed to use the threat of invading Cuba and Puerto Rico as a bargaining point to force Spain to withdraw her remaining troops from the mainland and recognize the South American governments. On December 20, 1824, Bolívar wrote to General Santander from Lima:

> It appears to me that the government should let Spain know that if in a definite period of time Colombia is not recognized and peace made, our troops will go immediately to Havana and Puerto Rico. It is more important to have peace than to liberate these two islands— "I have my own policy"—An independent Havana would give us much work to do while the menace would be worth more than the insurrection. This business, well conducted, could produce a great effect. But if the Spanish are obstinate we will move.[12]

A few months later, however, Bolívar indicated that he was reaching the end of his patience. He still preferred peace, but made it clear that "if it is necessary we will go to Havana."[13] Slowly, perhaps even reluctantly, in view of the hardships and suffering already endured in the struggle for independence, Bolívar was reaching the decision to assist the Cuban revolutionary cause.

Meanwhile, in Mexico, the government was reaching a similar decision to "go to Havana," and, together with Colombia, to free Cuba and Puerto Rico, and complete the expulsion of Spain from the Western hemisphere. President Victoria of Mexico authorized

---

* Arango, it will be recalled, had originally been an annexationist. But when United States policy doomed the annexationist cause, he became actively associated with the independence movement.

the formation of the *Junta Promotora de la Libertad de Cuba* (Junta for the Promotion of Cuban Liberty), to be composed of Cubans in Mexico and of Mexican volunteers.[14] Shortly after its formation, the Junta's membership included "the principal officers in the Mexican army and many of the most distinguished members of both houses of Congress."[15]

Having promised the Cuban revolutionary exiles in Mexico effective assistance in achieving the liberation of their native land, President Victoria dispatched an emissary to Bogotá "to propose that Mexico and Colombia should unite their forces and operate in concert to make Cuba independent under their joint protection."[16] The American press began to feature the news that forces from Mexico and Colombia might soon land on Cuban soil. Under the heading "Invasion of Cuba," the *National Gazette* of Philadelphia published a letter from an official in the Colombian Navy asserting that 10,000 men and a strong squadron were ready to liberate Cuba.[17] *Niles' Weekly Register* predicted that "the expedition to divest Spain of the possession of the island of Cuba will be easily accomplished since the people of this island are prepared to give a favorable reception to the invading forces which may soon be expected from Mexico and Colombia."[18]

No news could have been less welcome in Washington. The policy based on Adams's "law of political gravitation" was threatened with ruin. It was clear that an invasion of Cuba by the combined forces of Mexico and Colombia, assisted by the revolutionary forces in the island, would end Spanish rule in Cuba. At the same time, the liberation of the island would put an end to slavery in Cuba, for the Colombian and Mexican governments and the Cuban revolutionary movement favored emancipation. The prospect that an independent, free-labor Cuba, assisted in achieving its liberation by two of the Spanish American republics, would gravitate towards annexation to slaveholding United States (which had rejected every appeal for aid in gaining the island's independence) was so slim as to be non-existent.

No wonder the administration of President Adams was alarmed and took steps to prevent the liberation of Cuba. Its motivation was spelled out clearly by Henry Clay, Adams's Secretary of State. Clay had made political capital out of his role as a champion of the independence of the South American republics, and had spoken out effectively and movingly in their behalf. "I may be accused of an imprudent utterance of my feelings on this occasion, I care not," he had declared in the Senate in January, 1817, in calling for recognition of the South American republics. "When the happiness, the liberty of a whole people is at stake, and the people our neighbors, our brethren, occupying a portion of the same Continent, imitating our example and participating of the same sympathies with ourselves, I will boldly avow my feelings and my wishes in their behalf, even at the hazard of such an imputation."[19] But these words were conveniently forgotten in 1825 when "the independence, the happiness, the liberty" of the people of Cuba and Puerto Rico were "at stake." Then, in a series of letters to American Ministers abroad, Clay acknowledged, first, that since a Colombian-Mexican invasion of Cuba and Puerto Rico would be supported by their populations, it would end in the independence of the islands, and such an outcome would not be in the interest of the United States:

> The success of the enterprise is, by no means, improbable. Their [Colombia and Mexico] proximity to the islands, and their armies being perfectly acclimated will give to the united efforts of the [two] Republics great advantages. And, if with these be taken into the estimate, the important and well known fact that a large portion of the inhabitants of the Islands is predisposed to a separation from Spain, and would form a powerful auxiliary of the Republican armies, *their success becomes almost certain.*[20]

Continuing, Clay alluded to the danger to the Southern states of the abolition of slavery in Cuba, and raised the "scare" of the island becoming another Haiti:

> If Cuba were to declare itself independent, the amount and character of its population render it improbable that it could maintain its independence. Such a premature declaration might bring about a renewal of those shocking scenes, of which a neighboring Island was the afflicted theatre.[21]

The policy of the United States was clear, Clay wrote: *"This country prefers that Cuba and Porto Rico should remain dependent on Spain. This Government desires no political change of that condition.*"22

Toward this end the Adams administration made three major moves.

First it impressed upon Mexico and Colombia that the United States could tolerate no change in the status of the Spanish West Indies islands. When Joel R. Poinsett was sent to Mexico City as first Minister to Mexico,* he was instructed by Clay immediately to inform that government that the United States would not "remain indifferent" to the departure of an expedition from Colombia and Mexico for the liberation of Cuba and Puerto Rico. "Their [the United States] commerce, their peace and their safety are too intimately connected with the fortunes and fate of the Island of Cuba to allow them to behold any change in its condition and political relations without deep solicitude."23

The second move in the Adams-Clay strategy was to attempt to convince Spain that only by making peace with its revolted colonies and recognizing their independence could she keep Cuba and Puerto Rico. If Spain recognized the independence of Mexico and Colombia, these countries would have little incentive to invade Cuba. Alexander Everett, the new American Minister to Spain, was instructed to approach the government in the most conciliatory manner possible, but to express this view of the United States. Clay pointed out that if peace were not made, the insurgent armies on the continent could not be disbanded and would inevitably be used against the Spanish forces in the island. Such an invasion was bound to be successful, since it would be accompanied by mass uprisings of the people of the islands, long anxious "to throw off the Spanish authority." But he was to remind Spain: "It is due to the United States to declare that they have constantly declined to give any countenance to that disposition."24

---

* Poinsett, a South Carolinian, had spent a few days in Cuba in 1823 and had come away convinced that, for the present, the United States should be "satisfied that it should remain dependent on Spain." He was further convinced that an invasion by Mexico and Colombia would produce a massive slave uprising in the island, and that the United States should do everything in its power to prevent this "calamity." (Joel R. Poinsett, *Notes on Mexico, made in the Autumn of 1822 . . . by a Citizen of the United States*, Philadelphia, 1824, pp. 209–23; Memorandum of Poinsett, State Department, Special Agents, III, 24ff., National Archives.)

Spain upset the Adams-Clay program by rejecting Washington's proposal. The reply of Don Francisco de Zea, the Spanish First Secretary of State for Foreign Affairs, was categorical: "His Majesty at no time thought of ceding to any power the islands of Cuba and Porto Rico, and, so far from such a purpose, is firmly determined to keep them under the dominion and authority of his legitimate sovereignty." He added that His Majesty deeply appreciated the feelings expressed by the American Minister, but if the United States was truly concerned over Cuba remaining under Spain, it should guarantee its ownership by the Madrid government. In return the American consulate at Havana would be recognized.[25]

The United States flatly refused such guarantee which meant renouncing its hopes of annexing the island. But Everett tried to dispel Spanish uneasiness about American intentions. The United States, he said, disclaimed "all projects of aggrandizement in that quarter . . . the disturbance of the external repose of the island or the dismemberment of the Spanish Empire." Still Spain adamantly refused to yield.[26]

The third step in the American program was to appeal to the European powers supposed to have influence at Madrid, to apply pressure on Spain to grant independence to her revolted colonies. Clay sent letters to the U.S. Ministers to Russia, France and England instructing them to seek their support for the plan. They were to emphasize that Spain would benefit by recognizing the independence of the new states, since continued attempts to regain them would incur the additional loss of Cuba and Puerto Rico. An independent Cuba would result in abolition of slavery and a racial war such as had occurred in Haiti, which would have to be met by stationing in the island "a large force of Foreign powers." The European nations could avoid this by influencing Spain to make peace now. Finally, whatever the circumstances, the United States "could not see with indifference" the islands of Cuba and Puerto Rico pass into the hands of any other power.[27]

This move also failed. The French government made it clear that it had no hope of inducing the "exalted or fanatical" government of Spain to make peace or face reality. Russia made an ineffectual gesture towards influencing Spain, largely to please the American Minister, but reported no success.

England came up with a counter-proposal. Canning argued that it was not the new American states but the great maritime powers that presented the greatest danger to Spain's hold on Cuba. He proposed, therefore, that the United States, France, and Britain should jointly, or each separately, issue an announcement "disclaiming each for ourselves, any intention to occupy Cuba and protesting each against such occupation by either of the others." Thus guaranteed her domination of Cuba and relieved of worry over the island, Spain could make her peace with her revolted colonies.[28]

Canning's counter-proposal was totally unacceptable to the United States. Clay declared that the plan would not prevent invasion of Cuba by Mexico or Colombia, and thus failed to solve the most pressing problem of the moment. Nor was there a need for a United States promise to "abstain from taking advantage of the incidents which may grow out of the present war to wrest Cuba from Spain." "Because," Clay piously added, "their pacific policy, their known moderation, and the very measures which they have already voluntarily adopted to bring about peace, are sufficient guarantee of their forbearance."[29] This reply left out the real reason for rejecting Canning's counter-proposal: the desire of the United States to keep its hands free to acquire Cuba!

Before leaving the European phase of the Adams-Clay strategy, it is worth noting that despite the Monroe Doctrine, the United States was quite willing for European powers to become involved in a movement to prevent the independence of an American area. The Adams-Clay policy was nothing less than a call for European aid to keep Mexico and Colombia from aiding Cuba and Puerto Rico to achieve independence, and to finally rid the American continent of Spanish monarchical domination. As Dexter Perkins, the foremost authority on the Monroe Doctrine, points out, this policy revealed to Latin America, very early, the selfish purposes of the United States.[30]

Meanwhile, in Mexico, Poinsett was exerting himself to prevent an invasion of Cuba from getting under way. He played on "Mexican jealousy of Colombia," and informed Clay that if this was seriously "cultivated," it could bring the results the United States hoped for.[31] Stalling for time while Poinsett was engaged in this work, Clay, on December 20, 1825, handed identical notes to the Mexican and Colombian Ministers in Washington asking the "suspension for a limited time of the sailing of the Expedition against Cuba and Porto Rico" to allow Russia to continue her efforts to persuade Spain to grant the revolting states complete independence.[32] Copies of the notes were sent to the American Ministers in Mexico and Colombia instructing each to further this policy.

In both countries Clay's request for delay was received very coldly. In the Mexican Congress, a resolution was introduced early in 1826 condemning the American request and proposing "that the government be authorized in conjunction with that of Colombia to send an expedition against the Island of Cuba, in order to protect its independence from the government of Spain, and to assist the inhabitants who have given so many proofs of their desire to be free."[33] Alarmed by this response to his request, Clay dropped diplomatic language and instructed Poinsett to warn the Mexican government that the United States would not permit Spain's expulsion from Cuba. Poinsett delivered this warning in person to President Victoria who expressed surprise that the United States should object to Cuba becoming independent. Poinsett countered that his government feared that Mexico planned to annex the island. Thereupon, President Victoria assured the American Minister:

> that the government of Mexico had no intention to conquer or keep possession of that Island—that the object of the expedition which they contemplated, was to assist the revolutionists to drive out the Spaniards, and, in case they succeeded, to leave that people to govern themselves.

The American representative expressed regret that such a statement had not been made earlier since silence had given the United States a different impression of Mexico's intentions. But when President Victoria offered to repeat this in writing, if the United States withdrew its objections to an invasion for the sole purpose of establishing Cuba's independence, Poinsett refused point-blank. "Although it would certainly be desirable to receive such a pledge from this government," he notified Clay, "I objected to commit my government as to the future guarantee of the Independence of Cuba in the present stage of this affair."[34]

The concern over Mexico's intentions by the American representative was nothing more than double-talk. Poinsett already knew, from the discussions in the Mexican Congress, that the purpose of the invasion was to establish an independent Cuba. But he feared an invasion regardless of its purpose. "What I most dread," he had written to Clay, "is that the blacks may be armed and used as auxiliaries by one or both parties."[35] The truth is the American government was as much opposed to an invasion for the independence of Cuba as it was to one for the purpose of annexing the island to Mexico or Colombia.* Clay's correspondence, quoted above, reveals that what he opposed was an invasion which had as its objective the independence of Cuba, an outcome, he said frankly, which was practically inevitable in view of the strength of the Mexican and Colombian invading forces and the assistance they would receive from the Cuban revolutionaries.

Not only did Clay refuse the guarantee of Cuban independence President Victoria requested, but he made use of President Victoria's statement to renew pressure on Spain to recognize her revolted colonies. Everett was instructed to assure Spain that Mexico was intent on Cuba's independence but that the invasion could be halted once recognition were granted, and "all ideas of Independence which the inhabitants [of Cuba] may entertain would cease with the cessation of the state of war which has excited them." But when Spain again countered with the suggestion that the United States guarantee the island to Spain, the Secretary of State again rejected the suggestion.[36] Spain then turned a deaf ear to all American entreaties that it recognize its revolted colonies.

The shabby Adams-Clay diplomacy had failed in Europe: Spain had rebuffed it; England and France were unwilling, and Russia unable, to make Spain change her mind. But the United States

---

* In December, 1826, the Mexican representative at the British court suggested to James Gallatin, U.S. Minister to England, that Cuba be made independent under the joint protection of the United States and Great Britain. Gallatin relayed this proposal to Clay, but it was speedily rejected, since it would have ended American hopes of acquiring the island. (Gallatin to Clay, Dec. 16, 1826, Despatches from Great Britain, XXXIII, National Archives.)

warnings to Mexico and Colombia worked, since they had the backing of England as well. To avert armed conflict with the United States and England, Mexico and Colombia were forced to postpone a Mexican-Colombian expedition to liberate Cuba until the views of the proposed Congress of American States to be held at Panama should be known. As General Bolívar sorrowfully told a delegation of Cuban revolutionaries who met with him at Caracas:

> We cannot set at defiance the American Government, in conjunction with that of England, determined on maintaining the authority of Spain over the Islands of Cuba and Puerto Rico; although that determination will keep us in constant alarm and will occasion to us much expense, in order to repel any attempt which our tenacious enemy might make for those Islands.[37]

The Congress at Panama, then part of Colombia, was initiated by Simón Bolívar, the liberator of Venezuela, Ecuador, Colombia, Peru and Bolivia, with the design of forming a federation of the Spanish-speaking American Republics to defend their newly-gained independence. As Bolívar wrote in the "Manifesto" of December 7, 1824, convoking the Congress:

> After fifteen years of sacrifices devoted to the liberty of America, in order to obtain the system of guarantees which in peace and in war will be the shield of our new destiny, it is already time that the interests and the relations which unite among themselves the American republics, previously Spanish colonies, have a fundamental base which will make everlasting, if possible, the duration of these governments.[38]

At first the United States was not included among the states invited, but its attitude toward being included was sounded out in the spring of 1825. President Adams was not interested; he had taken the position, as far back as 1820, that "there is no community of interests or of principles between North and South America,"[39] and he still held to this view. But when formal invitations were received in the fall of 1825, outlining also the subjects to be discussed at the Congress, Adams had second thoughts. Among the articles submitted by Colombia was one which proposed that the Congress "consider the expediency of combining the forces of the Republics, to free the islands of Cuba and Puerto Rico from the yoke of Spain, and, in such case, what contingent each ought to contribute for this end."[40] From Poinsett in Mexico, who was following developments closely, the administration received a dispatch warning of the likelihood that this article would be adopted, and recommending the sending of delegates who, by voicing the strong opposition of the United States, could prevent the Congress from undertaking this project.[41]

This caused President Adams to change his mind and to urge Congress to send two delegates to Panama.[42] His special message to Congress, March 15, 1826 stressed the necessity of having representatives present to look after the interests of the United States respecting Cuba and Puerto Rico. "The invasion of both those islands by the united forces of Mexico and Colombia is avowedly among the objects to be matured by the belligerent States at Panama." The nearness of Cuba to the Southern states, the presence there of a large slave population, the certainty of their liberation if Cuban independence were established by the new states, and the resulting menace to the Southern states, Adams emphasized, made it imperative that this government should be consulted in what was being planned at Panama. He pledged to Congress that the delegates of the United States would use their influence to restrain the new states from attacking Cuba and Puerto Rico. "It is unnecessary to enlarge upon this topic or to say more than that all our efforts in reference to this interest will be to preserve the existing state of things, the tranquillity of the islands, and the peace and security of their inhabitants."*[43]

---

* One other Caribbean country was mentioned in Adams's message—Haiti. Adams came out against American recognition of Haiti, one of the questions to be discussed at the Panama Congress. This stand aroused great bitterness in the Negro republic towards the United States. "My letters of the 26th of April from Port au Prince," Andrew Armstrong wrote to Henry Clay from Philadelphia, "inform me that the President's message on the Panama mission had been received there, and caused a great deal of ill feeling towards us, so much so, that at a large dinner where 'the prosperity of the U.S.' was proposed as a toast it was refused to be drunk, and reference was made to the message. It was, however, concluded that the toast should be drunk in *cold water*." (Armstrong to Clay, June 1, 1826, in Consular Letters, Cape Haitien, V, National Archives.)

Adams's stand on the Haitian recognition question was applauded by members of Congress from the slaveholding states. Senator Benton of Missouri explained the Southern view on recognition: "Our policy towards Haiti, the old Santo Domingo, has been fixed . . . for three and thirty years. We trade with her, but

Adams's message precipitated a broad discussion both in the newspapers and in Congress. *Niles' Weekly Register* threw its support behind participation in the Congress as a means of protecting American commercial interests from the competition of Great Britain,* but objected to sending delegates for the purpose of preventing an expedition to liberate Cuba. "It is an act of justice that Spain should be divested of this, the richest of her remaining colonies —and, certainly, it will be most agreeable to the people of the United States that it shall become an independent nation standing alongside of the new republics."[44] The Southern press, however, almost unanimously regarded the Congress as a threat to the institution of slavery, first, because of the proposed project of mounting an invasion against Spain in Cuba; secondly because the new Latin-American republics had abolished—on paper, at least—the practice of slavery; and, finally, because the abolition of the slave trade was also to be proposed at Panama. "We cannot, therefore, see any good to result from sending envoys to the Congress at Panama," concluded the *Southern Messenger*.[45] Even the argument of some Northern newspapers that it would be best for the slaveowners that the United States have someone present at Panama to take part in the discussions relating to Cuba, failed to move the Southern press.[46]

The Senate Foreign Relations Committee rejected President Adams's proposal to send delegates to the Congress. The Committee argued that the interest of the United States in Cuba and Puerto Rico forbade discussion of their destiny "with the new republics"

---

no diplomatic relations have been established between us. . . . And why? Because the peace of eleven states will not permit the fruits of a successful Negro insurrection to be exhibited among them. It will not permit black consuls and ambassadors to establish themselves in our cities, and to parade through our country, and to give their fellow blacks in the United States proof in hand of the honors which await them for a like successful effort on their part." (Thomas H. Benton, *Register of the Debates in Congress*, vol. VIII, p. 469.)

* " . . . these states are of incalculable importance to the United States and there is reason to fear that our great rival [Great Britain] in . . . [manufacturing] and [commercial] interests may have succeeded in establishing a predominant feeling in favor of herself, which it will be difficult for us to remove." (Vol. XXVIII, March 18, 1826. *See also* Francis L. Reinhold, "New Research on the First Pan American Congress Held at Panama in 1826," *Hispanic American Historical Review*, vol. XVIII, August, 1938, pp. 342–44.)

planning to invade them.[47] But in the debate in Congress, that very interest was urged by the Northern spokesmen as the reason why envoys should represent American views. "Ought we not . . . to send ministers to this Congress, to warn our brethren against such an undertaking [as an invasion of Cuba]?" Wood of New York appealed.[48]

The Southern Congressmen rejected the plea, and lined up in opposition to sending delegates. They placed great stress on the issue of avoiding "entangling alliances," but the Pittsburgh *Mercury* correctly sized up that argument: "The opposition of the South [to sending delegates] made much of this possible danger of entangling alliances, but it is now known that this was employed as a cover to their real purpose—the protection of slavery."[49]

Senator Haynes of South Carolina, spokesman for the opposition to Adams's proposal, bluntly stated the slaveholders' position toward the Panama Congress as a menace to the continued existence of slavery in the United States. He warned that the South would not "permit it [the slavery question] to be brought into question, either by our sister states, or by the Federal Government."[50] Rather than send delegates to Panama to warn against an invasion of Cuba, the Southern Congressmen advised the United States to let the Latin American Republics know immediately, in no uncertain language, that it would not stand for any move to free Cuba from Spain, and thus establish "a second Haiti to cast the shadow of its ominous gloom over our shores." And that if such an expedition should be attempted, the United States would use its "naval and military means to coerce the brigands and blacks into submission."[51]

This outrageous suggestion brought John Holmes of Maine to his feet to protest. He agreed that Cuba and Puerto Rico " must remain as they are,"* but if the invasion should occur and an insurrection

---

* However, Holmes conceded that the Latin-American republics had reason to feel bitter over the Adams-Clay maneuvers to prevent the liberation of Cuba. "Our dear friends, the Spanish Americans might well expostulate and complain thus: 'You advised us to refrain from an invasion of Cuba, lest it should prevent the mediation of Russia. We did refrain; Spain has gained time and recovered strength, and the mediation was a delusion! . . . How does it happen that your government is to defeat, as *far as in its power*, every enterprise of ours against Cuba and Puerto Rico?" (*Speech of Mr. [John] Holmes of Maine, Delivered in the Senate of the United States on the Mission to Panama, March, 1826, p. 18.*)

of slaves accompany it, the United States must under no circumstances interfere "against the insurgents."

My life for it, you could not maintain such a war—public opinion would not sustain you. A war out of the limits of the U[nited] States, a foreign war, to reduce men to servitude! Not an arm and scarcely a voice north of the Potomac, would be raised in your behalf. An administration which should attempt it, would seal its own destruction. No, Sir, the liberal and discreet politicians of the North, sympathise with their brethren of the slave-holding States. Our maxim is, that it is an evil, which *we* cannot remedy. The only relief we can give them, is to let them manage it *themselves,* and that any interference on our part will make it worse. But beyond this we will not go. To send our troops, the sons of freemen to a foreign country; to be the victims of the sword and the pestilence, for the purpose of suppressing an insurrection of the slaves, is a measure against which we shall ever protest—to which we will never submit. We could not if we would—the apostles of liberty, the advocates of universal emancipation would cry aloud, and denounce this war in favor of slavery! Their voices would be heard, even in the humble habitation of the slave, and you would soon find it necessary to withdraw your army [from Cuba and Puerto Rico] to preserve peace at home.[52]

After months of debate—the house discussion lasted four months (the Senate, in secret session, debated the issue for a briefer period)—participation in the Panama Congress was finally voted. All the states south of the Mason and Dixon line voted against the measure except Maryland and Louisiana.[53] The Pittsburgh *Mercury* commented: "The Southern opposers of the Panama Mission have practically formed a sectional slave party."[54]

In his instructions to the delegates to the Panama Congress, Clay once again announced the fixed determination of the United States to permit "no change in the possession of political charge of that island [of Cuba]" either by its transfer to another European power or "its annexation by a Spanish-American republic." An independent, self-governing Cuba was out of the question too. The "dis-

---

Congress had asked President Adams to lay before it the correspondence between the Government of the United States and the new States of America regarding the Panama Congress and related matters, hence the essence of the Adams-Clay strategy to prevent a Mexican-Colombian expedition to liberate Cuba in Puerto Rico was known.

cordant character of its population" made it inevitable that a successful uprising against Spain would be succeeded by the "tragic scenes, which were formerly exhibited in a neighboring island." Then the liberated Negroes of Cuba would seek to stir up the slaves in the United States to revolt for freedom. Would they not "be tempted, by the very fact of that independence, to employ all the means which vicinity, similarity of origin and sympathy could supply, to foment and stimulate insurrection, in order to join ultimate strength to their cause?"

This fear of contagion from the liberated slaves of Cuba required the United States to oppose any invasion of Cuba by Colombia and Mexico, and the delegates were told to secure the suspension of any military or naval expedition by holding out the possibility that the United States would side with the European powers against the two South American republics. It is worth spelling out this ultimatum in Clay's own words:

> The United States have too much at stake, in the fortunes of Cuba, to allow them to see, with indifference, a war of invasion, prosecuted in a desolating manner, or to see employed in the purpose of such a war, one race of inhabitants combatting against another, upon principles and with motives that must ultimately lead, if not to the extermination of one party or the other, to the most shocking excesses. The humanity of the United States, and their duty to defend themselves against the contagion of such a war and dangerous examples, would constrain them, even at the hazard of losing the friendship, greatly as they value it, of Mexico and Colombia, to employ all the means necessary to their security.[55]

Cuban scholars have long contended that the liberation of their island was frustrated by the effect on the Panama Congress of the determined United States opposition to a liberating expedition. The National Congress of Cuban Historians, meeting in 1947, declared: "This Yankee opposition was the primary reason for which there was not reached in the Congress of Panama a clear agreement on the independence of Cuba and Puerto Rico."[56]

But apologists for the Adams-Clay policy argue that the stand taken by the government of the United States had no effect because its delegates did not reach Panama until after the Congress had adjourned. (One delegate died while on his way.) The fact that the Congress failed to reach a decision on liberating Cuba was, therefore, in no way related to the role played by the United States.[57]

This viewpoint ignores the fact that the opposition of the United States to the independence of Cuba was well known at Panama though American representatives were not there to voice it. Poinsett, who was in close touch with the deliberations of the Congress, emphasized that "the plenipotentiaries were probably deterred from acting upon this very important subject by the language which has been held by the president [of the United States] with regard to these islands."*[58] Bolívar himself declared that the opposition of the United States to the Mexican-Colombian expedition had been made so clear by the time the Congress met as to have been "little less than insuperable."[59] General José Antonio Paéz, who was commissioned by Bolívar to lead the expedition if it materialized, wrote in his memoirs that the opposition of the United States made the venture impossible. "The government of the United States," he added, "and I say this with sorrow, thus blocked the independence of Cuba."[60] Finally, Martin Van Buren, Clay's successor as Secretary of State, instructed Minister Van Ness to explain to the Spanish government that the United States was chiefly responsible for savin Cuba and Puerto Rico for Spain before and during the Panama Congress:

> Cuba and Puerto Rico, occupying, as they do, a most important geographical position, have beeen viewed by the neighboring States of Mexico and Colombia, as military and naval arsenals which would at all times furnish Spain with the means of threatening their commerce and even of endangering their political existence. Looking with a jealous eye upon these last remnants of Spanish power in America, these two States had once united their forces, and their

---

* The reference was to Adams's message of March 15, 1826, discussed above, in which he set forth U.S. opposition to the Mexican-Colombia expedition. It is interesting to note that the message was widely circulated in Cuba by Captain General Vives tu discourage revolutionary activity. Reporting this fact, *Niles' Weekly Register* observed: "These things will be very acceptable to our brethren in the South, but they would do well to remember that that which is apprehended should be calculated upon, though it may not happen just now." (Vol. XXX, May 13, 1826, p. 186.) For evidence of Vives's fear of an invasion from Mexico and Colombia, *see* José L. Franco, editor, *Documentos para la Historia de Venezuela existentes en el Archivo Nacional de Cuba*, La Habana, 1960, pp. c–cii.)

arm, raised to strike a blow which, if successful, would for ever have extinguished Spanish influence in that quarter of the globe, was arrested chiefly by the timely interposition of this Government, who, in a friendly spirit toward Spain, and for the interest of general commerce thus assisted in preserving to his Catholic Majesty this valuable portion of his colonial possessions.[61]

"In this way," writes Evelío Rodríguez Lendián in his study, *El Congreso de Panamá y la Independencia de Cuba,* "was the great work of freeing Cuba frustrated. Had not the United States intervened, the liberating forces of Colombia and Mexico would have established Cuba as an independent nation. This would have anticipated our independence by 70 years . . . it would have avoided for several generations the cruel and prolonged struggle, the ruination and martyrdom, the sacrifice and the death on the scaffold."[62]

The shameful policy the United States had been pursuing in its effort to prevent a change in the status of Cuba helped to alienate not only the Cubans but the new Latin-American states as well. On October 15, 1826, after the Panama Congress, Dawkin, British Minister to Colombia wrote to George Canning that the United States was now an object of suspicion throughout Latin America. "The general influence of the United States is not in my opinion, to be feared. It certainly exists in Colombia, but it has been very much weakened even there by their protests against any attack on Cuba. . . ."*[63] The Latin American states saw that the United States government did not hesitate to seek European assistance when it wished to frustrate a program in the interest of the Spanish American nations, and that it was not above sacrificing the interests of its American neighbors to promote its own advantage.[64]

Thus the long list of grievances which Cubans have against the United States can be said to have begun as early as the decade 1820–1830. In 1849, there was published in New York a pamphlet by a Cuban, entitled *The United States Government Has Injured the Liberty of the People of Cuba.* The author conceded that not all Cubans had favored the independence of their island from Spain

* This hostility to the United States gave Canning an opportunity to strengthen British influence in Latin America, especially in Mexico, at the expense of the United States. (J.F. Rippy, *Rivalry of the United States and Great Britain over Latin America, 1808–1830,* Baltimore, 1929, pp. 172–75.)

during the great struggles for liberation during the 1820's, and that the opposition of the Creole planters who feared that independence would bring an end to the system of slavery in the island was partially responsible for Cuba's remaining under Spanish domination. But he went on:

> The chief cause why the Cubans have not broken the chains which oppress them, and why they have not risen to the rank of freemen, as all of them are anxious to do, is that the Government of the United States has riveted these very chains. There is not a statesman or diplomatist who does not know it. . . . An extensive scheme of conspiracy [*Soles y Rayos de Bolívar*] having proved abortive in consequence of inexperience, in 1823, the same task was pursued with zeal in the country, and the assistance of Colombia and Mexico was solicited, and with that aid the blow was preparing which was to have imparted freedom to Cuba and Porto Rico in 1826, when the American government being informed of that undertaking . . . the President made a special message on the 15th of March, 1826, and sent it to Congress, stating the undertaking, and giving assurance that he would not spare any effort tending to support the authority of Spain on the *ill-fated Islands* of Cuba and Porto Rico. . . . Thus was frustrated the undertaking. . . . The cause of Liberty, the cause of Humanity, and Civilization, the general interests of the West, the very conveniences of the United States, all, all, was forgotten: the Cabinet of Washington openly opposed that holy crusade for the complete American Redemption, and did not permit the regeneration sparks of the purification flame which had been heroically kindled by Anglo-Americans themselves to pass over to the Archipelago of the West Indies.[65]

In July, 1854, the Havana correspondent of the New Orleans *Daily Picayune* reported his surprise at the widespread antagonism to the United States among the Cuban people. After investigating the problem, he acknowledged that there was a basic reason for this feeling:

> In sooth, her [Cuba's] proximity to your Government, at least, has been anything but a boon to her. Let us take a glance at history. In 1826 Colombia and Mexico prepared an expedition to invade the island and drive the Spaniards out. The American Government officially notified those powers that it would consent to no change in the political condition of Cuba, and the enterprise was abandoned. Is it any wonder that the Cubans recall this with indignation?[66]

chapter 9

THE SECOND REFORM MOVEMENT

By 1830, the decade of intense efforts for Cuban independence was over. The Spanish authorities still accused Colombia and Mexico of continuing to plan to invade the island, but this had little basis in fact. United States opposition had settled this question. Moreover, with the fall of the reactionary Bourbon government in France and the accession of Louis Phillippe to the throne in 1830, Ferdinand VII lost all possibility of French aid in reconquering his former colonies. Mexico and Colombia, no longer threatened by Spain, ceased giving assistance to independence activities in Cuba, and formal Spanish recognition, which followed in 1836, ended all Cuban hopes of aid from that quarter.

Independence hopes were replaced by new efforts to achieve reforms within the existing framework of Spanish absolutism, made doubly oppressive since 1825 when the Captain General was invested with "facultades omnímodas." The outstanding leaders of the second reform movement, José Antonio Saco, José de la Luz y Caballero, and Domingo del Monte, were young liberals, influenced by the ideology of the revolutionary period. They, and others associated with them, were products of the growth in cultural interests and educational facilities during the first decades of the nineteenth century. The economic societies and the colleges—products of the reform movement of the late eighteenth and early nineteenth century—diffusing knowledge of political economy, philosophy and chemistry and other studies, were the schools out of which the new reform leaders emerged. Saco was to become a distinguished political writer; Luz y Caballero a leading educator, and del Monte was to earn distinction as a literary critic and inspirer of Cuban literature.[1]

170

Still, it must be noted that the reform leaders belonged, through their social origins and their family connections, to the circle of the wealthy planter class, and that their ideology, in the main, reflected the views and interests of this class. Their program, like that of the first reform movement of the period 1790 to 1820, included demands for economic, political and social changes.

In 1818, as we have seen, the earlier reformers had won their basic economic demand—freedom of commerce—when Ferdinand VII opened the ports of Cuba to foreign vessels without monopolistic restrictions. High duties, however, still imposed a heavy burden on foreign trade, which the second reform movement sought to eliminate or lighten. To be sure, trade with Spain was now freer than before, but the bulk of the Cuban trade was with the United States and, to a lesser degree with Great Britain. (More sugar and coffee were exported to the United States than to Spain.) By 1833, the major part of the export trade and an increasing percentage of the import trade, namely flour, was with the United States.[2]

Naturally, the United States shared the desire of the Cuban reformers to remove discriminatory duties on the trade between Cuba and North America. "The great object of our government in relation to Cuba," Secretary of State Livingston wrote in September, 1832, "is a free and untrammeled trade, on its present footing, eased of the discriminatory duties. . . ."[3] U.S. pressure on the Spanish government resulted in some success, in that year, when the tonnage duty on foreign vessels in Cuban ports was reduced from $2.50 to $1.50.[4]

But this gain was short-lived. The Spanish merchants and bureaucrats, who needed still higher tariffs if they were to control the Cuban trade, vigorously protested. They succeeded in winning the support of the Spanish government which needed tariff revenues. Late in 1832, new discriminatory rates were laid on imports from the United States. Two years later, Spain raised the duty on American flour brought to Cuba in American vessels to $9.50 a barrel and $8.50 when imported in Spanish ships. Congress retaliated by raising the tonnage duties on Spanish vessels from the island and laid a special duty on Cuban coffee. Trade between Cuba and the United States was seriously injured—Cuban coffee production was practically ruined—even though Americans, by 1834, were handling so large a percentage of the carrying trade between Cuba and the United States as to have a virtual monopoly.[5]

The Cuban reformers, representing the interests most affected by this tariff war, demanded an end to this conflict, and the elimination of all obstacles standing in the way of a direct commercial interchange with the United States. Instead of the usual procedure, under which Spanish ships took on cargoes in the United States of flour, lard and other products, carried them to Spain, and then re-exported them to Cuba, with Cubans paying extra duties and unnecessary haulage charges, which vastly increased the cost, Cuban reformers called for the right of American exporters to ship their merchandise direct to Cuba.[6]

In the political sphere, the reformers advanced, as an ultimate goal, the demand raised a quarter of a century before: assimilation or autonomy or both, that is, the enjoyment by Cubans of the rights held by citizens in the Peninsula including the right of representation in the Cortes. More immediately, however, they called for an end to the "facultades omnímodas," under which the island was ruled by martial law as if it were under seige, "placing even the most innocent activities under the scrutiny of the military, exercising a strict censorship over all discussions in the press, outlawing public meetings, and forbidding not only such 'inciting words' as independence and abolition of slavery, but even any public reference to political reform."[7] The reformers called for limitation on the powers of the Captain General, restricting his now absolute control over the army, postal service, the press, the slave traffic, the prisons, and all forms of activity in the island.

In the social sphere, the reform demand differed from its predecessor. The first reform movement had called not only for continuation of slavery but for the expansion of the slave trade. The young reformers of the 1830's, while continuing to uphold the system of slavery, opposed the continuance of the slave trade.

Why this change?

The reformers, as we have pointed out, represented basically the interests of the powerful Cuban sugar and coffee planters. In the period of the first reform movement, all the sugar and coffee was produced by the hand labor of the slaves. But in 1819, steam power was introduced to grind the sugar cane. This did not yet materially affect the character of the industry as a whole; in 1830, only a small group of mills, mainly those in the vicinity of Matanzas and Cárdenas, possessed steam engines. Moreover, the work on the coffee plantations in no way varied from before; it still depended exclusively on slave labor. Thus, by the overwhelming majority of the Cuban producers, slavery was still considered indispensable for their prosperity. But there emerged a small but influential minority of more far-sighted planters who realized that the introduction of the steam engine in sugar production foreshadowed the day when the illiterate African slave would be replaced by a new type of worker: a wage-earner, literate, and therefore able to master the techniques of processing sugar by machinery. While they could not yet predict in 1830 precisely when this transformation would occur, this small group comprehended the folly of adding more African slaves when signs indicated that the future needs of the sugar industry would require a different type of labor. The correct program for Cuba, as they saw it, was to maintain slavery, but to end the further importation of slaves.[8]

The more far-sighted planters were convinced, furthermore, that the Spanish rulers had a sinister motive in promoting the slave trade despite their own laws against it. Increasing the slave population until it vastly outnumbered the whites would make the latter more dependent on Spanish rule. The Cuban whites would cling to Spain for protection against insurrection of "savage blacks," and the absolute Spanish domination of the island would be guaranteed.[9] Hence the planters who sought relief from this absolutism logically turned against the slave trade.

Nothing here said, however, should leave the impression that this represented the majority viewpoint of the slaveholding planter class. The planters desirous of halting the illicit slave traffic came mainly from the old Creoles whose plantations were well stocked with slaves, and who felt no urgent need for a fresh labor supply, unlike those who were operating new sugar plantations with an undersized labor force. The older planters were also opposed to the slave traffic because, among the other reasons, it prevented a rise in the price value of the slaves they already owned. The capital of these planters might easily be doubled by the end of the slave trade, which would inevitably increase the value of the existing slave labor force. Small wonder that they supported the demand of the reform movement to terminate the traffic.[10]

But the most pressing motivation behind the reform demand for abolition of the slave trade was the fear that increasing the majority of the Negroes in the island would end in a revolution such as had swept Haiti. Even Arango y Parreño, the early reform leader and champion of the slave trade, became frightened by this danger in his later years. From 1828 to 1832 he addressed repeated *comunicaciones* to the Spanish government urging extinction of the slave traffic. They were filed away and never known outside of official circles.[11] But in the June, 1832 issue of *Revista Bimestre Cubana,* appeared José Antonio Saco's article, "Análisis Sobre Brasil," the first public discussion of the slave-trade problem.

Saco did not treat it from the humanitarian point of view "because this is not respected when the interests speak," but pointed out that continuation of the slave trade endangered the future of Cuba and suggested the advantages to be derived from increasing the white population through immigration. Cuba must not become another Haiti, he said, and pictured the "miserable national existence" that would ensue upon a revolutionary upheaval of the numerically superior Negroes.[12]

In no sense did Saco advocate the abolition of slavery in Cuba. Nor did he envisage a future for Cuba in which there would be a place for the Negro. He merely called attention to the dangers inherent in the continuation of the slave trade. Nevertheless, his pamphlet incensed the Spanish officials and merchants and the vast majority of the Cuban planters. The government of Spain, deriving large revenues from the wealth of the Cuban sugar plantations, was in no mood to consider Saco's plea. Neither were the Captains General who received a percentage for each slave smuggled into Cuba, nor the Spanish merchants in Cuba who derived enormous profits from the illicit slave trade. And the Cuban planters, who joined with the Spanish merchants in connivance in the trade, united with them in opposing Saco's suggestion. Only the most enlightened elements of the island, those who could see beyond the immediate present, and the Creole youths, "sincerely applauded the enlightening thought [of Saco]."[13]

In 1833, an event occurred in Spain which gave a measure of hope to the Cuban reformers who believed that better things were possible under Spanish rule. Ferdinand VII died and was succeeded by his daughter Isabel II, under the regency of Maria Cristina. In order to ensure her daughter's throne, the latter was forced to identify herself with the liberal camp. She reopened the universities and declared a political amnesty which brought back from abroad the many thousands Ferdinand had driven into exile. The liberal revolution was climaxed by the institution of a new constitution which, while more conservative than that of 1812, provided for constitutional government, and a call was issued for elections to the Cortes.

The optimism of the Cuban reformers was quickly dashed. On one point both absolutists and constitutionalists agreed: Spain could hold her remaining colonies only by exercising a despotic power. To apply this policy in Cuba, Miguel Tacón was sent as Captain General in June, 1834. An ultra-conservative monarchist who had suffered defeats in the colonial wars, Tacón was to become the most loathed of all the Captains General in Cuba's colonial history. Although his predecessors, Vives and Mariano Ricafort, had not been distinguished for liberalism, they had sought the support of the wealthy Creole planter class, believing that by encouraging them to identify their interests with those of the Metropolis they would resist any revolutionary trend.

With the arrival of Tacón on the island in 1834, the policy of toleration toward the planter class came to an abrupt end. Tacón viewed all Cubans, regardless of class, as putting Cuban interests foremost, and these he considered fundamentally antagonistic to the interests of the Metropolis. Suspicious of all Cubans, he surrounded himself with *Peninsulares* only and a few representatives of foreign governments. The voice of the Creole planter class that had hitherto played such an important part in Spain's colonial policy in Cuba now went unheard as Tacón vented his hatred against all Cubans without distinction.

Tacón is symbolic of the military despotism to which Cuba was subjected. He was the first to exploit to the full the omnipotent powers conceded the Captain General in 1825. (Ricafort delegated much of his absolute authority to minor officials.) The emergency that had produced this grant had passed, but the powers remained to be invoked at will. Tacón proved what awful powers they could be. His four years of rule were marked by a ruthless proscription of all who opposed his will, and imprisonment and exile for all who questioned the *status quo*. Reform sentiment, economic, political and social, was extirpated.[14]

One of the first to feel the weight of Tacón's despotic hand was José Antonio Saco. During the last years of Vives's administration and throughout that of his successor, Ricafort, Saco had been publishing articles in which he laid bare the evils of Spanish domination. Among other things, he charged that the Cuban administrative posts were used to reward the Court's political favorites. But Saco did not suffer for his views until he touched on the most dangerous theme of all: the slave trade. His pamphlet against its continuation aroused, as we have seen, widespread antagonism. Tacón was personally affected since, as Domingo del Monte pointed out, he took his half-ounce of gold for every slave landed on the island illicitly.[15] It is hardly surprising then that the pamphlet was condemned. On July 17, 1834, Saco was exiled from Havana to Trinidad, and from there expelled to Spain. Here, supported by wealthy reformist friends, he attacked Tacón and called for an end to the despotic "facultades omnímodas."

In 1836, during the height of Tacón's tyranny, the Cuban reformers were given their long hoped-for chance to bring their case before the Spanish government. The liberals in Spain had finally succeeded in restoring the Constitution of 1812 which provided for Cuban representation in the Cortes. Against the wishes of Tacón, elections were held in three Cuban cities. When the exiled Saco was elected deputy by Santiago de Cuba, Tacón twice annulled the elections, whereupon Saco was elected a third time. The other two deputies, elected from Havana and Puerto Príncipe, were also liberal reformers.

The two deputies proceeded to Spain to meet Saco, with whom

they prepared a manifesto to present to the Cortes calling for tariff reforms, effective enforcement of the anti-slave-trade law, an end to the rule of Tacón, abolition of the "facultades omnímodas," and the initiation of a program leading eventually to autonomy for Cuba. But they never got the opportunity to present the memorial. The Cuban deputies were not even permitted to take their seats in the Cortes. Agustín Argüelles, the great liberal of 1810–12, rationalized their exclusion on the grounds that the admission of American deputies in 1810 and 1812 had led to the loss of the greater part of Spanish America.

The infuriated Saco led his fellow-deputies from Cuba in the preparation of a famous protest. Published in Madrid, on February 21, 1837, the *Protesta de los Diputados electos por la Isla de Cuba a las Cortes generales de la nación* minced no words; it warned that this reactionary political move would only drive a deep division between Cubans and Spaniards, and unless reversed immediately would create an unparalleled bitterness against the Spanish government.[16]

But the protest went for naught. A Royal Decree of April 25, 1837 announced that the island of Cuba would now be governed under *leyes especiales* ("special laws"),* and its provinces would no longer furnish deputies to the Cortes. The disdainful attitude toward the Cubans was revealed in the wording of the Decree acknowledging that it might be ". . . distasteful to the wicked, who under the semblance of desiring liberty which they do not understand, aspire to some other object, damnable and prejudicial to their own safety and interests. . . ." In other words, reformism was merely a cloak for independence and abolition. This attitude is also reflected in the express provision of the decree forbidding freedom of the press. The Captain General was granted discretionary power to censor all written or printed material, and especially to watch the admission of material printed in other countries.[17]

Thus, Cuba was deprived of representation in Spain, put outside the constitution, and placed even more firmly under the iron-handed rule of the military government. The world witnessed the irony

---

* The promise that there would be special laws adopted for Cuba was never fulfilled.

and absurdity of simultaneous constitutionalism in Spain and absolutism in Cuba.*

Since there was no way for Cuban reformers to bring their grievances to the Spanish Cortes, the majority of them abandoned all political activity. Unable to return to Cuba, unwilling to remain in Spain, even if he had been allowed to stay, Saco took up residence in France where he began work on his monumental history of slavery. Before he left for what was to be permanent exile from Cuba, he issued from Madrid a new warning to the Creole proprietors in his native land urging the complete ending of the slave trade. He pointed out that the trade was increasing, and that abolition of the traffic would not, as the Creole proprietors feared, ruin or endanger the agriculture of the island. Saco analyzed three of the most common arguments employed by the slaveowners to justify the slave trade: first, that only African slaves could withstand the hard labor on the sugar plantations; second, that only Africans could resist tropical climate and infirmities; third, that free labor was too expensive in Cuba. He answered each of these arguments in turn, giving specific examples. Whites had accustomed themselves to plantation work; whites born on the island could, and did, withstand tropical heat and diseases; white labor had proved less expensive when compared with the mortality and maintenance costs of slave labor. Moreover, he warned the proprietors that the slave trade was doomed to disappear under the pressure of world opinion. The slaveowners should awaken to that fact and make the necessary adjustments now and with foresight.[18]

Saco's arguments aroused little response from the Creole planters. Nevertheless, he was to continue to influence Cuban events with his pen. He had become Cuba's acknowledged spiritual leader in exile.

Not all Cubans accepted the deprivation of their constitutional

* Another example of this contradiction related to the slavery issue, A Royal Decree of March 29, 1836 abolished whatever remained of slavery in the Peninsula; but when it was proposed that the decree be discussed in the Cortes and there acted upon, the motion was turned down on the ground that even though the matter referred to the Peninsula and not to the colonies, such a discussion would only alarm the slaveowners of Puerto Rico and Cuba. (José Antonio Saco, *Historia de la esclavitud de la raza Africana en el Nuevo Mundo y en especial en los países Americano-hispanos*, Habana, 1938, vol. II, p. 156.)

rights without protest. In Oriente, a rebellion broke out led by General Lorenzo, governor of the Eastern Department, which proclaimed the re-establishment of the Constitution of 1812 in the island. At first the uprising had the support of the Creole planters in Oriente, and threatened to gain control of the entire area. In Santiago, the center of the uprising, Spanish rule ceased.[19]

Tacón organized a military expedition to put down the revolt. But he did not depend on armed might alone to smash the threat to Spanish rule. He already knew enough about the Cuban planter-slaveowning class to predict that their support for General Lorenzo would weaken when they realized that a revolutionary situation in Oriente could spark a slave rebellion. As the Cuban historian Manuel Villanova points out, Tacón counted on "the group of Cuban *hacendados* who saw in the constitutional regime a menace to the existence of slavery."[20] To give the *hacendados* time to reconsider the support they had offered General Lorenzo, Tacón did not hurry his troops towards Oriente.

Tacón's evaluation of the situation proved correct. When the planters saw that the rebellion was leading to all-out war, they abandoned the revolt and demanded of Lorenzo that he take "measures which he judges conducive to put us in harmony with the present Administration of the rest of the island." They gave this reason for their abandonment of the revolt: "When harmony is lacking among the authorities the people are also divided in opinions, the parties are in ferment, *property is put in danger*, security ceases, lives are jeopardized, and, in one word, *anarchy threatens*."[21] No wonder the Spanish Minister Calatrava said that the existence of slavery in Cuba was worth an army of 100,000 men for maintaining its loyalty to Spain.[22]

Once again the wealthy Creole planters had demonstrated that they were prepared to accept an oppressive Spanish tyranny rather than risk the loss of their slaves in a revolution.

Saco put his finger on the crux of the whole question when he wrote:

> In Cuba, where there is no other alternative but life or death, a revolution must never be attempted, except when its triumph shall be as certain as a mathematical demonstration. In our present cir-

cumstances, the *political revolution* is necessarily accompanied by a social revolution and the social revolution is the complete ruin of the Cuban race.[23]

Even after the constitutional revolt in Oriente split apart, Tacón had no easy time suppressing the uprising. However, he obtained valuable assistance from an interesting development which foreshadowed future events in Cuban history. American-owned plantations and sugar mills, and the Juraguá Iron Company's mines and the British-owned copper mines were located in the neighborhood of Santiago. Fearing that the uprising might damage these properties, and concerned lest it spread and overthrow Spanish rule throughout the island, consular officers of the United States, Britain and France called for warships of their respective countries to put in at Santiago in support of Tacón. The naval aid of the three countries was of considerable assistance to Tacón in suppressing the internal revolt in Oriente. The three powers demonstrated that, despite their rivalry, they could co-operate wholeheartedly when faced by an internal threat to Spanish rule in Cuba. This was expressed by Nicholas P. Trist, United States Consul in Cuba since 1833, in a report to Secretary of State Forsyth:

> We [the United States, England and France] may have differed in the past over the precise influence each should exercise in this island, but I am happy to report that when the crisis was faced by this government, the danger to its authority being even greater than you may have learned from reports reaching Washington, there was no thought of using the situation to achieve a special advantage. The only thought was to maintain the authority of the government and to assure the continuation of Spanish rule in the island. This, fortunately, has been achieved.

In concluding his dispatch, Trist praised Tacón's administration in Cuba. The island was "flourishing & will, I am firmly convinced, continue to improve in every respect so long as Tacón shall remain at the helm."[24] That the liberty of the Cubans was hardly "flourishing" did not trouble the United States Consul!

Had any Cuban liberal read Trist's dispatch he would have hardly been surprised by the Consul's praise of Tacón's regime. Ever since Tacón had arrived in Cuba to inaugurate his reactionary regime, Trist, much to the disgust of the Cuban liberals, had given him ardent co-operation. His enthusiasm for the despotic Captain General became more understandable when protests began arriving in Washington, charging that Trist was participating in the slave trade in collusion with Tacón and a syndicate which shared its profits with Queen Mother Maria Cristina of Spain.

In August, 1835, reluctantly yielding to British pressure, Spain ratified a new treaty which was supposed to put teeth in the law of 1817 abolishing the slave trade. Spain promised to take more efficient measures against the participation of her subjects in the slave trade. The only result of the Treaty of 1835, however, was to change the character of the slave trade without essentially reducing it. (In 1835, the year of the new treaty, an estimated 19,000 slaves were landed illicitly on the island of Cuba and the number rose to 42,240 in 1837.[25]) Ships were no longer openly fitted out in Cuban ports. The slavers simply changed from the Spanish to the American flags. Since the British could not search American ships—the United States was then the only power refusing to concede the right of search—the American flag was used by slave ships in African waters. (To a lesser extent the Portuguese flag was also used.) "From the fall of 1836 onwards," notes a student of the African slave trade, "an increasing number of Spanish-owned slavers were navigated to Africa under the American flag and with legitimate American papers aboard . . . and by 1839 made up a large proportion of all the slavers sailing to Cuba."[26]

Trist took good advantage of the fact that the Stars and Stripes gave immunity to slave traders, and, as the voluminous evidence in his case indicates,[27] connived at, aided, and abetted by all means in his power, the slave-trading syndicate to which Tacón and the Spanish Crown belonged. The syndicate bought American ships (built in Baltimore), sent them to Africa with a token American citizen aboard, loaded them with Negroes. On the return voyage their ownership was transferred to the American whenever a British cruiser appeared. Trist signed ship's papers in blank form for these vessels; he even authenticated the papers of the numerous Portuguese vessels clearing in and out of Havana for Africa. Of the 71 slavers known to have put in at Cuban ports in 1838, Trist provided papers for 61.[28]

Public indignation in the United States over the use of the American flag to shield the slave trade led to an investigation of Trist. The accused Consul defended himself by diverting the issue, accusing the British of using the slave trade question as a screen to gain control of Cuba and abolitionize it.[29] This charge, of course, attracted approving attention from the slaveholding forces in Congress. Trist, proved guilty in an investigation conducted in Havana by Alexander H. Everett, former Minister to Spain,* was recalled as Consul, but this was done on general grounds. On July 15, 1841 a letter was sent to Trist informing him that President Tyler, though without forming any judgment on the particular charges against him, had decided to make a change at Havana. Thus no official condemnation was pronounced on his use of the American flag to assist the Cuban slave trade.**[30]

At this point in Cuba's history, the second reform movement was already a thing of the past. The reform cause was dead—so dead, in fact, that it did not stir again until almost twenty years later. Yet, though the second reform movement failed, it was not without lasting significance. The cynical smashing of Cuban hopes of sharing in the liberal era in Spain, along with the brutal despotism of Tacón's rule, deepened the division between Cubans and Spaniards. Although many leading Cubans, having lost hope of moderating Spanish oppression, followed Saco into exile, others were to remain in the island and continue the struggle. In his poem, José Jacinto

---

* Actually, Everett's report was only a slap on the wrist. "The consul might," he wrote in summing up, "without impropriety, and in the full discharge of his duty, ought to have taken more active measures to prevent the illegal use of the American flag. . . . His omission to do so has not been the result of indifference, or any more corrupt motive; but of a settled conviction that any measures which he could take for the purposes alluded to would be entirely ineffective, from the impossibility of procuring such evidence as would be available in a court of justice." (Everett to Forsyth, July 21, 1840, 36th Cong., 2nd Sess., *House Exec. Doc. No. 115*, pp. 471–95.) For an unconvincing defense of Trist, *see* J. Fred Rippy, "Nicholas Philip Trist," *Dictionary of American Biography*, vol. XVIII, pp. 645–46.

** Trist was made chief clerk of the State Department, and, at the end of the Mexican War, was sent to Mexico to negotiate peace.

Milanés of Matanzas voiced the sentiments of those who would continue the battle for Cuba:

> I am a son of Cuba
> I am tied to her by a powerful destiny.
> I go with her. It is imperative
> that I follow her
> whether the path be
> perilous or pleasant.

> Because of her I go,
> without obstacles or delays,
> either under the yoke or suffering
> from vengeance;
> I will go with her while I
> weep because she is a slave,
> I will go with her until I
> can sing her freedom.* [31]

---

* José Jacinto Milanés (1814–1863) was Secretary of the Railroad Company of Matanzas until he became mentally ill. Self-taught, he mastered several languages.

chapter 10

CUBAN SLAVE SOCIETY

In the latter part of Tacón's administration, an event occurred which foreshadowed major developments during most of the next decade. In 1837, the liberal *Club de los Habaneros* organized the *Conspiración de la Cadena Triangular y Soles de la Libertad* (Conspiracy of the Threefold Chain and Suns of Liberty) to abolish slavery and free the island. Tacón's informers betrayed the conspiracy, and it was suppressed. But for the next eight years Cuba entered a period in which the struggle against the slave trade and slavery dominated the scene.

Though the forces mobilized in this struggle were primarily Cuban, a powerful factor was British pressure for the complete suppression of the slave trade and for modification of Cuba's domestic labor system. British agitation in Cuba was the product of English abolitionism and empire interests. On August 28, 1833, in response to incessant petitions by the anti-slavery societies, Parliament finally passed the Emancipation Act abolishing slavery in the British Empire.*

Although the act was intended to be gradual, its object had been completed in the British West Indies by the late 1830's.[1]

The emancipation of slaves in the sugar-producing British West Indies raised the cost of production in those islands, while Cuba retained its cheap slave labor. North American and European merchants who formerly purchased their staples in British Jamaica, now came to Havana for Cuban sugar.[2] The only hope of an eco-

---

* British planters in the West Indies were given a compensation of twenty million pounds. All slaves were converted into apprentices. For field hands the term of apprenticeship was six years, and for all others, four years. Extension of this period was made impossible.

184

nomic revival in the British West Indies lay in an immediate end to the slave trade, and as soon as possible, to slavery itself in Cuba. A British Commission in the 1840's frankly declared that if the Cuban slave traffic continued, the ruin of the British West Indies "would be complete and immediate."[3] In the same period the Captain General of Cuba informed his home government that England was not merely driving for a complete suppression of the slave traffic but for a total emancipation of the island's slaves. The motive was to destroy Cuba's advantage over the British West Indies in the production of sugar.[4]

For all England's efforts to curtail the illicit slave traffic in Cuba, the slave trade, for several reasons, actually increased after the Treaty of 1835. For one thing, the new treaty differed little from that of 1817. To be sure, the right to search suspected ships and to detain them on *prima facie* evidence was an advance; formerly, suspected ships could only be detained if slaves were found aboard. Yet, as David Turnbull pointed out after a visit to Cuba, it was easy to dispose of *prima facie* evidence such as water-barrels and dock arrangements. ". . . any ordinary ship's carpenter can perform this operation on a very short notice. . . ."[5] In effect, the Treaty of 1835 merely changed the character of the slave trade without reducing it; the American and Portuguese ships took over from Spanish slavers. In the Webster-Ashburton Treaty of 1842, the United States agreed to suppress the use of the American flag in the slave traffic, but American ships continued to bring slaves to Cuba. The profits were so large that American speculators, especially wealthy New Yorkers, were willing to take the risks.[6]

One has merely to glance at the economic structure of Cuba to understand why the illicit traffic continued and even increased. The era of Cuban prosperity, initiated by the Haitian revolution of the 1790's, was stimulated afresh by the abolition of slavery in the British West Indies. By the 1840's, sugar was the basis of this prosperity. (By 1851 sugar accounted for 84 percent of Cuba's exports.[7]) Coffee had ceased to have much significance, for the greater portion of the coffee estates had been abandoned or turned over to sugar production. The devastating hurricanes of 1843 and 1845 undoubtedly figured in this, but the principal cause of the slow demise of the Cuban coffee industry was the tariff imposed by the United States in 1834 in retaliation against discriminatory tariffs in Cuba on American flour. Thereafter, the United States bought most of its coffee from Brazil.[8]

The tobacco industry was also prospering, both in the exportation of the raw leaf and the finished cigar, but the small tobacco farmers were not heavy users of slave labor. The Cuban sugar industry alone was responsible for the continual infiltration of African slaves. The number of sugar plantations rose from 510 in 1827 to 1,400 in 1846, but the size of the plantations also increased in the trend toward greater establishments with heavy investments in land, steam-powered machinery and slaves.[9] Capital and credit could come from Cuba, Spain and the United States, but in Cuba there was no internal source of slaves comparable to the border states of the South, and natural increase was low because few women were imported from Africa. (A traveller in the island noted that "not a single female was to be met with in the plantations."[10]) Hence the only way to increase the slave labor force to meet the requirements of expanding sugar production was to recruit it in Africa.[11] To be sure, the cost of slaves kept mounting, but the price of sugar more than kept pace and not only paid for additional mechanization but swelled the fortunes of the great Creole planting families.*[12]

When the United States tariff of 1842 caused a drop in sugar prices, the planters answered it by producing still more sugar. Thus, in periods of high or low prices, sugar production rose and so did the requirement for an increased labor force.[13] This demand of the Cuban planters for slave labor—save for the small group whose plantations were well stocked with slaves and who hoped to double their capital when the slave traffic closed—had proved to be too great to be influenced by Saco's practical arguments for

---

* Cuba was predominantly a sugar country not only in terms of the wealth but also in terms of social prestige. Many "sugar noblemen" bought titles from the Spanish Crown at a standard price of $25,000. Even the sugar planter who was heavily in debt—and many were—occupied a place of social importance in Cuba. (F. Wurdiman, *Notes on Cuba. . . . By a Physician,* Boston, 1844, p. 149; Leland H. Jenks, *Our Cuban Colony,* New York, 1927, p. 25; Maturin M. Ballou, *History of Cuba,* Boston, 1854, pp. 140–41.)

terminating the slave trade, and it was to prove too strong to be overcome by British efforts to halt the traffic.

Ignoring her treaties with Great Britain, Spain refused to put an effective stop to fresh importations of Africans into Cuba. Indeed, the Spanish authorities quite openly connived in the traffic. The corrupt Queen Mother in Madrid was financially involved in a slave-smuggling company; the Spanish Captains General in Cuba received up to an ounce of gold (or about fifty dollars) for each slave they cleared into the island, and their subordinate officials also received a "cut" in appreciation of their "co-operation."[14]

Thus a large network of interests was involved in the accelerating Cuban slave traffic. There were the Cuban sugar planters who demanded a constantly replenished labor supply; the Spanish and American investors in slave ships to Africa who gained enormous profits in Cuba; the Spanish Crown which shared the profits of the slave-trading syndicate; the Captains General who deposited hundreds of thousands in London banks, earned by their connivance in the traffic during their terms in Havana;* and there were the scores of poorly paid functionaries whose main income came from slavers' bribes.[15]

The working class, Negro and white, came out on the losing end, of course. An estimate of the labor force of Cuba in 1846 reveals that out of a total population of 896,294 there was a working population of 431,258, divided as follows:

	Urban	Rural	Total
WHITE	58,806	54,504	113,310
FREE NEGRO	47,162	18,252	65,414
SLAVE	44,951	207,583	252,534
TOTAL	150,919	280,339	431,258[16]

The number of white workers does not mean that they occupied a significant position in Cuba's economy. That economy was based primarily on slave labor, and this reduced work opportunities for

* Captain General Roncali deposited approximately half a million pesos in London after a brief stay in Cuba. (Herminio Portell Vilá, *Historia de Cuba en sus relaciones con los Estados Unidos y España*, La Habana, 1938–41, vol. I, pp. 477–78.)

free labor and made it impossible for it to organize into trade unions to improve conditions.* For one thing, agriculture, which alone could employ a vast number of white workers, mainly employed slaves. For another, slavery bred a contempt for work and created a society in which there was no respect for labor. "It is the presence of slavery," Turnbull noted, "which in the island of Cuba, as in every country where it exists,** throws every personal exertion into discredit. Because labour is the lot of slavery, the pride of the freeman is alarmed lest the line of demarcation should not be broad enough between him and the slave, and he therefore abstains from working altogether."[17] "The result," he noted, "is that the Church, the Bar, medicine, cattle-raising, and the Army are the only careers and occupations which have attracted our youth; and, since many have not been able to find employment, the necessary consequence is that a considerable number are idle."[18]

Twenty years later, the problem of white vagrancy had become even more aggravated. Juan J. Reyes, in his 1851 study of vagrancy in Cuba, reported that unemployed whites wandered through the provinces stealing and living off the land. This would continue as long as these workers looked "not only with repugnance, but also with horror on that kind of labor which habit commonly associates with slaves." So long as slavery existed, it was "necessary to confess that the path which leads to vagrancy is determined and many times inevitable."[19]

Most sugar plantations were managed by overseers *(mayordomos)* for absentee owners. The only object of the overseer, in which he was encouraged by the planter, was to show a large profit. Brutal exploitation was the order of the day. During the

* In his study, "The Development of Organized Labor in Cuba," Charles Albert Page notes "the complete absence of any organizational basis" among the free white workers of Cuba in the mid-nineteenth century. (unpublished Ph.D. thesis, University of California, Latin-American Studies, 1952, p. 15.) However, there appears to have been a Fishermen's and Sailors' Guild organized in Nuevitas in 1855. (*ibid.*, p. 179.)
** This is illustrated graphically in a report by Thomas Ewbank, a traveller in Brazil. "Ask a respectable native youth of a family in low circumstances why he does not learn a trade and earn an independent living; ten to one but he will tremble with indignation and inquire if you mean to insult him! 'Work! Work!' screamed one; 'we have blacks to do that!'" (Thomas Ewbank, *Life in Brazil*, New York, 1856, p. 184.)

cutting season, when the success of the crop depended upon speedy day and night operation, slaves were often worked to death.[20] Turnbull described the two faces of Cuban slavery. Domestic slaves were treated well and this was what the visitor saw in Havana; but the field hands, left to the mercies of the *mayordomos,* were wretchedly treated, he could affirm "as the result of personal inquiry and minute observation. . . ."* "In no quarter," he wrote in 1840, "unless perhaps in Brazil, which I have not visited, is the state of slavery so desperately wretched as it is at this moment on the sugar plantations of the queen of the Indies, the far-famed island of Cuba."[21]

Most travellers who, like Turnbull, went into the interior of the island, reported that the slaves on the sugar plantations were miserably housed, fed, and clothed. The average life duration of these slaves did not exceed ten years. The travelers were appalled by the frequency of suicide among the slaves. (Self-inflicted death by suspension, strangling, or, as a last resort, by folding back the tongue, appeared to be common.) They could understand why when they saw the tin masks, shackles and pronged collars that many slaves, despite the law forbidding shackling of slaves, were forced to wear for acts of minor insubordination.[22]

Cuban Negroes were divided into *bozales,* recent arrivals in the island; *ladinos,* imported before the legal though not actual suppression of the slave trade in 1820; *emancipados;* and *criollos,* born on the island. Of all the Negroes in Cuba the lot of the *emancipados* was perhaps the most bitter. *Emancipados* were Africans taken from captured slave ships. According to Article 7 of the Treaty of 1817, they were to receive from the Mixed Commission a certificate of emancipation, and then be delivered to the government in whose territory the Commission pronounced sentence. Thus, if the *emancipados* were captured off the coast of Cuba by either British or Spanish ships, they were to be delivered to the government of

---

* Apart from conveying an erroneous impression of the real conditions of the slaves in Cuba, the better treatment of the slaves in Havana who were the personal servants, male and female, of the absentee landowners was another instrument of control over slavery. It fostered division among the slaves and supplied the owners with spies and traitors useful in detecting plots to overthrow the slave system.

Cuba, which was obligated to place them under its patronage; to give them employment for a period of from five to seven years as servants or free workers, and to guarantee their liberty at the end of the term. The planters, in return for the services of the *emancipados*, were to feed and clothe them, instruct them in religion, teach them a trade, and set them free at the end of the term.[23]

But no sooner were the first slave cargoes captured off the coast of Cuba in 1824, and the Negroes declared free by the Mixed Commission and placed under the patronage of the Cuban government, than reports began to circulate of gross abuses. English consuls in Havana, instructed to enforce the obligations of the Treaty of 1817, charged that the Captains General were selling the *emancipados* to the slaveowners; that the planters, instead of teaching them a trade or working them as free men as provided by law, treated them exactly as slaves. According to Saco, the *emancipado* was more a slave than the slave himself, for the slaveowners tended to squeeze all the labor possible in the five to seven years the *emancipados* were under their control. The few *emancipados* who survived the seven years' indenture, came to their "freedom" broken in health, and incapable of sustaining themselves in Cuban society.[24]

Soon a lucrative business developed in substituting *emancipados* for dead or missing slaves and the provision that they be freed after seven years was forgotten. The majority of the *emancipados* became permanent slaves.[25] British pressure to end this vicious violation of the Treaty of 1817 brought little result. The most Spain was willing to do was to issue, on April 14, 1824, a pious hope that *emancipados* be given to persons of good character so that they might be more certain of learning a trade which would make it possible "that later they could live on their own." Planters were charged with treating the *emancipados* well and told to establish a register wherein the name of the *emancipado* and the plantation was recorded. In this way, the government could check on his condition.[26]

Soon complaints were heard of false names and details being entered in the register. In practice, the planters continued to retain the *emancipados* as slaves and could resell them after their period of service was over. The British sought to solve the problem by proposing that when slaves were captured, the Negroes be put at liberty at once. But the Cuban authorities refused. They argued that an increase in the number of free Negroes in the island would undermine the slave system, and that the granting of immediate freedom to slaves from Africa "would represent a dangerous example to the other slaves of the island." When the British proposed that all *emancipados* be returned to Africa, the government of Cuba objected that it was too expensive, and stressed the un-Christianlike nature of the suggestion, for it would mean returning them to the "darkness of paganism." "But the real reason," writes one student of the subject, "was that a sizeable income was derived from turning over the *emancipados* to the slaveowners for a period of seven years. Since this arrangement represented a source of revenue for the authorities and a source of labor for the proprietors, there was not the least demand in Cuba for the return of the *emancipados* to Africa."[27]

Despite assurances in the Treaty of 1835 that the *emancipados* would be freed after their seven years' service, this did little to improve their worsening conditions. A register of all the *emancipados* was to be kept at the office of the Captain General with full identifications. This register was to be placed at the disposal of the Mixed Commission every six months, so it could ascertain the number, location, and condition of the *emancipados* and see to it that the treaty was being enforced. But the British members of the Commission complained that only rarely could they persuade the Captain General to turn the register over to them, and that usually the register was not kept up-to-date or else kept in such a manner that the records could not be clearly distinguished.[28]

The Negro people of Cuba, unfortunately, had few writers to describe the life of their enslaved brothers and sisters and to speak up for their rights. One such work, however, does exist. It was published in London in 1840 under the title: *Poems by A Slave in the Island of Cuba Recently Liberated; Translated by R. R. Madden, M.D., with the history of the Early Life of the Negro Poet, Written by Himself.*[29] In his introduction, Madden, a leader of the British and Foreign Anti-Slavery Society, told how he had been presented with the collection of poems and the autobiography when he was in Cuba in 1838. Some of the poems had been published in the island, but only such "as were of a publishable kind in a country like Cuba, where slavery is under the especial protection, and knowledge under the ban of the censors of the press."* Madden had translated into English a number of the poems which were unpublished "or unpublishable in Cuba," as well as the narrative of life under slavery. (The originals in the Spanish language were deposited with the Secretary of the British and Foreign Anti-Slavery Society.) Although Madden could not disclose his name, he mentioned that the author was in his forty-second year, and had been born in Cuba of a father and mother who had lived and died in slavery, had labored on a sugar plantation and had obtained his liberty at the age of 38 by purchasing it for $800. As a free Negro, he lived in Havana and gained his livelihood by

---

* This, of course, was the main reason for the absence of descriptions of life under slavery by the Cuban Negroes themselves. In the United States, slaves who escaped to the North and freedom were able to publish narratives of life under slavery—one of the most important being that by Frederick Douglass, an escaped slave—but in Cuba, where no haven existed for a fugitive slave except the mountain wilderness, this was impossible.

Recently, an event occurred in Cuba which threw some light on conditions under slavery. During the presentation of diplomas to 3,500 *alfabetizados* (men and women who had learned to read and write during the Revolutionary government's campaign to wipe out illiteracy in Cuba), Maria de la Cruz Senmanat was one of those who received a diploma. What was unusual in this remarkable ceremony was the fact that she was 106 years old, and had been born a slave on May 3, 1855. The following excerpts from her conversation with Dr. Fidel Castro during the ceremonies, which were broadcast on television, are significant:

"Did you know the times of slavery?"

"Of course I did. I was born in the sugar mill, Senmanat, at Santa Cruz del Norte, in the province of Havana. When I wanted to learn to read and write from the coachman of the family that took me from the sugar mill to Havana, the housekeeper found a cardboard with letters that I used to hide underneath the seat where I used to sit to embroider, and to think of my mother who remained working in the house of the owners of the sugar mill. He used to ask me, what is this letter? When the colored people were found learning, they were punished, called 'dogs,' and put into stocks. . . ."

Dr. Castro urged the former slave to write the story of her life, and she promised to do so.

"Dr. Castro: 'Remember now, that you have a commitment with the people to write your life-story.'

"Maria de la Cruz Senmanat: 'And I will write it.'" (*Revolución*, June 19, 1961.)

hiring himself out as an occasional servant. In a copy of the work in the New York Public Library, the Negro author is listed, in pencil, as Juan Francisco Manzano.

The autobiographical material is interesting for the light it throws on the cruel treatment of the slaves and their hunger for freedom. After describing how the owner of the sugar plantation on which he was a slave had told him he could not hope to purchase his freedom no matter how hard he worked, the author writes: "As for me, from that moment that I lost my hopes, I ceased to be a faithful slave; from an humble, submissive being, I turned into the most discontented of mankind. I wished to have wings to fly from that place, and to go to Havana, and from that day my only thoughts were in planning how to escape and run away."

His poems present a vivid picture of Cuban slavery. The poem entitled "The Slave Merchant" contains these bitter passages:

> The Cuban merchant prosecutes his trade
> Without a qualm, or a reproach being made
> . . . . . .
> What wrongs the poor have suffered by his trade.
> To him, what boots it, if the sale is good,
> How many perished in the fray of blood!
> How many peaceful hamlets were attacked,
> And poor defenceless villages were sacked!
> How many wretched beings in each town
> Maimed at the onslaught, or in flight cut down!
> How many infants from the breast were torn,
> And frenzied mothers dragged away forlorn!
> To him, what boots it, how the ship is crammed;
> How many hundreds in the hold are jammed;
> How small the space! What piteous cries below!
> What frightful tumult in that den of woe!
> Or how the hatches when the gale comes on,
> Are battened down, and ev'ry hope seems gone;
> What struggling hands in vain are lifted there,
> Or how the lips are parched that move in prayer,
> Or mutter imprecations wild and dread,
> On all around, the dying and the dead;
> What cares the merchant for that crowded hold,
> The voyage pays, if half the slaves are sold.[30]

The long poem, "The Sugar Estate," pictures the visit of a British abolitionist to a Cuban plantation. He is taken in hand by the planter who is home to meet him, instead of being in Havana as usual.* The planter assures the Englishman that what he may have heard of the condition of the slaves has no relation to the actual facts.

> You see them yonder in that field of cane,
> They have no cause, believe me, to complain;
> They want for nothing, have no wish on earth,
> Except for work—of which there is no great dearth,
> I only wish the poor but fared elsewhere,
> One-half as well as all our slaves do here.
> Observe—the field is not so very far—
> How full of mirth and glee our Negroes are!
> How well they look! how pleased to work! You see
> What happy creatures even slaves can be!
> We spare no pains indeed to make them so,
> It is, no doubt, our interest so to do,
> Besides, you know, humanity itself
> Has claims upon us, quite apart from pelf.

Left to himself, the Englishman explores the sugar estate, and discovers that the condition of the slaves differs sharply from the lyrical description of his host:

> Jamaica bondsmen in "the good old times,"
> Of our West Indian cruelties and crimes,
> Were pretty hardly worked, both old and young,
> Yet here is an amount of labour, wrung
> From Cuban slaves, just double that of ours,
> And nearly twice the sum of working hours;

* In the course of the poem, a slave declares:
> Our despot does not live on his estate.
> He loves the town, and there he goes the gait
> of other fools, and thinks that all grandees
> Should lead a life of luxury and ease.
> He finds Havana stored with ev'ry vice,
> Can feed his pampered senses or entice.
> There in his squalid splendour, he can move,
> Exhaust the passions and imagine love;
> Plume up his haughty indigence in smiles,
> And waste a harvest on a harlot's wiles.

For here the grasping master still must have
Just thrice the produce from each working slave.

. . . . . .

What does it matter here, how many lives
Are lost in labour, while the planter thrives,
The Bozal market happily is nigh,
And there the planter finds a fresh supply.
'Tis cheaper far to buy new strength, we're told,
Than spare the spent, or husband out the old;
'Tis not a plan by which a planter saves,
To purchase females, or to rear up slaves.

Talking with the overseer, the Englishman obtains a clear picture of how slavery operates:

We purchase slaves to cultivate our plains,
We don't want saints or scholars to cut canes;
We buy a Negro for his flesh and bone,
He must have muscle—brains, he need have none.
But where, you ask me, are the poor old slaves?
Where should they be, of course, but in their graves!
We do not send them there before their time,
But let them die, when they are past their prime.
Men who are worked by night as well as day,
Somehow or other, live not to be grey
Sink from exhaustion—sicken—droop and die,
And leave the Count another batch to buy;
There's stock abundant in the slave bazaars,
Thanks to the banner of the stripes and stars!
You cannot think, how soon the want of sleep
Breaks down their strength, 'tis well they are so cheap,
Four hours for rest—in time of crop—for five
Or six long months, and few indeed will thrive.

With twenty hours of unremitting toil,
Twelve in the field, and eight indoors, to boil
Or grind the cane—believe me, few grew old,
But life is cheap, and sugar, sir—is gold.[31]

"But life is cheap, and sugar, sir—is gold." In one line the Negro poet epitomized the whole system of Cuban slavery. Small wonder he wrote in one of his poems entitled, "To Cuba":

Cuba, of what avail that thou art fair!
Pearl of the seas, the pride of the Antilles!
If thy poor sons, have still to see thee share
The pangs of bondage, and its thousand ills;
Of what avail the verdure of thy hills?
The fair bloom the coffee plain displays
Thy canes' luxuriant growth; whose culture fills
More graves than famine, or the sword finds ways
To glut with victims calmly as it slays.

Cuba, oh, Cuba, when they call thee fair!
And rich and beautiful, the Queen of the isles!
Star of the West, and ocean's gem most rare!
Oh, say to them who mock thee with such wiles
Take of these flowers, and view these lifeless spoils
That wait the worm; behold the hues beneath
The pale cold cheek, and seek for living smiles,
Where beauty lies not in the arms of death,
And bondage taints not with its poisoned breath.[32]

In translating and publishing these poems, Madden hoped that
he had "done enough to vindicate in some degree the character of
Negro intellect. At least the attempt affords me an opportunity of
recording my conviction, that the blessings of education and good
government are only wanted to make the natives of Africa in-
tellectually and morally, equal to the people of any nation on the
surface of the globe."[33] It is, indeed, part of the tragedy of Cuba
in this period that such evidence could not be made available to
the inhabitants of that island. But when, as we shall presently see,
a great Negro poet was executed in Cuba for voicing far less
vigorous hatred of tyranny, it is hardly surprising that the remarkable verses and autobiography of the "recently liberated"
slave could not be published in his native land.

To have published these poems would, of course, have demolished
one of the most powerful devices of control over slavery—namely,
the fostering of a belief in the innate inferiority of the Negro
people. The ideologists for the wealthy sugar planters—so-called
ethnologists, sociologists and historians—asserted that the Negro
was not really a man but a kind of beast who had obtained the
power of speech; because of innate inferior racial characteristics,

he could not raise himself to the level of the white man and was incapable of exercising the rights and duties which an organized society demanded. His sole function was to fulfill the God-ordained role of slave to the white man. As Arango y Parreño put it, "there had always been slaves in the world and there always would be." The Negro was an inferior being, he insisted, condemned by the inexorable designs of God to be a slave for the superior race, and as long as there existed men of black skin there would be slavery.*[34]

The myth of the racial inferiority of the Negro became a fixed tenet in Cuban society of the nineteenth century, and was supported by the leading social thinkers in the island. The Negro, by the color of his skin, went the argument, was condemned in all social systems to occupy the lower and most exploited stratum of society. His color alone made it impossible for him to enjoy the fruits of liberty. Giving him freedom was to consign him to destruction since he could never rise out of a status of inferiority. Joaquin S. Suárez, a Cuban *hacendado* who belonged to the reform circle whose ideology reflected the class interests of the wealthy planters, insisted that the Negro's skin color subjected him to perpetual slavery. "It constitutes a point of incontestible doctrine," he wrote, "that it is impossible for the Negro and white races to live in any other way unless it is under the condition of oppressor and oppressed, of slave and master, and that consequently every project of emancipation would be as bad for the one as it would be disastrous for the other."[35] The Cuban historian Pedro J. Guiteras, in his *Historia de la Isla de Cuba* approvingly summed up the racist ideology of the Cuban slaveowners:

> The Negro who was declared free by the benevolence of the master would not identify himself with the mass of society. His color being permanent would continue as an element to separate him from the white race, because the indelible mark of race remains constant and invariable in spite of all the opinions and philanthropic sentiments; and according to the state of opinion

* Arango saw only one way out of this inevitable fate for the Negro, and that was "the whitening of our Negroes" through intermixing with lower-class whites. In this way, over a period of time, the inferior Negro racial traits would disappear and the blacks would be able to rise out of their predestined state as slaves since they would no longer be Negroes. (Francisco Arango y Parreño, *Obras*, Habana, 1888, vol. II, pp. 338, 340, 376, 654.)

where slavery exists as well as where it has been wiped out . . . it is impossible for the Negro to rise by his own efforts to the condition of the white man, no matter what may be his personal merits. . . . The truth is that the emancipated Negro has not been able to equal the hopes corresponding to the lovers of humanity.[36]

In the eyes of these racist ideologists—and in Cuba all spokesmen for the slaveholding class before 1868 were generally racists[37]— there was no place for the Negro in Cuban society. "Cuban nationality," Saco emphasized again and again, "is formed by the white race."[38] The only disagreement among the racist spokesmen for the *hacendado* class was whether the Negro was to remain in Cuba as an inferior, enslaved being, deprived of all natural human rights, or be eliminated entirely from Cuban soil. The more conservative ideologists of slavery adhered to the first while some reformers advocated the second. Thus the reformer Domingo del Monte wrote: "The task of all Cubans of hearts and of noble and sacred patriotism ought to be, first, to end the slave trade, and then go on little by little to the suppression of slavery without convulsions and violence, and, in the end, *to clean Cuba of the African race*. This is what reason will understand, self-interest, politics, religion and philosophy, in short, Cuban patriotism, require."[39] Saco underwrote this thesis to the full. "I desire," he said over and over, "not by violent nor revolutionary means, but temperate and pacific ones, to bring about the diminishing, the extinction if it were possible, of the Negro race in Cuba."[40]

Fundamentally, this reactionary concept of eliminating the Negro from Cuban life was rooted in fear. The ideologists for the slaveowners argued day in and day out that the Negro was not a man but a beast of burden predestined by God and nature to slave for the superior white race. But they knew inwardly he was a man, and that like other men he craved freedom and was only awaiting an opportunity to strike out for it. Saco realized this and his solution was to eliminate the Negro entirely, for "in the island of Cuba there have always been dangers of slave rebellions since the time that slavery was introduced into this island."[41]

The slaveowners, however, rejected this solution. They sought to meet the problem by a massive and intricate system of control.

As part of this system, the slave himself was propagandized about his innate inferiority from childhood to the grave, and often came to accept the concept of the inferiority of his entire people. As "Placido," the martyred Negro poet, wrote in condemning this vicious aspect of the system of slave control:

> The Negro is born and from then on
> for lack of culture
> In a chaos of bitterness
> becomes afflicted and blind.[42]

The core of this system was the Spanish garrison, ever ready to drown in blood every move of the slaves to liberate themselves. To supplement this military power, there were guards and police, patrols and armed men on horseback who roamed the countryside. Regulations for slave conduct saw to it that united action by slaves was impossible. The slaves of one work crew were prohibited from contact with another. They were kept isolated within the confines of the plantations and farms on which they worked. Overseers, unhampered by any judicial restrictions, punished any infraction of these rules and any protest, individual or collective. In short, Cuban society in the slave era, like all slaveholding societies, was in a state of constant military preparation for internal warfare. The Cuban historian Ramiro Guerra y Sánchez has brilliantly analyzed it:

> Slavery created, in fact, a state of permanent war between the white and the Negro, because the former deprived the latter of the natural right to liberty, and in case of protests or rebellion, punished him implacably to the point of causing death under the whip. Slavery was basically a perpetual state of war. The white believed that the right was on his side through the refuge of a traditional law—he had acquired the property of the servant whose destiny was to submit, obey, work and die. The Negro, as ignorant and savage as he might be, felt differently. His hostility against the master was defensive; therefore just. And the ends which the problem proposed, deprived the slave of all hope of liberation while the master kept his power. The Negro had no other solution than to try to destroy the white. What is certain is, when history judges the facts impartially as a whole without racial prejudices, that from the beginnings of the [nineteenth] century was produced in Cuba a

double longing for liberation: a longing for political and economic liberty on the part of the slave and the Cuban white, a longing for civil liberty and social equality on the part of the slave and the free Negro. There is no moral reason nor any other kind of reason to place the aspiration of the political liberty of the white on a plane superior to the longing for civil liberty of the Negro. The white Cuban had as an enemy, the oppressor of the metropolitan power. The slave had the white as the enemy, be he Spanish or Cuban, because both were in agreement on maintaining slavery. Only the racial prejudice of the whites and the inferiority complex created by slavery, by laws and customs in many Negroes, has permitted the continuation of considering as crimes the rebellions of the slaves to exterminate the masters and free themselves.[43]

Despite its elaborate machinery of control, the Cuban slaveholding class lived in constant fear and was often subjected to panics arising from doubt of its ability to maintain its power. Both these feelings were amply justified. Local spontaneous uprisings of slaves occurred in various districts in 1832, 1835, 1836, 1837, and 1838. All were suppressed with the usual terror; but, as T. R. Gray, American Consul in Trinidad pointed out in describing the suppression of the 1838 slave revolt in that city, "no one can say how soon it will be resumed."[44]

The slaveowners did not have long to wait. The rising tide of struggle against slavery reached unprecedented heights in the 1840's.

chapter 11

THE RISING TIDE OF ANTI-SLAVERY

Throughout the 1830's, the Captains General of Cuba complained to the home authorities of the activities of the British Consuls over the *emancipado* program and other aspects of the enforcement of the Treaties of 1817 and 1835. These activities, they charged, endangered public order and disturbed the slave population. Infected with "English ideas of liberty," the Negroes were coming to expect support from Great Britain, the most powerful nation in the world, whenever they struck out for freedom. Such "wild notions" served to encourage slave revolts.[1]

These protests were as nothing compared with those that arose in the fall of 1840. On November 3, 1840, David Turnbull, the famous English abolitionist, arrived in Havana as British Consul, and precipitated a series of events unprecedented in the history of Cuba.

Turnbull already knew the island well from his years of service on the anti-slave trade Mixed Commission. He had many friends among the Cuban liberals, including José de la Luz, Martínez Serrano, Domingo del Monte, Vicente and Rafael Castro. In 1838, he had been made a member of the Royal Patriotic and Economical Society of Havana. Enrique José Varona described him as "a man of iron, active and vigilant as few men were, he knew all that went on in Cuba."[2]

Turnbull was already famous as the author of *Travels in the West. Cuba; with Notices of Porto Rico, and the Slave Trade*, based on his observations as agent of the English Anti-Slavery Society. The book, published in London early in 1840, minced no words about the author's abolitionist sentiments. Turnbull reported the status of the slave in Cuba to be "desperately wretched"; that of

201

the *emancipados* to be "worse than ordinary slavery"; and the slave trade to be "on the increase in spite of the exertions that are made to suppress it."[3] This, of course made him unwelcome to the Cuban slaveholders and the authorities in the island who grew rich on the illicit slave trade. They were especially alarmed by the passage in his book which declared flatly: "The British authorities in Havana ought clearly to be acting as one man in discountenancing slavery, as well as in the suppression of the slave trade."[4] Moreover, the Spanish authorities were angered by Turnbull's charge that the Government protected the slave trade "as a growing check on the known desires of the Creoles for independence," in order more easily to maintain the people in obedience to Her Catholic Majesty.[5]

Turnbull's book, however, qualified him in the eyes of Lord Palmerston, Minister of Foreign Affairs, for the office in Cuba.[6] He was appointed British Consul at Havana and Superintendent of Liberated Africans (*Negros libertos*).* Turnbull took with him as Vice-Consul another British abolitionist, Francis Ross Cocking.

At the news of Turnbull's appointment Captain General Tacón immediately communicated his disapproval to the First Secretary of State in Spain. He warned that official of the dangers of Turnbull's presence in the island: "His ideas are those of a reformer of the kind who in exchange for maintaining a principle for protection of the Negroes, are surely capable of sacrificing the white race." He urged that Spain immediately declare him *non grata* and request his replacement. The communication was forwarded to the Spanish Minister in London with orders to take up the matter verbally with Lord Palmerston and urge him to appoint another Consul to replace Turnbull.[7] Palmerston brusquely rejected the suggestion.

Meanwhile, Turnbull and Cocking arrived in Havana and got a cold reception from the slaveowners and their allies. The slave interests were up in arms. The Royal Board of Promotion of Agricul-

---

* This position was not recognized in any of the diplomatic treaties between Spain and England. Turnbull himself noted that the office "is one of recent creation, arising out of the necessity of providing for the present comfort and future freedom of the Negroes captured by our cruisers, and brought with the slaver to the Havana, preparatory to her condemnation." (*Travels in the West. Cuba: with Notices of Porto Rico, and the Slave Trade*, London, 1840, p. 42.)

ture and Commerce, in a letter to the Captain General, warned that the principles upheld by Turnbull would be circulated "to the freed Negroes and thereon to the slaves, creating elements of distress in a country which by the soft nature of its inhabitants allows the slaves in the towns to participate in the domestic comforts and has relaxed discipline among those destined to cultivate the land." The preaching of the doctrine of freedom where it would be heard by people to whom freedom was unattainable would "create irretrievable evils, as was the case of the bloody Negro insurrection in nearby Santo Domingo." Concluding, this semi-official organization of businessmen demanded that Turnbull be expelled from the island as a menace to the prosperity and security of Cuba. Captain General Tacón did not go that far, but seeing his lucrative income from the slave trade menaced, he refused to recognize the new British Consul.[8]

But Turnbull was not to be intimidated. He knew that his ideas on the slave trade and slavery were endorsed by Palmerston, and he proceeded to do something about them. He had barely taken over his post when he insisted that the government of Cuba immediately enforce the treaties of 1817 and 1835 and put a stop to the slave trade. As a first step, he proposed that Spain formally agree to strengthen the powers of the Mixed Commission.[9] Next, Turnbull proposed a census of the slaves to determine which had entered Cuba after 1820, making it clear that since these Negroes had been brought into the island illegally, the owners of the slaves should be ordered to free them.

These two proposals, if adopted, would practically end slavery in the island. Since the average span of a slave in the cane fields and on the coffee plantations seldom exceeded 20 years, and since the great majority of the slaves were in these areas of production, it was obvious that, in 1840, almost all the slaves brought into Cuba before 1820 were dead. Thus, if those brought in after 1820 were liberated, and enforcement of the slave trade treaties were made effective, slavery in Cuba would be practically finished. There would remain only a handful of old slaves and a very few born in the island.[10]

Spain rejected both of Turnbull's proposals. The Spanish Council of State indignantly denied that the anti-slavery treaties were not enforced, and insisted that the increase of slaves in Cuba came not from the African trade but from marriage and the breeding of slaves "as in the United States"—an obvious falsehood. As for Turnbull's second proposal, the Council of State argued that if the Negroes brought in after 1820 were liberated and allowed to operate on their own, ignorance, laziness, and licentiousness would overrun Cuba as it had done Haiti and Jamaica, and this "would ruin the production of sugar." "We view with sadness such a suggestion from our old ally and friend," the Council of State concluded.[11]

In Cuba the mere mention of a census of all slaves illegally imported since 1820 caused consternation. Before word arrived that the British proposal had been rejected in Madrid, the Board of Promotion warned that "since the great wealth of the country as well as the small, lesser wealth depends upon the number of working arms to support them, from the moment Mr. Turnbull's system were established, production would entirely stop, thus leaving the territory abandoned to the disaster of general misery and the commotions of the Negro against the white."[12] The *Ayuntamiento* (Municipal Council) of Havana warned that if Spain granted England power to establish a tribunal in Cuba with authority to decide the status of illegally imported slaves, rebellion would be likely and the island would be irretrievably lost to the mother country. There was no alternative, for "left to themselves, free Negroes, in the ignorance and stupidity in which we maintain them for our convenience,* would retrograde naturally to a savage state and soon the island of Cuba would suffer the same fate of Española (Haiti)." The white population would not stand by idly and allow Spain "to sacrifice 400,000 whites for a measure that would make even unhappier 500,000 colored people."[13]

Though the slaveholders and their allies rejoiced at the rejection of the British proposals, they were fearful that weak Madrid might yet be pressured into accepting Turnbull's radical abolition meas-

---

* Thus the truth emerged in the moment of panic and it was admitted by the slaveholders that the Negro was not innately inferior but was kept in a state of ignorance for the profits of the slave interests.

ures. Their mistrust of the home government appeared to be justified when Tacón was relieved in 1841 by Captain General Gerónimo Valdés, who, while not an abolitionist, believed in enforcing the treaties on the slave trade and in encouraging Chinese and white immigration as the first step toward gradual abolition of slavery. No sooner had he taken over command in Cuba than Valdés infuriated the slaveowners and their allies by recognizing Turnbull officially as the British Consul. Next, he announced his intention to punish severely anyone found guilty of importing slaves into the island, and let it be known that no bribery would sway him.* Finally, he informed the slaveowners that the formerly ignored provisions in the slave codes protecting the slaves against abuse would be enforced.[14]

Valdés's policy had a dual effect on developments in Cuba. The slaveowners and their allies regarded these measures as the prelude to Spanish capitulation to Britain's demands, and thus the only way to maintain slavery was to be annexed by the United States, where slavery flourished under government protection. Simultaneously, in the United States, Southern members of Congress, alarmed by news of Turnbull's activities and the growing movement for gradual emancipation of Cuban slaves, raised an outcry for United States action against Turnbull and Valdés.[15] As we shall see in the next volume, a conspiracy for the annexation of Cuba to the United States spread during the early months of Valdés's administration.

The other effect was to stimulate the Negroes in Cuba into action. Seeing that Spain was yielding to British pressure, the anti-slavery elements in the island, among whom the free Negroes were most important, intensified their activity. In the summer of 1841, there were unsuccessful but large-scale slave uprisings in sugar mills and coffee plantations. And in October, 1841, fifty slaves building a mansion in Havana battled Spanish troops.[16]

The panic-stricken slaveowners attributed these uprisings to Turnbull's abolitionist activities, particularly after they saw a copy of the July 14, 1841 issue of the *British and Foreign Anti-Slavery Reporter*. An article by Turnbull contained the following:

---

* Valdés was said to be the only Captain General of the period who failed to enrich himself through the slave trade.

I have the great pleasure to inform you that the principles of abolition of slavery are already taking roots in this city and in Matanzas. At the present moment there are great hopes of obtaining results favorable to humanity and freedom and, if carefully dealt with, they must precisely bring about good results, in spite of the opposition against which we have to fight—the harmful influence of the traffic in Negroes. I say, therefore, without fear of being contradicted, that all the employees of Her Majesty appointed to any post in this Island should be in favor of abolition. This is also the opinion and the general desire of all those who favor it in this city; those who are small in numbers but influential by wealth. It seems incredible that all these men could do so much good. Their example would give strength to the rising principles of abolition throughout the country; their vigor and activities, based upon principles, would seek and find every day and hour the means to block the horrible progress of slave traffic in this market. Such men are necessary in the tribunal of the Mixed Commission of this city.[17]

The article was among the documents submitted in a demand for Turnbull's expulsion from the island. The British were accused of using their Consul in Havana as an agent for destroying the prosperity of Cuba in order to achieve the economic recovery of Jamaica, which had been rendered a wasteland by "the fanaticism of the antislavery society."[18] Although Valdés rejected the appeal for Turnbull's expulsion, he shared the common opinion that Turnbull was responsible for the recent slave uprisings. He assured the slaveowners they had no reason to fear that Spain would yield to Great Britain's demand for liberation of all slaves illegally imported since 1820. In fact, he had been informed by Madrid that Spain would never consent to any measures threatening the existence of slavery in Cuba.[19]

The slave interests had barely time to rejoice when Spain did yield to the relentless British pressure. Orders were issued to Valdés to prepare for the emancipation of all slaves introduced fraudulently since 1820. Valdés did not dare to publish the order. Instead, he pleaded with Madrid to reconsider, warning that Spain would lose Cuba to the United States if it insisted on his carrying out these orders.[20]

Meanwhile, Palmerston was acting to implement Spain's reluctant decision. He had already rejected pleas from the Spanish Minister Plenipotentiary in London requesting the removal of Turnbull, bluntly declaring that

> It is not the government of Spain which has the right to request from the British government the dismissal of Her Majesty's Consul to Cuba for having complied with his duties, but it is the British Government that has the right to request from Spain the dismissal of all the employees in Cuba, starting from the Governor himself, because they all protect notoriously and openly all the slave merchants in violation of the obligations of the treaty of the Spanish Crown. . . . It is impossible for the British government to behold indifferently how a treaty concluded between Great Britain and a foreign power is violated in the way in which the Treaty of 1835 with Spain is daily and publicly broken by the employees of the Spanish Crown.[21]

Two steamers loaded with munitions were dispatched to join the British Antilles squadron. The vessels arrived in Havana with instructions to support Turnbull in pressing Valdés to carry out the slave census. But the Captain General persuaded Vice-Admiral Parker that any attempt to carry out a register of slaves would cause a dangerous commotion in the island. The matter was postponed until further instructions were received.[22]

The knowledge of what had been passing back and forth between Madrid and Havana leaked out. The consequences were not long in coming. The annexationists frantically stepped up their activities. Now that their interests in preserving slavery were threatened, the *Peninsulares* were ready to join with the Creoles in the annexationist movement. But news came from England which slowed up this development. A change of ministry occurred and Lord Aberdeen replaced the aggressive abolitionist Palmerston. On February 12, 1842, Aberdeen promised Madrid that the British government would not, for the moment, press the demand for a registry of illegally possessed slaves. At the same time, while refusing to dismiss him, Aberdeen instructed Turnbull to stop pursuing the matter further in Cuba.[23]

Furious at this turn of events, Turnbull began organizing a revolt against Spain with abolition of slavery as one of the first measures to be enacted by the new independent government of Cuba. One wealthy Creole who had been approached by Turnbull testified:

> I attest on my word, the most solemn oath if necessary, that having been solicited by the English Consul Mr. Turnbull, he said to me that the powerful and influential abolitionary societies of England at whose head was Prince Albert, tendered to the natives of this island whatever necessary of money, arms, vessels and men might be wanted to acquire their independence from Spain, provided they would at the same time undertake the emancipation of the slaves. A seductive proposition which I repelled at the moment on the ground that, although the principle of the liberty of all men is based on the immutable and holy law of nature, it is unhappily in opposition in our present circumstances to the other natural principle not less sacred of self preservation; and I ended by proposing that if the philanthropic principles of said societies were true and rational, they would use their power in liberating first the whites from the heavy tyranny of Spain, and afterwards the manumission of the slaves in a gradual and prudent manner to the benefit of both races would be entertained. . . . I am cognizant of the fact that the said Consul called and made similar propositions to several persons, natives of this country, whom he thought influential and disposed to admit his dazzling offers, which were rejected by all.[24]

Turnbull did, however, find a few white Cubans who supported abolition and were not so frightened by the prospect of emancipation as to be willing to forego an opportunity to free their native land. He also obtained the support of a large group of Negroes, led by a free Negro, José Miguel Mitchell. Turnbull remained in Havana, while his Vice-Consul Cocking and Mitchell made several trips into the interior to recruit followers. The Cuban planter-reformer Domingo del Monte reported that Turnbull and Cocking were "offering independence to the Creoles on condition that they will unite with the colored people in effecting a general emancipation of the slaves, and in converting the Government into a *black Military Republic*, under British protection." (It was typical of even the reformers in Cuba to associate abolition of slavery with a "black Military Republic.") He reported further that they had "proposed to the Venezuelan General, Mariano, who resided at Kingston, Jamaica, to take command of an invading army. This is to be seconded . . . by an insurrection of the slaves and free men of color, supported by the white Creoles." Turnbull was said to have arranged with British officials in Jamaica not to interfere with the expedition, which was to be composed largely of Negroes.[25]

Although del Monte, who sought to incite the government of the United States to action against Turnbull's plans, exaggerated the scope of the conspiracy, the evidence indicates that it was a formidable one. But, as often happened in Cuban history, it was smashed before it got started. The free Negro, José Miguel Mitchell, was arrested and condemned to death by the Permanent Executive Military Commission. (The sentence was commuted to ten years' imprisonment in Africa.) No charges were brought against Turnbull and Cocking, probably because the Spanish authorities did not want to publicize the extent of the conspiracy, but Valdés demanded the removal of the British Consul. "I believe a sacred duty of my position to beg with great emphasis from Your Excellency," he wrote to the Spanish First Secretary of State, "to secure his removal because I have proof that he spreads his intrigues not only by advising the freedom of Negroes but also works among the whites inducing them to independence, for which he tells them that they must strive. . . ." He accused Turnbull of provoking the slave insurrections in 1841, of encouraging *emancipados* to resort to the British Consulate, and of abusing his powers in other ways to advance the cause of independence with emancipation as its first objective.[26]

Complying with Valdés's petition, presented by the Spanish Minister, Aberdeen removed Turnbull from his post. Still undaunted, but fearing for his safety, Turnbull left the island on June 8, 1842.* In his letter of farewell to Captain General Valdés, May 26, 1842, Turnbull made it clear that he stood by his principles, and while conceding that his "zeal for the cause of liberty" may have caused him to act "in an exacting way which sometimes has been the cause of provoking resistance," he had "not mistaken the path that inevitably must be followed in the not distant future."

---

* He had been replaced on June 5 by the new Consul, Joseph Tucker Crawford, who was empowered to exercise his functions over the whole island. Turnbull had been restricted to Havana. Turnbull, however, continued as "Superintendent of Liberated Africans."

However, I must point out that Cuba, Porto Rico, and Brazil are the only places outside of the United States, where the degrading spectacle of slavery continues to be offered. And if by tolerating those abominable practices, this new belief acquires additional strength, the consequence will be that slavery and the slave traffic will be soon swept away by the overwhelming torrent of public indignation.[27]

In his reply, Valdés made a sharp remark about the British attitude towards what Turnbull had called "the spirit of the century."

I will say only that if such spirit is humanitarian and eminently liberal, it could carry its beneficial influx to change the situation of the unfortunate people of Ireland and those in the colony of India. . . .[28]

As the ship carrying Turnbull left the harbor of Havana, the entire slave-owning population of Cuba heaved a sigh of relief. In Spain the news was greeted with similar rejoicing. "We have finally got rid of Turnbull," the Spanish Minister to London wrote joyfully.[29]

The rejoicing did not last. Turnbull did not remain away from Cuba for long. Having been appointed a member of the Anglo-Portuguese Mixed Commission, he went to New Providence and then to Jamaica. From there he made his way to Nassau, capital of the Bahamas, and gathering a number of free British Negroes, returned to Cuba on October 16, 1842, on a ship manned by the Negroes. The purpose of the visit was ostensibly to visit the plantations owned by British citizens who had emigrated to Cuba with their families and slaves from New Providence. Some of these slaves, Turnbull charged, had been free before leaving New Providence but had been re-enslaved in Cuba. Since he was still "Superintendent of Liberated Africans," it was his duty to see to it that they were set free. At the same time, Turnbull planned to tour the island in behalf of abolition and had brought with him a considerable collection of anti-slavery literature.[30]

This time Valdés did not bother with petitions to England. Turnbull was arrested as he arrived at Cárdenas and his Negro associates were shot down. Turnbull was escorted from prison, under military guard, put on board a British steamer, and notified that not only was he expelled but that he was "not again to visit the Island of Cuba under any pretext whatever."[31] Yielding to Spanish demands, the British abolished the position of "Superintendent of Liberated Africans."

The hatred of Turnbull was so intense among the Cuban slave-owners that they had him expelled as a member of the Royal Patriotic and Economical Society of Havana. However, this was only a temporary victory for the slave interests. A number of the Cuban liberals opposed to the slave trade, led by José de la Luz y Caballero, forced a reversal of the decision. Much to the disgust of the slaveowners, the British abolitionist was reinstated as a member.[32]

Even though Turnbull was out of the way, and his leading Negro associates either killed or imprisoned, the slave interests were still apprehensive lest the seeds he had sowed should ripen. The number of outbreaks of rebellion since 1838, though isolated, proved that the slaves were definitely restless, and Turnbull's agitation was bound to reach them. These apprehensions were given expression in the promulgation of the new slave code of November 14, 1842.

This code resembled that of 1789 in its provisions for religious instruction, recreation and care of the slave.* But though evidence had piled up that obligations placed upon the slaveowners were rarely lived up to, there was nothing added in the code of 1842 to compel such obedience. What was really new in the new code were the provisions for greater controls over the activities and movements of the slaves. Slaves of one plantation could not visit slaves of another without permission and written license of their owner or overseer. Any individual was authorized to detain a slave who lacked a license. Slaves were required to show docile obedience to constituted authorities and respect for white persons. Any slave discovering and reporting a conspiracy was promised liberty and a reward of 500 pesos.[33]

But the new slave code did little to allay the continual dread of uprisings, especially in districts like Cárdenas and Matanzas, where

---

* As in the code of 1789, the slaves were to be instructed in the Catholic religion, to be provided with adequate food, clothing and shelter, and hours of recreation. An ordinary working day was defined as ten hours, but in time of harvest, sixteen hours. As before, a master who mistreated his slave was obliged to sell him to another master.

the slaves far outnumbered the whites.* The slave interests feared
the day when the revolts on isolated estates would merge into a
general uprising. Since, under Valdés, the Spanish troops were kept
in the capital, such an uprising, if it spread, might become impossible to control.[34] Hence the slave interests petitioned Spain to
station troops in the heart of the sugar-producing region, so that they
could act the moment the slaves revolted.

But the request was unnecessary, for Spain replaced Valdés with
Leopoldo O'Donnell, who immediately mobilized the armed forces
to stamp out any uprising. Shortly after he arrived in the island,
this reactionary had an opportunity to put his iron-fisted policy into
practice. O'Donnell, incidentally, took bribes not only from the
slave traders but from the large slaveowners as well. When he re-
tired as Captain General in 1848, he had accumulated a fortune of
half a million dollars.[35]

On March 27–28, 1843, the dreaded prospect of a general slave
insurrection almost became a reality. It occurred in what was then
the richest sugar zone of Cuba, corresponding to the present province of Matanzas. The uprising began in the "Alcania" mill at
Cárdenas, and involved the whole crew of 250 slaves. The rebels
moved on to neighboring mills—"La Luisa," "La Trinidad," and
"La Aurora"—appealed to the slaves there to join them in a bid
for freedom, and added, mill by mill, their entire crews to the uprising. Then the slaves invaded a nearby coffee plantation—
"Moscú"—and a horse-breeding farm—"Ranchuelo." On the
same night, the slaves who were building the railroad between
Cárdenas and Júcaro, as if in response to a previously agreed-upon

* The percentage of the numerical superiority of Negroes over whites is difficult
to determine, for the exact figures were intentionally camouflaged by Spain. The
Spanish authorities manipulated census data to suppress evidence that the illegal
slave trade was increasing. At the same time, as part of the policy of tying the
white population closer to Spain, they released figures which showed that the
Negroes outnumbered the whites. Another factor operating against accurate
listing was the tax on slaveowners. In order to evade payments, the owners reported fewer slaves than they actually possessed.

The census returns for Cuba in 1850 gave a total population of 1,247,230:
605,560 white, 205,570 free Negroes, and 436,100 slaves. It is probable that the
ratio of Negroes to whites in 1843–44 was much greater. (Portell Vilá, *Cuba*,
vol. I, p. 476; Richard H. Dana, *To Cuba and Back*, Boston, 1859, pp. 221–22;
Hunt's Merchants' Magazine, vol. XXXVIII, 1850, p. 735.)

signal, also rebelled. But before the two groups could unite, a rapidly mobilized battalion of troops attacked the poorly-armed slaves. Scores of Negroes were massacred, and hundreds suspected of connivance with the rebels were flogged. The conspiracy failed.[36]

But in November of the same year another general slave uprising broke out. It began in the mill "Triumvirato" in Matanzas, and like the March uprising, spread as the crew invaded nearby mills, adding their slaves to the revolt. Again the rebels were attacked by troops, and once again the revolt was crushed with brutal reprisals.[37]

The O'Donnell technique of terror was again applied in December, 1843. A slave betrayed the plans of a conspiracy in the Trinidad mill in Matanzas. O'Donnell's immediate investigation ended in the execution of sixteen slaves at the mill. The crews of the neighboring mills were forced to witness the executions.[38]

The wave of terror reached its climax in one of the most shameful pages of Cuban history—the suppression of the *Conspiración de la Escalera*.

chapter 12

LA ESCALERA

In January, 1844, a large-scale conspiracy in Matanzas was discovered. For almost three years, secret meetings had been taking place, attended by free Negroes and slaves and a handful of white Cubans to organize a revolutionary uprising aimed at social betterment for the free Negroes and liberation for the slaves. The insurrection was to start in Matanzas, and the rebels were to lead the slaves from the plantations of Havana where they would be joined by free Negroes and slaves in the capital. The goal was the establishment of a republic in which slavery would be abolished and Negroes would enjoy full equality with whites.[1]

The insurrection never got beyond the planning stage. After it was exposed by informers, Captain General O'Donnell seized upon it to terrorize all who sought freedom for the slaves so that never again would they dare to raise their heads. Thousands, including foreigners, were arrested on the basis of mere rumor and treated cruelly even before being brought to trial. In Matanzas alone the Permanent Executive Military Commission "tried" more than 3,000 persons, most of them free Negroes. All told, 4,039 individuals were arrested; 2,166 were listed as free Negroes, 972 as slaves, 74 as whites, and 827 were not classified.[2]

Torture was authorized to obtain confessions. Suspected Negroes were bound to ladders and lashed until they confessed—hence the name "la Escalera" (the Staircase). A wealthy Cuban slaveowner, Miguel Aldama, who witnessed this barbaric punishment, was impressed by the courage of the victims. After denouncing the conspiracy as horrifying and the punishment as necessary, he went on to characterize the authorities as "ruffians" and the Negroes as

214

"true martyrs of liberty. Together, all as one, they swore to win or die, and they took an oath that not even the cruel whip has been able to break."[3]

The Military Commission condemned 78 to death, 1,292 to prison, and over 400 to exile. How many died under the lash has never been determined although a conservative estimate would be 300.[4] The authorities issued a public report whitewashing the torturers and asserting that many of the victims had died of "diarrhea." "Thus diversion was added to the crime," observes Sergio Aguirre.[5]

On June 9, 1844, six months after the conspiracy was discovered, United States Consul Robert B. Campbell wrote from Havana: "The government are still engaged in finding and arresting the suspected parties of the intended insurrection."[6] And six months later, Negroes were still being seized and tried. Kennedy, the British judge of the Mixed Commission, wrote on February 24, 1845: "It is truly distressing to hear the account of cruelties and oppressions committed on this unhappy class of persons during the last year."[7]

What had started as a movement to crush the rebellious slaves had soon reached out to the free Negroes and even to white liberals who dared to oppose slavery or the slave trade. This was a logical consequence of the pattern of terror, for the slave interests knew that free Negroes gave support and leadership in the movement to abolish slavery, and that white Cubans from the professional and small farmer classes sympathized with this movement. By the time *La Escalera* was over, the best leaders of the free Negroes, either by execution or deportation,* had been eliminated and scores of white liberals had been imprisoned or driven into exile.**

Among the free Negroes who were executed were the dentist Andrés Dodge, the musician José Miguel Román, and the talented poet Gabriel de la Concepción Valdés, known as "Plácido." "Plácido," a free Negro, had become famous for his poems written

---

* Following the revolts of 1844 a decree was issued ordering the expulsion of all free men of the colored race who had come from another country.

** José de la Luz Caballero and Domingo del Monte were accused of complicity. Both were out of the country at the time, but De la Luz returned to face his accusers, and he was finally acquitted. However, it should be noted that though he opposed the continuation of the slave trade, De la Luz had only words of praise for O'Donnell's bestial suppression of the *Escalera* conspiracy.

to celebrate anniversaries and birthdays, and on the surface there was nothing revolutionary in these verses. But underneath there was always an affirmation of his hatred of tyrants and love for freedom. In his poem in honor of Isabel II, "Plácido" wrote:

> As before the altar of Supreme
> Jove
> Hasdrubal swore hatred against
> the Romans
> And showed them the fierceness of
> Mars.
> I, before God, swear eternal
> hatred against all tyrants.[8]

So great was the nervous fear of rebellion in Cuba that such lofty expressions by a Negro could not be tolerated. "Plácido" was arrested on the trumped-up charge of being Turnbull's agent, and of having been selected as President of the Republic to be set up by the conspirators. Though the evidence against him was obtained by torture, he was executed.

Three decades later, the American Negro leader, Henry Highland Garnet, addressing a meeting in New York's Cooper Institute which had been called by the Negro people of New York in support of the Cuban struggle for independence, declared:

> You cannot forget, Cubans, the immortal mulatto poet of your country, the brave and heroic Plácido. Like yourselves, you know that he loved liberty, and freely offered himself on her sacred altar. He was accused of being concerned in an attempted insurrection, and was condemned to die the death of a traitor. When he was led forth to death, he cried:
>
> > "O, Liberty! I hear thy voice calling me
> > Deep in the frozen regions of the North, afar,
> > With voice like God's, and vision like a star."[9]

Turnbull was blamed by the Spanish authorities as the prime mover of the conspiracy and of having stirred the otherwise contented slaves and free Negroes into rebellion. A military commission investigating the plot came to the conclusion that his "subversive activities" were not only the cause, but that he had personally conceived and planned the conspiracy, and had even arranged for an expedition of Negroes from Jamaica to aid the revolt once it had begun.[10]

Most Cuban historians accept the findings of the military commission.[11] Moreover, Mario Hernández Sánchez-Barba, the Spanish historian, in his recent article, "David Turnbull y el problema de la esclavitud en Cuba," also accepts them. Having examined the huge three volumes of testimony of the "conspiración de la gente de color" in the Spanish archives, Hernández concludes that the conspiracy began during Turnbull's regime as Consul in Havana, that Turnbull sent his personal envoys, the Negroes, Miguel Flores and Luis Guigot, to the meetings of the conspirators and helped formulate the initial plans for the unprising.[12]

Like everything else connected with this conspiracy, however, it is impossible to state definitely just what Turnbull's role was. Indeed, it is still difficult to determine, more than a century later, if the conspiracy of 1844 had actually been organized or whether it was invented by O'Donnell and the slave interests to rid the island of those who might lead a movement against slavery. Some Cuban historians, among them Vidal Morales and Francisco González del Valle, label the conspiracy a mirage, provoked by the suspiciousness of the Spanish authorities. Others, like Pérez Cabrera, consider that no conclusion is warranted; while a third group, of which José Manuel Ximeno is most representative, hails the conspiracy as the most important organized in Cuba up to that time, and "the first major Cuban conspiracy of a secessionist nature with ramifications all over the Island."[13]

There is no doubt, however, that many innocent people perished in the barbaric repression. Nor is there any doubt that the slaves in the region of Matanzas and Cárdenas were seething with rebellion, and that free Negroes and anti-slavery white Cubans had established contacts with the slave population.[14] There is no doubt either that before he was expelled, Turnbull had left behind an organization to continue the movement to end slavery in Cuba,[15] though to ascribe the entire conspiracy to this courageous humanitarian is to belittle the desire of the Negro population to achieve freedom and equality. Finally, whether or not the insurrection was set to take place or was exaggerated out of all proportion in order to justify the repression, there can be no doubt that *La Escalera* had a decisive influence on Cuban history.

Cuba, during *La Escalera*, was correctly characterized as a "naked, unsophisticated Military Despotism."[16] But the slaveowners were satisfied. Even though O'Donnell removed Cubans from all public offices on the ground that they could not be trusted to exercise the necessary firmness, his policies were applauded by the Cuban slaveowners and their allies. In a memorial to Madrid, signed by several hundred landowners, merchants and citizens of Havana, the Captain General was praised for having ferreted out the slave conspiracy and wiping out the conspirators "in a very thorough manner." His conduct had given "the highest satisfaction," and had "saved the country from the greatest peril that ever confronted it." The petition asked that he be continued in command of the island.[17]

This provides a key to Cuban history of this period. On many questions, the interests of the Creole *hacendados* and Peninsular merchants clearly conflicted. The *hacendados* resented their exclusion from political life and opposed the policies which benefited Spanish business men and hindered the free development of Cuban trade. What united Creole *hacendados* and Peninsular businessmen was their common interest in preserving slavery and their common fear of a successful slave uprising. As the petition to Madrid makes clear, this bond was stronger than the antagonisms separating the two classes.[18] Undoubtedly the Cuban slaveowners would have agreed with the Spanish Ambassador in Washington who warned that there must be no lessening of the omnipotent powers of the Captain General in Cuba, and that all reforms for the island be denied: "If the present system is not maintained the island will be lost and the colored race will triumph."[19]

One immediate effect of *La Escalera* was that harsher slave regulations were adopted. The decree of May 31, 1844 added further restrictions on the movements of slaves and imposed severer punishment on those suspected of disturbing activities.[20] The Cuban authorities were now less than ever disposed to set the *emancipados* free according to the terms of the treaties. The British government repeatedly accused O'Donnell of re-selling the *emancipados* into slavery after their period of service was over. One gets a clear glimpse into the operations of this vicious practice from Lord Palmerston's letter of August 3, 1846 to Sir Henry Lytton Bulwer, British Minister in Madrid:

> By despatch recently received from her Majesty's Commissioners at Havana . . . it appears that the practice of reselling Emancipados, which has been going on for some time past under the sanction and direction of the Captain General of Cuba was the public topic of conversations. . . .
>
> It is also stated that upwards of 5,000 of these unfortunate persons have been re-sold at rates varying from 5 to 9 ounces of gold (for example, 50 emancipados were sold to the Gas Company of Havana for a period of five years to serve as lamp-lighters), by which means a profit of upwards to six hundred thousand dollars has been made by persons in the Government House . . . and that 400 Emancipados have been transferred to the Marqués de las Delicias, Chief Judge of the Mixed Court, and the greatest slave proprietor of the Island, to be held by him for the benefit of the Countess Guerega, wife of General O'Donnell . . . a direct and flagrant violation of the treaty engagements. . . .
>
> You will express the confident hope that the Government of Spain will give positive and peremptory orders to General O'Donnell to obtain . . . full and complete liberty for these nominally emancipated Negroes. . . .[21]

O'Donnell did not deny these charges; he justified them, declaring that the conspiracy of 1844 proved how dangerous it was to increase the size of the free Negro population.[22]

Thus the condition of the Cuban slaves worsened precisely at the time that abolition received a serious setback. The repression of *La Escalera* demonstrated to the slaves that the time was not ripe for a mass liberation movement. It was to be many years before they dared attempt other uprisings. The ranks of the free Negro and white Cuban leadership of the anti-slavery struggle had been so decimated by the repression that it took almost two decades for it to recover.

However, one consequence of *La Escalera* was that, for the first time, a clamor arose against the continuance of the slave trade. Ramón de la Sagra, representative of the Peninsular element in Cuba, noted in 1845 that while for twelve years his agitation against the slave trade had been met on all sides "with silence and indifference," after *La Escalera* his views received attention, especially in the country districts where the slaves outnumbered the whites so overwhelmingly.[23] Thus, a group of planters in Matanzas, noting that there were at least 600,000 slaves in the district whom they feared were infected with emancipatory ideas from Haiti and Jamaica, petitioned for the cessation of the contraband trade which threatened "all our hopes of security and future well-being."[24]

The petition was supported by the exiled Saco who published, in 1845, his *La Supresión del tráfico de esclavos en la Isla de Cuba*, in which he again argued against the internal and external dangers of continuing the slave trade, and again suggested the need to increase the number of whites in Cuba through immigration. With keen insight, he pointed out the significance of the recent slave revolts and plots. "Slave risings have occurred at all times; but they have always been partial, confined to one or two farms, without plan or political result. . . . Very different is the character of the risings which at brief intervals have occurred in 1842 and 1843; and the conspiracy last discovered is the most frightful which has ever been planned in Cuba, at once on account of its vast ramifications among slaves and free Negroes, and on account of its origin and purpose." In the future, it would not be necessary for the Negroes to rebel all at once; sporadic, partial movements "repeated here and there" would be enough to destroy credit and confidence; force an exodus of capital and an emigration of white Cubans; the economic ruin of the island would be intensified year by year "until there comes the most terrible catastrophe."

"If the slave trade continues," he prophesied, "there will be in Cuba neither peace nor security. . . . Cuba, in order to face the future, must not only instantly and forever terminate all slave traffic, but protect by obligation the colonization of whites."[25]

Although Saco was accused by some slaveowners of being "in the pay of the British," this pamphlet made a greater impression than any of his previous appeals for abolition of the slave traffic.

Meanwhile, Great Britain was intensifying her pressure on Spain. The British public had been shocked by reports of the wholesale arrests and executions accompanying *La Escalera*. The arrest of many British citizens as suspects added fuel to the indignation. The British press bitterly assailed O'Donnell; the London *Morning Advertiser* demanded that England intervene to clean up the "slaughter-house flowing with human blood." The British government was not slow to take action. Lord Aberdeen informed Spain that England would use force, if necessary, to implement the anti-slave trade provisions of the Treaty of 1835.[26]

These reactions created a favorable climate for a new measure against the slave trade, and, on March 4, 1845, the Cortes approved "The Law of Abolition and Repression of the Slave Trade." This subjected pilots, captains, owners of cargoes, and others engaged in the slave trade to six years in prison, and eight years if they resisted. It also provided for the punishment of any public official who, given proven knowledge of a disembarkation, did nothing to halt it. Unfortunately, this important advance was nullified by Article 9, prohibiting the pursuit of contraband slaves within the bounds of the sugar plantations or refineries. Officials were obliged to take action when notified that a slave expedition was being prepared or had landed, "but in no case, nor at any time, shall it be possible to proceed against or disturb slave proprietors in their possession of slaves under pretext of their origin." This meant, of course, that once the slaves had been introduced illegally into the plantations, there was no legal way to recover them or to proceed against their owners. Thus while the immediate effect of the Treaty of 1845 was to reduce the slave traffic somewhat,* the Article 9 loophole kept the door open for future importations.[27]

It was typical of Spain that she should appear, on the one hand, to yield to British and Cuban reform pressure, while, on the other,

---

* Actually, the reduction in the traffic was due more to fears aroused among slaveowners by the revolts of 1842–43 and the conspiracy of 1844 than to the new law. In any event, documents presented to the British Parliament demonstrate that in the years following *La Escalera*, the slave traffic diminished notably. A reported 10,000 *bozales* had arrived in 1845, but in 1846 this number had diminished to 1,350; to 1,700 in 1847; and to 1,500 in 1848. (Documents presented to the British Parliament by Mr. Hutt, cited in Armas y Céspedes, *De la esclavitud en Cuba*, La Habana, 1921, pp. 120–22; Hubert S. Aimes, *A History of Slavery in Cuba, 1511–1868*, New York, 1907, p. 170.) Thus it can be said that though *La Escalera* had left the abolitionist movement in Cuba seriously weakened, with its leadership either wiped out or driven underground, not all abolitionist exertions had been in vain.

she should assure the slaveholders that no one would touch the slaves illegally brought into their plantations. Indeed, Spain went out of her way to convince the slaveholders that the Act of 1845 did not give Britain greater powers of intervention in the Cuban slave traffic. On the contrary, she informed them triumphantly that Britain had promised to minimize the intervention of her Consuls. The new act, Spain continued, was intended solely for the security of the slave interests, for it would remove dangers of a slave rebellion.[28]

Despite these assurances, the action of the Cortes aroused the hostility of many Cuban slaveholders and the slave trading merchants. Speaking for these interests—as well as for himself personally—O'Donnell, in a series of communications to Madrid, expressed the belief that the law of 1845 would ruin the economy of the island, and lead to its separation from the mother country. In ten years, he predicted, Cuba would experience a vast shortage of labor, for there would be no way to replace those slaves now working on the plantations.[*] Soon the whites would outnumber the Negroes, and when this happened, "the guarantee of conserving the territory and its dependence on the Metropolis will come to an end."[29]

O'Donnell's warning alarmed the Spanish government and it appointed a Committee, the Colonial Section of the Royal Council, to examine the subject further. The Council agreed with O'Donnell that the preservation of Spanish dominion in Cuba would depend on maintaining a higher ratio of Negroes to whites. (6 Negroes to 4 whites was the proper ratio.) To maintain it, the Council proposed a system of breeding slaves, after the manner of the United States. To encourage slave-breeding, the owners who would increase the number of females on their plantations would be exempt, wholly or in part, from capitation taxes on slaves. It also proposed a higher tax to be levied on domestic slaves, to encourage putting them to work in the fields. And, "in order to conserve for a longer time the

---

* O'Donnell was convinced that white immigration would not work, and that it would not be possible to breed more slaves because even on plantations of from 400 to 700 slaves there existed not one female slave. (Arthur F. Smith, "Spain and the Problem of Slavery in Cuba, 1817–1873," unpublished Ph.D. thesis, University of Chicago, 1958, pp. 112–13.)

life and health of the slaves," the hours of labor, set forth in the slave codes, should be reduced. But this revision should be made secretly and be kept a secret, and to be communicated only verbally to the slave owners, *"because it would be very dangerous if the slaves understood that it was necessary to restrain the cupidity of their owners, and because the abolitionist societies would give to these regulations the interpretation most convenient for them."* The Council also recommended that more reliance be placed on Oriental labor, pointing out that "the good qualities of the Chinese have already been proved in the Philippines." Finally, the Council proposed that all free Negroes under fifty be exiled or forced to work on a sugar plantation. Exile would eliminate a "potentially dangerous" element from Cuban society, while driving the free Negroes to the plantations would increase the labor force and keep them under supervision.[30]

What a commentary these proposals are on the brutish mentality of the men who advanced them! When the rest of Europe was moving in the direction of abolishing slavery, the Spanish government, in order to preserve its hold over Cuba, was recommending ways of maintaining and strengthening its system of human bondage, including the hideous practice of slave-breeding! What a commentary, too, on the nature of slavery in Cuba that the proposals lightening the labor of the slaves be carried out secretly! What, finally, can be said of men who bluntly recommended the re-enslavement of free Negroes?

Actually, only one of the recommendations was ever adopted in Cuba—the use of other labor than Negro slaves. Before *La Escalera*, Saco and a few others had stressed the importance of gradually replacing Negro slave labor with free white labor, but had made little impression. After the terror produced by the slave uprisings of 1843 and the plot of 1844, the subject began to be discussed more seriously. Saco's pamphlet of 1845 condemning the slave trade and arguing in favor of free white labor was followed by other publications treating the same theme. In February, 1845, a Royal Decree directed Spanish consular agents abroad to prepare passage for immigrants to Cuba. Within a year, 500 Spanish and European agricultural colonists, aged 18 to 40, were to be brought to the island at government expense, the colonists to repay half the costs incurred within a term of three years after receiving employment. In return, the colonists were to contract to remain in Cuba for this period. It was thought that these colonists would be employed in tobacco and coffee cultivation, and in the industrial side of sugar production, such as administrative work on the *haciendas,* or as artisans.[31]

A few white contract agricultural laborers were imported, but they had little effect on the agricultural system.[32] So those who were seeking a way to stave off future slave revolts looked elsewhere. In 1847, the first Chinese contract laborers were introduced. The contract term of eight years was subject to voluntary renewal. A number of prominent planters subscribed for the laborers. In 1849, Indians from Yucatan, numbering 135, arrived in Havana. The price of each Chinese laborer was fixed at 125 pesos, and that of the Yucatecan Indian at around 100 pesos.

The Chinese and Yucatecan workers were bought, sold and transferred like slaves, and treated as slaves. Both groups were so brutally handled that many committed suicide, and the Mexican government put an end to the emigration.[33]

The Chinese and the Yucatecan Indians proved as disappointing as the white immigrants. (Many died of disease and overwork before the expiration of their contracts.) But these moves to replace Negro labor demonstrated how frightened were the slave interests of Cuba by the events of 1842–1844.

They were not the only ones frightened. In the United States a wave of hysteria overspread the slaveholding South. Its spokesmen in the government reflected these fears. Early in 1843, the State Department received an alarmist communication "from a highly respected source," namely the Cuban planter Domingo del Monte, to the effect that England intended to seize Cuba, free the Negroes and establish a *"black Military Republic* under British protection." He pleaded with the United States to block these efforts. Secretary of State Daniel Webster, frightened by this report, referred it to Robert B. Campbell, the U.S. Consul at Havana, for investigation, impressing upon him "the absolute necessity of absolute secrecy in everything that relates to the inquiries you are directed to make." Webster added that if the report should prove true, the

Spanish authorities might "securely rely upon the whole naval and military resources of this country to aid . . . in preserving Cuba," for:

> If this scheme should succeed, the influence of Britain in this quarter, it is remarked, will be unlimited. With 600,000 blacks in Cuba, and 800,000 in the West India Islands, she will, it is said, strike a death blow at the existence of slavery in the United States . . . and even to prevent the free passage of the commerce of the United States over the Bahama banks, and through the Florida channel.[34]

Campbell reported the story to be without foundation, though he characterized the activities of the British abolitionists in Cuba as "troublesome."[35] John Quincy Adams's observations on the affair are extremely interesting, since no one had more intimate knowledge of U.S. intentions towards Cuba. He felt that it all added up to the fact that England, determined to abolish the slave trade, was putting pressure on Spain to live up to treaties in which she had undertaken to end the traffic. But certain American interests, notably the slaveholders and their northern allies, wanted to take advantage of the situation, and, by the bogey of a "Black Republic," forestall England's designs on Cuba. Adams, now a staunch foe of the slavocracy, described Webster's instructions to Campbell as "putrid with slavery and the slave trade." As he saw it, the "Black Republic" scare reflected a spirit of encroachment in the United States. "My heart sinks for the cause of human freedom," he wrote in his diary.[36]

Campbell's reassuring report did not end the alarm in Washington. From Jamaica, the State Department was receiving regular dispatches from R. M. Harrison, U.S. Consul, warning of the desire of the freed Negroes to effect a junction with the Negroes of Haiti, capture Cuba, and then descend upon the southern United States with the aim of liberating the enslaved Negroes there. He called attention to a society established in Jamaica, under the auspices of Baptist missionaries, which had for its object the liberation of the slaves of Cuba as the first step in gaining the "entire emancipation of the Slaves of the U[nited] States without regard to the means, provided it can be effected." While some officials in the State De-

partment dismissed these reports as "unduly alarmist," the South-
erners took them seriously. And they were especially alarmed by
Harrison's dispatch of June 14, 1843, in which he reported that
the "notorious Turnbull," who had been ordered out of Cuba by the
Captain General, had arrived in Jamaica, ostensibly as the head
of an English-Portuguese Commission for recaptured Africans, but
with the real intention of effecting, from Jamaica, a slave insurrection in Cuba.[37] Simultaneously came the report from Cuba telling
of the arrest of José Miguel Mitchell, Turnbull's protégé, as the in-
stigator of a plot for an invasion of free Negroes from Jamaica,
to aid a Cuban revolt.

The Tyler administration was now convinced that Great Britain
planned to use its full power to end slavery in Cuba, and it was
equally determined to exert its full power to prevent this. When the
Spanish Minister to the United States, Argaiz, asked President
Tyler and his Secretaries of State and Navy to make a naval demonstration in Cuban waters of American support of Spanish authority,
the response was immediate. Commodore Chauncey was sent to
Cuba at the head of a naval squadron to make sure that the reported
British plans did not materialize. And Consul Campbell, in Havana,
offered co-operation to the Captain General in "defending the city"
against an invasion from Jamaica.[38] Abel P. Upshur, who had succeeded Webster as Secretary of State, advised Argaiz "that the
Spanish authorities should execute anyone attempting rebellion in
Cuba, or if a foreign government protected him, as Britain did
Turnbull, the people of Cuba should lynch him, and then it would
be interesting to observe who objected."[39]

When Washington Irving, American Ambassador to Spain, con-
veyed the information to the Spanish Foreign Minister about the
readiness of the United States naval forces in the vicinity of Cuba
to defend it against all foreign intervention, and to guarantee the
security of slavery in the island, the reply was one of extreme
gratitude:

> "Mr. González Bravo," the famous author wrote to Upshur, "ex-
> pressed himself aware that the interests and feelings of the Spanish
> and United States governments were identical on most subjects
> connected with Negro slavery; and that our policy was fair and

friendly towards Spain in regard to her West India colonies, and he appeared to be much gratified by my avowal of the determination of our government to maintain Spain in the possession of Cuba, by force of arms if necessary, and to consider it a cause of war for any other power to attempt to possess itself of the island. He expressed no apprehensions about the present state of Cuba, but on the contrary, a full confidence that the vigorous measures which the Spanish government were about to take, would be efficacious in putting the island in a state of security."[40]

The "vigorous measures," of course, were those instituted by Captain General O'Donnell, who more than followed Upshur's advice, executing not only anyone attempting, but even anyone suspected of attempting, to rouse the slaves to rebellion. This reassured Upshur, but not the Southern slaveholders, who were appalled by the scope of the conspiracy disclosed in the *Escalera* persecutions. "*La Escalera,*" notes Basil Rauch, "made the apparition of a Negro republic, under British protection and dangerously close to the cotton states, seem real and imminent."[41]

It was to be expected that the outstanding ideologist of slavery, John C. Calhoun, would reflect the slaveowners' attitude in his policy toward Cuba when he assumed the post of Secretary of State on March 6, 1844. Calhoun believed that Upshur had not gone far enough to frustrate British attempts to abolish slavery in Cuba. "The danger is great & menacing," he had written to Upshur in August, 1843, "involving in its consequences the safety of the Union and the very existence of the South." He wanted the Secretary of State to approach France and to suggest that "our gov't & that of France . . . enter into a guaranty of its (Cuba's) possession to Spain against the interference of any other power."[42]

When he became Secretary of State, Calhoun's alarm over British aims intensified. In the department, he found a note from Mr. Packenham, British Minister to the United States, communicating a dispatch from Lord Aberdeen to the effect that the British government had no intention of disturbing the domestic tranquillity of the slaveholding states of the Union, but "that Great Britain desires, and is constantly exerting herself to procure the general abolition of slavery throughout the world." In his reply to Packenham, Calhoun informed England that as long as she

confined her policy to the abolition of slavery in her own possessions and colonies, no other country had a right to complain. . . .
But when she goes beyond, and avows it as her settled policy and
the object of her constant exertions to abolish it throughout the
world, she makes it the duty of all other countries, whose safety
or prosperity may be endangered by her policy, to adopt such
measures as they may deem necessary for their protection.[43]

The sensational news of *La Escalera* confirmed the worst fears of
Calhoun and the slaveholders for whom he spoke. They were now
convinced that the British attempt "to procure the general abolition
of slavery" was already in operation in Cuba. It would no longer
do to support Spain in her possession of Cuba while waiting for the
"apple" to ripen and fall into the possession of the United States.
The time was arriving to take steps for the annexation of Cuba. Not
quite yet, to be sure, for first there was the annexation of Texas and
Oregon to carry out, and there was still an immense part of Mexico
to be seized and brought within the United States. Once these
matters were disposed of, the annexation of Cuba could be next on
the agenda.

La Escalera was thus a turning point in the history of Cuba and
its relations with its North American neighbor. Annexationism
surged in Cuba and the United States with a common objective—
the protection and preservation of human slavery.

REFERENCE NOTES

chapter 1 THE CONQUEST OF CUBA

1. Vilhjalmur Stefanson, with the collaboration of Olive Rathbun Wilcox, editor, *Great Adventures and Explorations*, New York, 1947, p. 195.
2. *Ibid.*
3. Bartolomé de las Casas, *Historia de las Indias*, Mexico, 1951, vol. I, chapter XLV.
4. J. Alden Mason, *Use of Tobacco in Mexico and South America*, Chicago, 1924, p. 3.
5. Marius André, *Columbus*, New York, 1928, p. 139.
6. Cornelius Osgood, *The Ciboney Culture of Cayo Redondo, Cuba*, New Haven, 1942, p. 26.
7. Fernando Portuondo, *Curso de Historia de Cuba*, La Habana, 1941, p. 62.
8. Antonio Bachiller y Morales, *Cuba Primitiva*, La Habana, 1883, pp. 52–110; Irene A. Wright, *The Early History of Cuba*, New York, 1916, pp. 8–13.
9. Quoted in André, *op. cit.*, p. 142.
10. *The Golden Conquistadores*, Introduction and Commentaries by Irwin R. Blacker, Edited by Harry M. Rosen, Indianapolis, 1960, p. 98.
11. César Rodríguez Expósito, *Hatuey, El Primer Libertador de Cuba*, La Habana, 1944, p. 98.
12. *The Golden Conquistadores, op. cit.*, preface.
13. José Martí, *The Age of Gold*, San José, Costa Rica, p. 150.
14. Expósito, *op. cit.*, p. 84.
15. Las Casas, *op. cit.*, vol. I, pp. 62–64; Expósito, *op. cit.*, pp. 95–98.
16. Expósito, *op. cit.*, pp. 112–20.
17. Wright, *op. cit.*, p. 48.
18. George Edward Ellis, "Las Casas and the Relation of the Spaniards to the Indians," *Narrative and Critical History of America*, edited by Justin Winsor, Boston and New York, 1884, p. 319.
19. *Ibid.*, pp. 305, 327; Wright, *op. cit.*, pp. 32–34; Hudson Strode, *The Pageant of Cuba*, New York, 1936, pp. 34–35.
20. Willis Fletcher Johnson, *The History of Cuba*, New York, 1920, vol. I, pp. 73–74.
21. Silvio Arturo Zavala, *New Viewpoints on the Spanish Colonization of America*, London, 1943, p. 25.
22. Silvio Arturo Zavala, *La encomienda indiana*, Madrid, 1935, pp. 26–35.
23. Silvio Arturo Zavala, *De encomienda y propiedad territorial en algunas regiones de la América española*, Mexico, 1940, pp. 30, 85.
24. *Ibid.*, p. 77; Lowry Nelson, "The Evolution of the Cuban Land Sys-

tem," *Land Economics*, vol. XXV, November, 1949, pp. 365–70; Wright, *op. cit.*, pp. 38–48.

25. Gonzalo Fernández de Oviedo y Valdés, *Historia general y natural de las Indias*, Madrid, 1851–55, pp. 164–68.
26. *Ibid.*, pp. 168–79.
27. Fernando Ortiz Fernández, *Cuba Primitiva*, La Habana, 1922, pp. 65–67.
28. Wright, *op. cit.*, pp. 146–47.
29. *Ibid.*
30. María Virtudes Morán, "Church and State in Cuba," unpublished M.A. thesis, Columbia University, May, 1950, p. 9.
31. Wright, *op. cit.*, p. 178.
32. David Weeks, "The Agrarian System of the Spanish American Colonies," *Journal of Land and Public Utility Economics*, vol. XXII, February, 1947, pp. 153–68.
33. Wright, *op. cit.*, pp. 137–40; Johnson, *op. cit.*, vol. I, pp. 126–27.
34. Wright, *op. cit.*, p. 140.
35. Ortiz, *op. cit.*, p. 151.
36. Wright, *op. cit.*, p. 188.
37. *Letters from the Havana, During the year 1820, Containing an Account of the Present State of the Island of Cuba, and Observations on the Slave Trade*, London, 1821, p. 6.
38. Ramiro Guerra y Sánchez, *Manual de la historia de Cuba, económica, social y política*, La Habana, 1938, pp. 44–45, 53–54.

chapter 2 ECONOMIC DEVELOPMENT OF CUBA, 1520–1790

1. Don Jacobo de la Pezuela y Lobo, *Diccionario geográfico, estadístico, histórico de la isla de Cuba*, Madrid, 1863–66, vol. II, p. 26.
2. *The Golden Conquistadores, op. cit.*, p. 98.
3. Pezuela, *op. cit.*, vol. II, pp. 63–64.
4. *Ibid.*
5. H. E. Friedlander, *Historia económica de Cuba*, Habana, 1944, pp. 67–75.
6. *Ibid.*, pp. 84–89.
7. Fernando Ortiz Fernández, *Cuban Counterpoint: Tobacco and Sugar*, New York, 1947, pp. 280–81. Translated from the Spanish by Harriet de Onís. All references to Ortiz hereinafter are to this work.
8. *Ibid.*, pp. 218–19.
9. Pezuela, *op. cit.*, vol. II, p. 242.
10. William C. Atkinson, *A History of Spain and Portugal*, London, 1960, pp. 166–69.
11. Clarence Harvey, *Trade and Navigation between Spain and the Indies*, Cambridge, Mass., 1918, pp. 34–62.
12. Wright, *op. cit.*, pp. 211–12.
13. Ortiz, *op. cit.*, pp. 216–17.
14. Johnson, *op. cit.*, vol. II, p. 21.
15. Wright, *op. cit.*, p. 258.

16. Don Jacobo de la Pezuela y Lobo, *Historia de la Isla de Cuba*, Madrid, 1868–1878, vol. I, p. 543.
17. Pezuela, *Diccionario*, *op. cit.*, introduction.
18. Friedlander, *op. cit.*, pp. 82–83.
19. Ortiz, *op. cit.*, p. 217.
20. *Ibid.*
21. Friedlander, *op. cit.*, pp. 63–74.
22. Elías Entralgo, "Monopolio del Tabaco: sublevación de los vegueros," *Curso de introducción a la historia de Cuba*, La Habana, 1938, pp. 115–22.
23. Friedlander, *op. cit.*, pp. 180–85.
24. Nelson Vance Russell, "The Reaction in England and America to the Capture of Havana, 1762," *Hispanic American Historical Review*, vol. IX, August, 1929, p. 312.
25. Friedlander, *op. cit.*, p. 79.
26. *Ibid.*, pp. 95–99; Herminio Portell Vilá, *Historia de Cuba en sus relaciones con Los Estados Unidos y España*, La Habana, 1938–41, vol. I, p. 79.
27. Pezuela, *Diccionario*, *op. cit.*, vol. II, p. 56.
28. Ortiz, *op. cit.*, pp. 55–60, 67–70, 77.
29. Hubert H. S. Aimes, *History of Slavery in Cuba, 1511 to 1868*, New York, 1907, p. 35.
30. Portell Vilá, *op. cit.*, vol. I, p. 77.
31. Roy F. Nichols, "Trade Relations and the Establishment of United States Consulates in Spanish America, 1779–1809," *Hispanic American Historical Review*, vol. XIII, August, 1933, p. 290.
32. U.S. Congress, *Journals of the Continental Congress, 1774–1789*, Washington, D.C., 1904–1937, vol. XX, p. 698.
33. Luis Marino Pérez, *Guide to the Materials for American History in Cuban Archives*, Washington, D.C., 1907, pp. 29–32.
34. Nichols, *op. cit.*, p. 291.
35. Arturo Morales Carrión, *Puerto Rico and the non-Hispanic Caribbean: A Study in the Decline of Spanish Exclusivism*, Rio Piedras, Puerto Rico, 1952, pp. 67–70.
36. Friedlander, *op. cit.*, pp. 112–14.

chapter 3 THE SOCIAL STRUCTURE OF CUBA, 1520–1790

1. Aimes, *op. cit.*, p. 37n.
2. Apology of Fernando VII, December 19, 1817, from the preamble of the Treaty of September 24, 1817, with Great Britain, in Jose María Zamora y Coronado, *Biblioteca de legislación ultramarina*, Madrid, 1845, vol. III, pp. 126–27.
3. Arthur F. Smith, "Spain and the Problem of Slavery in Cuba, 1817–1873," unpublished Ph.D. thesis, University of Chicago, 1958, pp. 7–8.
4. Johnson, *op. cit.*, vol. II, p. 55.
5. Wright, *op. cit.*, pp. 195–96.
6. *Ibid.*, p. 151.

7. *Ibid.*, pp. 197–98.
8. Ortiz, *op. cit.*, p. 84.
9. *Journal of Negro History*, vol. XIV, January, 1929, pp. 63, 71, 84, 99.
10. Zamora, *op. cit.*, vol. III, pp. 130–36.
11. *Cf.* Smith, *op. cit.*, p. 43.
12. Johnson, *op. cit.*, vol. II, p. 212.
13. *Cf.* Francisco Arango y Parreño, *Obras*, Habana, 1888, vol. I, p. 127.
14. *Ibid.*, pp. 132–33.
15. Smith, *op. cit.*, p. 48.
16. *Letters from the Havana*, *op. cit.*, p. 37.
17. Ortiz, *op. cit.*, pp. 57–58.
18. *Ibid.*, p. 287.
19. José Antonio Portuondo, *Bosquejo Histórico de las Letras Cubanas*, La Habana, 1960, p. 11.
20. Raúl Cepero Bonilla, *Azúcar y Abolición:Apuntes para una historia crítica del Abolicionismo*, La Habana, 1948, pp. 18–20.
21. Smith, *op. cit.*, pp. 50–52.
22. Raimundo Cabrera y Bosch, *Cuba and the Cubans*, Philadelphia, 1896, pp. 64–67.
23. Salvador de Madariaga, *The Rise of the Spanish American Empire*, New York, 1947, pp. 160–65.
24. Cabrera, *op. cit.*, pp. 69–71.
25. *Ibid.*
26. Portuondo, *op. cit.*, p. 12.
27. *Ibid.*
28. *Ibid.*, pp. 12–13.
29. Johnson, *op. cit.*, vol. II, p. 254.
30. *Ibid.*, vol. III, pp. 243–44.
31. Herminio Portell Vilá, *Juan de Miralles, un habanero amigo de Jorge Washington*, La Habana, 1947, pp. 12–19.
32. Portell Vilá, *Historia de Cuba*, *op. cit.*, vol. II, pp. 36–75. All references hereinafter to Portell Vilá are to this work.
33. Arthur P. Whitaker, editor, *Latin America and the Enlightenment*, New York, 1942; Bernard Moses, *The Intellectual Background of the Revolutions in South America, 1810–1824*, New York, 1926.
34. Portell Vilá, *op. cit.*, vol. II, pp. 64–76.
35. Philip S. Foner, editor, *The Complete Writings of Thomas Paine*, New York, 1945, vol. I, pp. 448–49.

chapter 4 THE ERA OF THE GREAT AWAKENING, 1790–1808

1. *Cf. Anales y memorias de la Real Junta de Fomento y de la Real Sociedad Económica de la Habana*, La Habana, 1856, vol. II, pp. 203–87.
2. Pezuela, *Historia de la isla de Cuba*, *op. cit.*, vol. II, p. 256; Rafael Montoro, *Historia de la Sociedad Económica*, La Habana, 1936, pp. 23–30; Friedlander, *op. cit.*, pp. 130–31.
3. Cabrera, *op. cit.*, pp. 47, 59.
4. *Actas de las Juntas Generales de la Real Sociedad Económica de*

Amigos del País, celebrada en los días 17, 18 y 19 de diciembre de 1837, pp. 19–35.
5. Portell Vilá, *op. cit.*, vol. I, p. 285.
6. Medardo Vitier, *Las ideas en Cuba proceso del pensamiento político, filosófico y crítico en Cuba*, La Habana, 1938, vol. I, p. 47; Gerardo García Castellanos, *Panorama histórico, ensayos de cronología cubana, desde 1492 hasta 1933*, La Habana, 1934, p. 220.
7. Ludwell Lee Montague, *Haiti and the United States, 1714–1938*, Durham, North Carolina, 1940, p. 5.
8. Alexander Humboldt, *The Island of Cuba*, translated by J. S. Thrasher, New York, 1856, p. 271.
9. Friendlander, *op. cit.*, pp. 121–22.
10. Aimes, *op. cit.*, p. 59.
11. Robert G. Caldwell, *The López Expeditions to Cuba, 1848–1851*, Princeton, New Jersey, 1915, p. 21.
12. Sergio Aguirre, *Lecciones de Historia de Cuba. Primero Cuaderno*, La Habana, 1960, pp. 85–86.
13. *Journal of Negro History*, vol. XIV, January, 1929, p. 96.
14. José Antonio Saco, *L'Esclavage à Cuba et la Revolution d'Espagne*, Paris, 1869, from the preface by Leon-Pierre Adrien Montlue, p. 6; Aguirre, *op. cit.*, p. 85; Aimes, *op. cit.*, p. 60.
15. Guerra, *op. cit.*, p. 188.
16. José Antonio Saco, *Historia de la esclavitud de la raza Africana en el Nuevo Mundo y en especial en los países americo-hispanos*, Habana, 1938, vol. III, p. 17. Hereinafter cited as *Historia*.
17. *Ibid.*, pp. 18–20; Portell Vilá, *op. cit.*, vol. I, pp. 36–37.
18. Domingo Amunátegui Solar, *La emancipación de Hispano América*, Santiago, Chile, 1936, pp. 1–9.
19. Pérez, *op. cit.*, p. 56; Nichols, *op. cit.*, pp. 293–94.
20. Pedro J. Guiteras, *Historia de la isla de Cuba*, New York, 1865–66, vol. I, p. 64.
21. Nichols, *op. cit.*, pp. 294–95.
22. *Ibid.*, p. 296.
23. Portell Vilá, *op. cit.*, vol. I, p. 125.
24. Nichols, *op. cit.*, p. 297.
25. J. B. Church to Col. Jacob Morton, April 30, 1799, and George C. Morton to Secretary of State Madison, Havana, April 21, 1801, Consular Letters, Havana, I; Josiah Blakely to Pickering, May 13, 1799, and Blakely to Madison, May 14, 1801, Consular Letters, Santiago, I, National Archives, Washington, D.C.
26. Nichols, *op. cit.*, p. 301.
27. Humphreys to Pickering, Madrid, November 16, 1799, Diplomatic Despatches, Spain, National Archives; Nichols, *op. cit.*, p. 301.
28. Morton to Madison, Jan. 9, 20, March 17, May 24, 1802, Consular Letters, Havana, I, National Archives.
29. Nichols, *op. cit.*, p. 305.
30. Gray to Madison, Dec. 5, 1803, Consular Letters, Havana, I, National Archives.

31. Hill to State Department, Nov. 1, 1805, Consular Letters, Havana, I, National Archives; Nichols, *op. cit.*, p. 311.
32. Humboldt, *op. cit.*, p. 271; Benjamin Allen, *A Story of the Growth of E. Atkins & Co., and the Sugar Industry in Cuba*, n.p., 1925, p. 8.
33. George C. Morton to Secretary of State Madison, April 21, 1801, Consular Despatches, Havana, I, National Archives.
34. Humboldt, *op. cit.*, pp. 218–19.
35. Nichols, *op. cit.*, pp. 293–94.
36. T. Lothrop Stoddard, *The French Revolution in San Domingo*, Boston, 1914, pp. 122–64.
37. *Cf.* prologue of José Antonio Saco, *Contra la anexión*, La Habana, 1928, vol. I, p. xv; José Antonio Saco, *La Esclavitud en Cuba y la revolución en España*, Madrid, 1868, pp. 2–15.
38. For a detailed analysis of these three currents in Cuban political thought throughout the nineteenth century, see Luis Estévez y Romero, *Separatismo, Anexionismo, y Autonomismo*, New York, 1898.
39. Aguirre, *op. cit.*, pp. 34–37.

chapter 5   THE "EVER-FAITHFUL ISLE," 1808–1820

1. William Robertson, *The Beginnings of Spanish-American Diplomacy*, New York, 1910, p. 236.
2. Jorge Gelabert Megret, "Cuba during the Wars of Independence, 1810–1824," unpublished M.A. thesis, New York University, 1957, pp. 26–28. In Spanish.
3. Cabrera, *op. cit.*, p. 395.
4. Gelabert Megret, *op. cit.*, pp. 34–35.
5. *Ibid.*, pp. 32–33.
6. Francisco J. Ponte Domínguez, *La Masonería en la independencia de Cuba*, La Habana, 1944, pp. 5–13.
7. Quoted in *Letters from the Havana*, *op. cit.*, pp. 48–49n.
8. Gelabert Megret, *op. cit.*, pp. 32–33.
9. John A. Mackay, *The Other Spanish Christ*, New York, 1933, p. 60.
10. *Ibid.*, p. 61.
11. Gonzalez del Valle, "El Clero en la Revolución Cubana," *Cuba Contemporanea*, vol. XVIII, October, 1918, p. 191.
12. José L. Franco, *Antonio Maceo: Apuntes para una Historia de su Vida*, La Habana, 1951, vol. I, p. 28.
13. Portell Vilá, *op. cit.*, vol. I, p. 148; Gelabert Megret, *op. cit.*, pp. 38–39; Aguirre, *op. cit.*, pp. 38–39.
14. José Alvarez de Toledo, *Manifiesto o satisfacción pundonorosa a todos los buenos españoles europeos y a todos los pueblos de la América por un diputado de las cartas reunidas en Cádiz*, Philadelphia, 1811, pp. 35–37.
15. Portell Vilá, *op. cit.*, vol. I, p. 48.
16. Rafael María de Labra, *América y la Constitución Español de 1812*, Madrid, 1914, pp. 127–29; Saco, *Historia, op. cit.*, vol. III, pp. 83–85.
17. Aimes, *op. cit.*, p. 64.

18. Ramiro Guerra y Sánchez, *Cuba, Centro de Rivalidad Internacional en el Caribe*, La Habana, 1952, vol. III, p. 30.
19. Shaler to Smith, June 5, 1811, Consular Despatches, Havana, II, National Archives.
20. Saco, *Historia, op. cit.*, vol. III, p. 90. Emphasis mine. P.S.F.
21. Aimes, *op. cit.*, pp. 67–69.
22. Saco, *Historia, op. cit.*, vol. III, pp. 90–112.
23. *Ibid.*, pp. 115–18; Aimes, *op. cit.*, 70–71.
24. Cabrera, *op. cit.*, pp. 398–400; Atkinson, *op. cit.*, pp. 264–65.
25. Cabrera, *op. cit.*, p. 399.
26. William Z. Foster, *Outline Political History of the Americas*, New York, 1951, pp. 142–43.
27. Saco, *Historia, op. cit.*, vol. III, pp. 83–85.
28. Ramiro Guerra y Sánchez, *Antecedentes y Significación de la Guerra de 1868*, La Habana, 1942, p. 6.
29. José de Ahumada, *Memoria Histórica Política de la Isla de Cuba*, La Habana, 1918, p, 255.
30. Portell Vilá, *op. cit.*, vol. I, p. 163; Aguirre, *op. cit.*, pp. 75–76.
31. Shaler to Smith, Havana, October 24, 1810, Consular Despatches, Havana, II, National Archives.
32. Portell Vilá, *op. cit.*, vol. I, pp. 163–64.
33. Saco, *Historia, op. cit.*, vol. III, pp. 83–85.
34. Gelabert Megret, *op. cit.*, p. 46; Cabrera, *op. cit.*, p. 397.
35. Elías Entralgo, *Los Problemas de la Esclavitud. Conspiración de Aponte*, La Habana, 1934, pp. 46–47; Clemente Lainer, "Cuba et la Conspiration d'Aponte en 1812," In *Revue de la Société Haitienne d'Histoire, de Géographie et de Géologie*, vol. XXIII, pp. 26–27.
36. Rogue E. Garrigó, *Historia Documentada de la Conspiración de los Soles y Rayos de Bolívar*, La Habana, 1939, vol. I, pp. 108–09.
37. Entralgo, *op. cit.*, pp. 48–64.
38. *Ibid.*, pp. 78–96.
39. *Ibid.*, pp. 102–05, 227.
40. Cited in Gelabert Megret, *op. cit.*, pp. 59–60.
41. *Ibid.*, p. 47.
42 Cepero, *op. cit.*, pp. 32–33.
43. *Ibid.*
44. José L. Franco, *Política continental americana de España en Cuba, 1812–1830*, La Habana, 1947, pp. 34–36.
45. *Ibid.*, p. 329.
46. Aguirre, *op. cit.*, p. 41.
47. Aimes, *op. cit.*, p. 91.
48. Guerra, *Manual, op. cit.*, p. 239; Pezuela, *Historia, op. cit.*, vol. IV, p. 50.
49. Aguirre, *op. cit.*, pp. 42–43.
50. C. K. Webster, *The Foreign Policy of Castlereagh, 1812–1815, Britain and the Reconstruction of Europe*, London, 1931, pp. 413–23; Saco, *Historia, op. cit.*, vol. III, pp. 122–24.
51. Saco, *Historia, op. cit.*, vol. III, p. 125.

52. Pezuela, *Diccionario, op. cit.*, vol. II, p. 285; Saco, *Historia, op. cit.*, vol. III, pp. 307–19.
53. Smith, *op. cit.*, pp. 92–95; Aimes, *op. cit.*, pp. 77–78.
54. *Letters from the Havana, op. cit.*, pp. 132–33.
55. Humboldt, *op. cit.*, p. 280.
56. Gelabert Megret, *op. cit.*, pp. 59–60.
57. *Letters from the Havana, op. cit.*, p. 52.

chapter 6 THE INDEPENDENCE MOVEMENT, 1820–1830

1. *Niles' Weekly Register*, vol. XVIII, May 6, 1820, p. 176; May 27, 1820, p. 263.
2. *Letters from the Havana, op. cit.*, pp. 50–51; Cabrera, *op. cit.*, pp. 403–04.
3. *Letters from the Havana, op. cit.*, p. 51.
4. *Niles' Weekly Register*, vol. XVIII, Aug. 5, 1820, p. 415.
5. Saco, *Historia, op. cit.*, vol. III, p. 144.
6. Juan Bernardo O'Gavan, *Observaciones sobre la condición de los Esclavos Africanos*, Madrid, 1821.
7. Aimes, *op. cit.*, p. 97; Saco, *Historia, op. cit.*, vol. III, pp. 43–44.
8. Saco, *Historia, op. cit.*, vol. III, pp. 1–31.
9. *Ibid.*
10. Smith, *op. cit.*, p. 60.
11. J. M. Phillippo, *The United States and Cuba*, London, 1857, p. 413.
12. French E. Chadwick, *The Relations of the United States and Spain—Diplomacy*, New York, 1909, pp. 224–25.
13. Richard B. Kimball, *Cuba and the Cubans; Comprising a History of Its Present Social, Political, and Domestic Conditions; also Its Relation to England and the United States*, New York, 1850, p. 56.
14. James Morton Callahan, *Cuba and International Relations*, Baltimore, 1899, p. 15.
15. *La Verdad*, June 15, 1849.
16. Cepero, *op. cit.*, pp. 33–34.
17. Manuel Villanova, quoted in *ibid.*, p. 34.
18. Ramiro Guerra y Sánchez, José M. Pérez Cabrera, Juan J. Remos, Emeterio S. Santovenia, editors, *Historia de la Nación Cubana*, La Habana, 1952, vol. III, p. 80.
19. Pezuela, *Diccionario, op. cit.*, vol. II, pp. 285–87.
20. Smith, *op. cit.*, pp. 41–42.
21. Gelabert Megret, *op. cit.*, pp. 62–64.
22. Johnson, *op. cit.*, vol. III, p. 319; Portuondo, *op. cit.*, pp. 17–18.
23. José L. Franco, editor, *Documentos para la Historia de Venezuela Existentes en el Archivo Nacional de Cuba*, La Habana, 1960, p. xcv.
24. Aguirre, *op. cit.*, pp. 77–79.
25. Gelabert Megret, *op. cit.*, pp. 70–71.
26. Franco, *Documentos, op. cit.*, pp. xcv–xcvi.
27. Cepero, *op. cit.*, pp. 32–37.
28. *Niles' Weekly Register*, vol. XVII, June 17, 1820, p. 286.

29. O. Pulgarón, *Apuntes Históricos Sobre la Masonería Cubana*, Guanabacoa, Cuba, 1933, pp. 12–15.
30. Forsyth to Adams, November 20, 1822, Diplomatic Despatches, Spain, XXI, National Archives.
31. Gray to Daniel Brent, Havana, October 31, 1821, Consular Despatches, Havana, III, National Archives.
32. Garrigó, *op. cit.*, vol. I, p. 153.
33. *Ibid.*, vol. II, p. 165.
34. *Ibid.*, p. 171.
35. *Ibid.*, pp. 165–69.
36. *Ibid.*, p. 173.
37. *Ibid.*, p. 174.
38. *Ibid.*, pp. 176–78.
39. *Ibid.*, p. 246.
40. *Ibid.*, Doc. No. 68. Emphasis in original. P.S.F.
41. *Ibid.*, vol. I, pp. 108–09; Cepero, *op. cit.*, p. 33.
42. Franco, *Documentos*, *op. cit.*, pp. xcv–xcvi.
43. Garrigó, *op. cit.*, vol. II, Docs. Nos. 68, 69.
44. Franco, *Documentos*, *op. cit.*, p. xlvi.
45. Garrigó, *op. cit.*, vol. II, pp. 190–210.
46. Franco, *Documentos*, *op. cit.*, p. xcvi.
47. Aguirre, *op. cit.*, pp. 77–79.
48. *Niles' Weekly Register*, vol. XXX, May 13, 1826, p. 186.
49. Johnson, *op. cit.*, vol. III, Chapter I.
50. Franco, *Documentos*, *op. cit.*, pp. xcvi, 224.
51. Vol. XXX, p. 159.
52. Franco, *Documentos*, *op. cit.*, p. c; Aguirre, *op. cit.*, pp. 78–79.
53. Justo Zaragoza, *Las Insurrecciones en Cuba*, Madrid, 1872, vol. I, p. 534.
54. Cepero, *op. cit.*, p. 33; Aguirre, *op. cit.*, p. 80.

chapter 7 EMERGENCE OF UNITED STATES POLICY TOWARD CUBA, 1800–1823

1. Merrill D. Peterson, *The Jefferson Image in the American Mind*, New York, 1960, Preface.
2. *Cf. Senate Report No. 351*, 35 Congress, 2nd Session, p. 1.
3. Reprinted in Antonio Núñez Jiménez, *La Liberación de las Islas*, La Habana, 1959, p. 458.
4. *Senate Report No. 351*, 35 Congress, 2nd Session, p. 1.
5. Madison to Anderson, Jan. 14, 1807, Instructions to Consuls, I, 208, National Archives.
6. Anthony Merry to Mulgrave, November 3, 1805, quoted in J. F. Rippy, *Rivalry of the United States and Great Britain over Latin America, 1808–1830*, Baltimore, 1929, p. 72.
7. Jefferson to Madison, August 16, 1807, Thomas Jefferson Papers, Library of Congress, Manuscripts Division.
8. Andrew A. Lipscomb and Albert Ellery Bergh, editors, *The Writings of Thomas Jefferson*, Washington, 1904, vol. IX, p. 327.

9. Isaac J. Cox, *The West Florida Controversy, 1790–1813*, Baltimore, 1918, pp. 290–92; Isaac J. Cox, "The Pan American Policy of Jefferson and Wilkinson," *Mississippi Valley Historical Review*, vol. I, 1914, pp. 222–23.
10. Morales Carrión, *op. cit.*, p. 68.
11. Lipscomb and Bergh, editors, *op. cit.*, vol. XII, p. 274.
12. Madison to Jefferson, April 24, 1809, James Madison Papers, Library of Congress, Manuscripts Division.
13. Lipscomb and Bergh, editors, *op. cit.*, vol. XII, p. 277.
14. James Gallatin to Madison, Sept. 17, 1810, James Madison Papers, Library of Congress, Manuscripts Division.
15. Gaillard Hunt, editor, *The Writings of James Madison*, New York, 1900, vol. VIII, pp. 121–22.
16. Reprinted in Núñez Jiménez, *op. cit.*, p. 458.
17. Roy F. Nichols, "William Shaler, New England Apostle of Liberty," *New England Quarterly*, vol. IX, 1933, pp. 76–77.
18. Portell Vilá, *op. cit.*, vol. I, p. 167.
19. Shaler to Smith, October 24, 1810, Consular Despatches, Havana, II, National Archives.
20. Shaler to Smith, June 11, 14, *ibid.*; Portell Vilá, *op. cit.*, vol. I, p. 167.
21. Shaler to Monroe, Havana, December 6, 1811, enclosing "nota," December 1, 1811, Consular Despatches, Havana, II, National Archives; Portell Vilá, *op. cit.*, vol. I, pp. 162–63.
22. Shaler to Monroe, Havana, December 6, 1811, Consular Despatches, Havana, II, National Archives.
23. Portell Vilá, *op. cit.*, vol. I, pp. 161–67.
24. Shaler to Monroe, December 8, 27, 1811, Consular Despatches, Havana, II, National Archives; Portell Vilá, *op. cit.*, vol. I, p. 170.
25. John Crane Pine, "The Role of United States Special Agents in the Development of a Spanish-American Policy, 1810–1822," unpublished Ph.D. thesis, University of Colorado, 1955, pp. 109–10.
26. Joseph B. Lockey, "An Early Pan-American Scheme," *Pacific Historical Review*, vol. II, 1933, pp. 440–47.
27. Carlos M. Trelles y Govín, *Un precursor de la independencia de Cuba, José Alvarez de Toledo*, La Habana, 1926, pp. 8–13, 153–60; Isaac Joslin Cox, "Monroe and the Early Mexican Revolutionary Agents," *Annual Report of the American Historical Association for the Year 1911*, Washington, 1913, vol. I, p. 203; Dallas to Monroe, Nov. 25, Dec. 23, 1811, Miscellaneous Letters, Dept. of State; Toledo to Graham, Jan. 4, 7, 1812, *ibid.*; Toledo to Monroe, Jan. 7, 1812, *ibid.*; Monroe to Dallas, Nov. 23, 1811, Domestic Letters, Dept. of State, XVI, 38; Toledo to Monroe, Nov. 16, 1811, Mexico, Filibustering Expeditions against the Government of Spain, 1811–1816, Dept. of State; all in National Archives.
28. José L. Franco, *Política Continental Americana de España en Cuba, 1812–1830*, La Habana, 1947, p. 16.
29. William Kenneth Bunce, "American Interests in the Caribbean Islands,

1783–1850," unpublished Ph.D. thesis, Ohio State University, 1939, p. 88.

30. *American State Papers, Foreign Relations*, vol. V, pp. 408–30.
31. *Colombian Centinel*, July 11, 1810.
32. Vol. II, March 28, 1812, p. 71.
33. Richmond *Enquirer*, June 3, 1817.
34. Washington *National Intelligencer*, July 24, 1816.
35. Richmond *Enquirer*, June 22, 1810; Louisiana (Mo.) *Gazette*, Aug. 2, Dec. 2, 1817; Rev. Brendan C. NcNally, "Coverage and Attitude of U.S. Press Relative to Independence Movements in the Spanish Americas, 1810–1825," unpublished Ph.D. thesis, University of St. Louis, 1949, p. 250.
36. Washington *National Intelligencer*, April 19, 1814.
37. *Freeman's Journal* (Philadelphia) reprinted in New York *Herald*, April 28, 1814.
38. Reprinted in Washington *National Intelligencer*, May 24, 1817.
39. Washington *National Intelligencer*, July 24, 1816.
40. Philadelphia *Aurora*, Nov. 10, 22, 1817.
41. "Treason, Rebellion, Revolution," in vol. II, March 21, 1812, pp. 58–59.
42. Reprinted in Philadelphia *Aurora*, Aug. 7, 1817.
43. *Cf.* Kenneth Porter, "The Hispanic Policy of John Quincy Adams, 1817–1828," unpublished Ph.D. thesis, University of California, 1935; Charles Carroll Griffin, *The United States and the Disruption of the Spanish Empire, 1810–1822*, New York, 1937; Arthur P. Whitaker, *The United States and the Independence of Latin America, 1800–1830*, Baltimore, 1941.
44. Quoted in Griffin, *op. cit.*, p. 257.
45. Philadelphia, 1818, pp. 10 *ff.* There are only three copies of the pamphlet in existence; one in the Harvard University Library, a second in the University Library, University of Pennsylvania, and a third in the Library of the American Antiquarian Society.
46. Nicholas Biddle to James Monroe, Dec. 11, 1817, March 15, 1818, James Monroe Papers, Library of Congress, Manuscripts Division.
47. *Annals of Congress*, 14th Cong., 2nd Sess., vol. XXX, p. 738.
48. *The Maryland Censor*, vol. I, no. 1, August 19, 1818. (Copy in Library of Congress, Newspaper Division.)
49. Whitaker, *op. cit.*, p. 212.
50. Philadelphia *Aurora*, July 30, 1819.
51. Charles Francis Adams, editor, *Memoirs of John Quincy Adams, Comprising Portions of His Diary from 1795 to 1848*, Philadelphia, 1874–77, vol. IV, p. 118.
52. *Ibid.*, vol. IV, pp. 8–10, 20; Griffin, *op. cit.*, pp. 187–88.
53. *Bell's London Messenger* reprinted in Washington *National Intelligencer*, Aug. 28, 1819; E. H. Tatum, Jr., *The United States and Europe, 1815–1823*, Berkeley, California, 1936, pp. 16–18; Rippy, *op. cit.*, pp. 76–80.

54. *Niles' Weekly Register,* vol. XIII, May 22, 1819, p. 60; Portell Vilá, *op. cit.,* vol. I, p. 191.
55. *Niles' Weekly Register,* vol. XIII, May 22, 1819, p. 62.
56. Griffin, *op. cit.,* p. 215; William McCorkle to James Monroe, Aug. 25, 1819, James Monroe Papers, New York Library, Manuscripts Division.
57. Vol. XVII, Feb. 12, 1820, p. 13.
58. *Niles' Weekly Register,* vol. XVIII, March 4, 1820, pp. 1, 2.
59. John Bassett Moore, *A Digest of International Law,* Washington, 1906, vol. I, p. 583.
60. Forsyth to Adams, Madrid, November 20, 1822, Dept. of State, Diplomatic Despatches: Spain, XXI, National Archives.
61. Washington *National Intelligencer,* quoted in *Niles' Weekly Register,* vol. XVI, Feb. 27, 1819, pp. 3–4.
62. Herbert Aptheker, *American Negro Slave Revolts,* New York, 1943, pp. 264–78.
63. John Forsyth to Adams, Madrid, November 20, 1822, *op. cit.*
64. Portell Vilá, *op. cit.,* vol. I, pp. 178–82.
65. John Warner to C. A. Rodney, Feb. 20, 1822, James Monroe Papers, Library of Congress, Manuscripts Division.
66. James Biddle to Monroe, August 3, 1822, *ibid.*
67. Portell Vilá, *op. cit.,* vol. I, pp. 215–16; Rippy, *op. cit.,* pp. 80–82.
68. Charles Francis Adams, editor, *op. cit.,* vol. VI, pp. 70–74, 111–12; J. R. Poinsett to Monroe, May 7, 1823, and José de Castillo to Poinsett, April 16, 1823, James Monroe Papers, Library of Congress, Manuscripts Division.
69. Bunce, *op. cit.,* p. 128.
70. *Cf.* Vincent Gray to Daniel Brent, Havana, October 31, 1821, Dept. of State, Consular Despatches, Havana, III, National Archives.
71. *Niles' Weekly Register,* vol. XXIV, March 15, 1823, pp. 25–26; April 5, 1823, pp. 72–73; April 26, 1823, p. 113; May 24, 1823, p. 180; August 9, 1823, p. 356; Boston *American Statesman,* Jan. 23, 1823; General Barnard to Monroe, James Monroe Papers, Library of Congress, Manuscripts Division.
72. Charles Francis Adams, editor, *op. cit.,* vol. VI, p. 138.
73. Adams to Randall, April 29, 1823, Dept. of State, Instructions to Consuls, II, 283, National Archives.
74. Adams to Hugh Nelson, Washington, April 28, 1823, Dept. of State, Instructions, United States Ministers, IX, National Archives.
75. *Ibid.* See also *American State Papers, Foreign Relations,* vol. V, pp. 408 ff.
76. Núñez Jiménez, *op. cit.,* pp. 459–60.
77. Charles Francis Adams, editor, *op. cit.,* vol. VI, p. 138; Lipscomb and Bergh, editors, *op. cit.,* vol. XV, pp. 436–37.
78. S. M. Hamilton, editor, *The Writings of James Monroe,* New York, 1898–1903, vol. VI, pp. 311–12.
79. Dexter Perkins, *The Monroe Doctrine, 1823–1826,* Cambridge, Mass., 1932, pp. 200–02.

80. Lipscomb and Bergh, editors, *op. cit.,* vol. XV, pp. 478–79; *Letters and Other Writings of James Madison, Fourth President of the United States,* Philadelphia, 1865, vol. III, p. 340.
81. Charles Francis Adams, editor, *op. cit.,* vol. VI, p. 178.
82. Adams to Rush, Nov. 29, 30, 1823, William R. Manning, editor, *Diplomatic Correspondence of the United States Concerning the Independence of the Latin American Nations,* New York, 1925, vol. I, pp. 210–13.
83. William R. Manning, *Early Diplomatic Relations Between the United States and Mexico,* Baltimore, 1916, pp. 98–99.
84. James D. Richardson, *A Compilation of the Messages and Papers of the Presidents, 1789–1897,* Washington, 1900, vol. II, pp. 217–18.
85. Perkins, *op. cit.,* pp. 202–04.

chapter 8 THE UNITED STATES AND THE INDEPENDENCE OF CUBA, 1823–1830

1. *Niles' Weekly Register,* vol. XVIII, May 27, 1820, pp. 239–40; Aug. 5, 1820, p. 415.
2. Charles K. Webster, *The European Alliance,* Calcutta, India, 1929, p. 76.
3. *Niles' Weekly Register,* vol. XX, Nov. 23, Dec. 7, 1822; Washington *National Intelligencer,* Nov. 1, 1822.
4. New York *Evening Post,* Nov. 26, 1822.
5. *See also* Washington *National Intelligencer,* Dec. 9, 1822.
6. *Niles' Weekly Register,* vol. XXII, Nov. 27, 1824, p. 204.
7. Quoted in Portell Vilá, *op. cit.,* vol. I, p. 244.
8. Emeterio Santovenia, *Bolívar y las Antillas Hispanas,* Madrid, 1935, pp. 66–145; Portell Vilá, *op. cit.,* vol. I, pp. 197–212.
9. Santovenia, *op. cit.,* pp. 120–44.
10. Evelio-Rodríguez Lendián, "El Congreso de Panamá y La Independencia de Cuba," *Universidad de la Habana, Revista de la Facultad de Letras y Ciencias,* vol. XII, 1911, pp. 15–16.
11. *Ibid.,* p. 17.
12. Franco, editor, *Documentos, op. cit.,* p. xcviii.
13. *Ibid.*
14. Manning, *Early Diplomatic Relations, op. cit.,* p. 129.
15. Poinsett to Clay, Sept. 13, 1825, Dept. of State, Despatches from Mexico, I, National Archives.
16. Manning, *Early Diplomatic Relations, op. cit.,* pp. 99–101.
17. *National Gazette,* Dec. 16, 1825.
18. *Niles' Weekly Register,* vol. XXIX, Dec. 24, 1825, p. 259.
19. *Annals of Congress,* 14th Cong., 2nd Sess., pp. 724–43.
20. Clay to Middleton, May 10, 1825, Washington, Dept. of State, Instructions: U.S. Ministers, X, National Archives.
21. *Ibid.*
22. Clay to Everett, Washington, April 27, 1825, *ibid.* Emphasis mine. **P.S.F.**

23. Clay to Poinsett, March 26, 1825, Instructions to Ministers, X, National Archives.
24. Clay to Everett, April 27, 1825, Instructions to Ministers, X, *ibid.*
25. Francisco de Zea Bermúdez to Nelson, July 13, 1825, Despatches from Spain, XXV, National Archives; 32nd Cong., 1st Sess., *Executive Document No. 12*, pp. 14–16.
26. Everett to Francisco de Zea Bermúdez, Oct. 10, 1825, Despatches from Spain, XXV, National Archives.
27. Clay to Middleton, May 10, 1825; to Rufus King, May 11, 1825; to James Brown, May 13, 1825, Dept. of State, Instructions to Ministers, X, National Archives.
28. Brown to Clay, Paris, March 12, 1826, Diplomatic Despatches, France, XIII; Middleton to Clay, St. Petersburg, Sept. 8, 1825, *ibid.*, Russia, X; Canning to King, Aug. 21, 1825, *ibid.*, Great Britain, XXXII, National Archives.
29. Clay to King, Oct. 17, 1825, Instructions to Ministers, X, National Archives.
30. Perkins, *op. cit.*, pp. 202–07.
31. Poinsett to Clay, June 15, 1825, Dept. of State, Despatches from Mexico, I, National Archives.
32. Manning, *Diplomatic Correspondence, op. cit.*, vol. I, pp. 263–64.
33. Resolutions enclosed in Poinsett to Clay, Jan. 28th, 1826, Despatches from Mexico, I, National Archives.
34. Poinsett to Clay, Feb. 1, 1826, *ibid.*
35. Poinsett to Clay, Oct. 29, 1825, *ibid.*
36. Clay to Everett, April 13, 1825, Instructions to Ministers, XI, National Archives.
37. Quoted in *The United States Government Has Injured the Liberty of the People of Cuba*, New York, 1849, p. 19.
38. Joseph B. Lockey, *Pan Americanism, Its Beginnings*, New York, 1920, pp. 312–20.
39. Charles Francis Adams, editor, *op. cit.*, vol. V, p. 176.
40. *The Congress of 1826 at Panama* (International American Conference), vol. IV, Historical Appendix, 1890, pp. 24–34.
41. Poinsett to Clay, May 31, June 23, 1826, Despatches from Mexico, I, National Archives.
42. Manning, *Early Relations, op. cit.*, p. 155.
43. Richardson, *op. cit.*, vol. II, pp. 329–40.
44. *Niles' Weekly Register*, vol. XXVII, April 30, 1825, p. 132; vol. XXIX, Jan. 7, 1826, p. 294.
45. Quoted in McNally, *op. cit.*, pp. 356–62.
46. *National Gazette*, Nov. 24, 1825; Richmond *Enquirer*, Dec. 2, 1825.
47. *American State Papers, Foreign Relations*, vol. V, p. 863.
48. Benton's *Abridgement of Debates in Congress*, vol. XIII, pp. 421–24.
49. Pittsburgh *Mercury*, Oct. 11, 1826.
50. Benton's *Abridgement of Debates in Congress*, vol. XIII, pp. 421–24.
51. *Speech of Mr. Hamilton of South Carolina on the Panama Mission, delivered in the House of Representatives, April 26, 1826*, Washington, 1826, pp. 22–24.

52. *Speech of Mr. (John) Holmes of Maine, Delivered in the Senate of the United States on the Mission to Panama, March, 1826*, p. 19.
53. H. B. Saul, "The Panama Congress and the Sectional Influence in the United States," unpublished M.A. thesis, Columbia University, 1920, p. 17.
54. Pittsburgh *Mercury*, April 26, 1826.
55. Clay to Anderson and Sergeant, Washington, May 8, 1826, Dept. of State, Panama Congress, 1826–1827, I, National Archives.
56. Núñez Jiménez, *op. cit.*, p. 461. Also Emilio Roig de Leuchsenring, *The American State Has Always Been an Enemy to Cuban Independence*, Havana, n.d., p. 56.
57. *Cf.* E. Burton, "Henry Clay," in Samuel Flagg Bemis, editor, *The American Secretaries of State and Their Diplomacy*, New York, 1928, vol. IV, pp. 148–49.
58. Poinsett to Clay, Sept. 23, Oct. 21, 1826, Despatches from Mexico, I, National Archives.
59. Vidal Morales y Morales, *Iniciadores y Primeros Mártires de la Revolución Cubana*, La Habana, 1931, vol. I, p. 97.
60. *Memorias del General José Antonio Páez, Autobiografía*, Madrid, n.d., pp. 455–56.
61. Van Buren to Van Ness, Oct. 2, 1829, Dept. of State, Instructions: United States Ministers, XIII, National Archives.
62. *Op. cit.*, p. 24.
63. H. W. V. Temperley, "The Later American Policy of Canning," *American Historical Review*, vol. XI, July, 1906, p. 793.
64. J. Fred Rippy in his introduction to Manuel Ugartés, *The Destiny of a Continent*, New York, 1925, p. xx; R. F. Arragon, "The Congress of Panama," unpublished Ph.D. thesis, Harvard University, 1923, pp. 620–45.
65. New York, 1849, pp. 18–19.
66. New Orleans *Daily Picayune*, July 10, 1854.

chapter 9   THE SECOND REFORM MOVEMENT

1. Guerra, *Manual, op. cit.*, pp. 296–324.
2. *Ibid.*, pp. 230–31.
3. Livingston to Shaler, Sept. 1, 1829, Special Missions, I, 92, National Archives.
4. Van Ness to Livingston, May 11, 1832, Despatches from Spain, XXX, *ibid.*
5. Senate Reports, 32nd Cong., 1st Sess., 318, pp. 1–3.
6. Portell Vilá, *op. cit.*, vol. II, p. 131.
7. Johnson, *op. cit.*, vol. III, pp. 13–17.
8. Cepero, *op. cit.*, pp. 9–10.
9. Portell Vilá, *op. cit.*, vol. I, pp. 477–78.
10. Aimes, *op. cit.*, p. 14; F. V. Aguilera, *Notes About Cuba*, New York, 1872, pp. 6–7.
11. Saco, *Historia, op. cit.*, vol. III, p. 150.
12. *Ibid.*, p. 151.

13. Fernando Ortiz Fernández in prologue to Saco's *Contra la Anexión*, La Habana, 1928, vol. I, p. xliv.
14. Cabrera, *op. cit.*, pp. 411–13.
15. Domingo del Monte, *La Isla de Cuba tal cual está*, a pamphlet written in Havana in 1836, published in New York or Madrid, and reprinted in Saco, *Historia, op. cit.*, vol. IV, pp. 269–97.
16. Signed by Francisco de Armas, Juan Montalvo and José Antonio Saco, and reprinted in *Información: reformas de Cuba y Puerto Rico*, New York, 1867.
17. Zaragoza, *op. cit.*, vol. I, p. 413.
18. José Antonio Saco, *La primera pregunta: La abolición del comercio de esclavos africanos arruinará o atrasará la agricultura cubana?* Madrid, 1837.
19. José de Ahumada, *op. cit.*, pp. 115–16.
20. Villanova, *op. cit.*, p. 339.
21. Cepero, *op. cit.*, p. 36.
22. Callahan, *op. cit.*, p. 173.
23. Saco, *Contra la Anexión, op. cit.*, vol. I, p. 47.
24. Trist to Forsyth, Havana, November 29, 1836, Dept. of State, Consular Despatches, Havana, II, National Archives.
25. Aimes, *op. cit.*, Appendix II, "Slaves Imported into Cuba."
26. Warren S. Howard, "The United States Government and the African Slave Trade, 1837–1862," unpublished Ph.D. thesis, University of California, Los Angeles, July, 1959, pp. 123–24.
27. *See particularly* Dept. of State, Consular Despatches, Havana, XIII–XVI, XVIII, National Archives, and *House Exec. Doc. 115*, 26th Cong., 2nd Sess.
28. Everett to Forsyth, July 21, 1840, Dept. of State, Consular Despatches, Havana, XIV, National Archives.
29. Trist to Forsyth, Feb. 20, Nov. 22, 1840, Dept, of State, Consular Despatches, XIII, XV, *ibid.*
30. Webster to Tyler, June 22, 1841; Webster to Trist, July 15, 1841, Instructions to Consuls, X, 40, 50, National Archives.
31. Portuondo, *op. cit.*, p. 23.

chapter 10   CUBAN SLAVE SOCIETY

1. Lowell J. Ragatz, *The Fall of the Planter Class in the British Caribbean, 1763–1833, a Study in Social and Economic History*, New York, 1928, pp. 454–55.
2. Captain Henry A. Murray, *Lands of the Slave and the Free: or Cuba, the United States, and Canada*, London, 1857, pp. 179–80; John G. Taylor, *The United States and Cuba: Eight Years of Change and Travel*, London, 1851, pp. 196–97.
3. Aimes, *op. cit.*, p. 172.
4. Al Ministro de Estado, La Habana, Septiembre 9, 1849, in *Boletín del Archivo Nacional*, Habana, vol. XVI, 1917, p. 278.
5. David Turnbull, *Travels in the West. Cuba; with Notices of Porto Rico, and the Slave Trade*, London, 1840, p. 388.
6. Philip S. Foner, *Business and Slavery: The New York Merchants and*

the *Irrepressible Conflict,* Chapel Hill, North Carolina, 1941, pp. 165–67.
7. Leland H. Jenks, *Our Cuban Colony,* New York, 1927, pp. 19–24.
8. *Ibid.,* p. 23; F. Wurdiman, *Notes on Cuba . . . By a Physician,* Boston, 1844, pp. 144–45; Richard H. Dana, *To Cuba and Back, A Vacation Voyage,* Boston, 1859, p. 117.
9. Portell Vilá, *op. cit.,* vol. I, pp. 350–51.
10. *The United States Government Has Injured the People of Cuba, op. cit.,* introduction.
11. Urbano Feijóo de Sotomaure, *La Isla de Cuba,* Paris, 1852, pp. 32–35.
12. Aimes, *op. cit.,* p. 157.
13. Portell Vilá, *op. cit.,* vol. I, pp. 350–51.
14. *Ibid.,* pp. 477–78; Murray, *op. cit.,* p. 173; Taylor, *op. cit.,* p. 414; *Annual Report of the American and Foreign Anti-Slavery Society,* May 6, 1851, p. 102.
15. Mariano Torrente, *Slavery in the Island of Cuba with remarks on the statements of the British press on the slave trade,* London, 1853, p. 47; Robert Baird, *Impressions and Experiences of the West Indies and North America in 1849,* London, 1850, vol. I, p. 179.
16. Charles Albert Page, "The Development of Organized Labor in Cuba," unpublished Ph.D. thesis, University of California, Latin American Studies, June, 1952, p. 4.
17. Turnbull, *op. cit.,* p. 266.
18. José Antonio Saco, *La vagancia en Cuba,* Habana, 1946, pp. 72–73.
19. Juan J. Reyes, *Memoria sobre las causas de la vagancia en la Isla de Cuba,* Habana, 1851, in Aimes, *op. cit.,* p. 262.
20. Wurdiman, *op. cit.,* pp. 144–49.
21. Turnbull, *op. cit.,* pp. 47–48.
22. R. R. Madden, *The Island of Cuba,* London, 1849, pp. 56–62; Wurdiman, *op. cit.,* pp. 149–55; Taylor, *op. cit.,* pp. 197–202; J. J. Ampère, *Promenade en Amérique, États Unis-Cuba-Mexique,* Paris, 1867, pp. 200–01; *Democratic Review,* vol. XLIII, New Series, 1859, p. 28.
23. Miguel Estorch, *Apuntes para la historia sobre la administración desde 3 de diciembre de 1853 hasta 21 de septiembre de 1854, del Marqués de la Pezuela en la isla de Cuba . . .,* Madrid, 1856, pp. 15, 17–18.
24. Ramiro Guerra y Sánchez, in *Historia de la Nación Cubana, op. cit.,* vol. III, pp. 80–82.
25. Smith, *op. cit.,* p. 65.
26. *Ibid.,* p. 66.
27. *Ibid.,* pp. 67–68.
28. Aimes, *op. cit.,* pp. 127, 232–33.
29. London, 1840, p. 86.
30. *Ibid.,* pp. 11–13.
31. *Ibid.,* pp. 30, 33–34, 43, 45, 49.
32. *Ibid.,* pp. 112–15.
33. *Ibid.,* introduction.

34. Francisco Arango y Parreño, *Obras,* La Habana, 1888, vol. II, pp. 376–78.
35. Saco, *Historia, op. cit.,* vol. IV, p. 249.
36. Quoted in Cepero, *op. cit.,* p. 98.
37. *Ibid.,* Chapter X, "Racismo y nacionalidad," pp. 93–104.
38. Saco, *Contra la Anexión, op. cit.,* vol. I, p. 224.
39. Quoted in Cepero, *op. cit.,* pp. 99–100. Emphasis mine, P.S.F.
40. Saco, *Contra la Anexión, op. cit.,* vol. I, p. 82.
41. Saco, *Historia, op. cit.,* vol. IV, p. 210.
42. Quoted in José L. Franco, *Antonio Maceo: Apuntes para una Historia de Su Vida, op. cit.,* p. 25.
43. Guerra, *Manual, op. cit.,* p. 442.
44. T. R. Gray to John Forsyth, Trinidad de Cuba, April 16, 1838, Dept. of State, Consular Despatches: Trinidad, National Archives.

chapter 11   THE RISING TIDE OF ANTI-SLAVERY

1. Aimes, *op. cit.,* pp. 127, 232–33.
2. Saco, *Historia, op. cit.,* vol. III, pp. 193–94; Guerra, *Manual, op. cit.,* p. 407.
3. Turnbull, *op. cit.,* pp. 48, 74–75, 128, 130, 133, 155, 160–62, 266, 279.
4. *Ibid.,* p. 43.
5. *Ibid.,* p. 155.
6. Morales, *op. cit.,* vol. I, pp. 228–29.
7. Mario Hernández y Sánchez-Barba, "David Turnbull y el problema de la esclavitud en Cuba," *Anuario de Estudios Americanos,* Sevilla, vol. XIV, 1957, pp. 33–34.
8. *Ibid.,* p. 274.
9. *Ibid.,* pp. 274–75.
10. *Ibid.*
11. Smith, *op. cit.,* pp. 91–93.
12. Hernández, *op. cit.,* p. 277.
13. Saco, *Historia, op. cit.,* vol. IV, pp. 127–35, 152, 164–65.
14. *Ibid.*
15. Hernández, *op. cit.,* p. 277.
16. Saco, *Historia, op. cit.,* vol. IV, pp. 176–78.
17. Quoted in Hernández, *op. cit.,* p. 282.
18. Mariano Torrente, *Cuestión importante sobre la esclavitud,* Madrid, 1841, pp. 4–7.
19. Saco, *Historia, op. cit.,* vol. IV, pp. 187–89.
20. *Ibid.,* pp. 194–98.
21. Hernández, *op. cit.,* p. 284.
22. Guerra, *Manual, op. cit.,* p. 402.
23. *Ibid.,* p. 404.
24. Consular Despatches, Havana, 1853, XXX, National Archives. The testimony is a translation and is marked, "Habana, Oct. 12, 1853. Attested to by Wm. H. Robertson, U.S. Consul in Havana."
25. Webster to Campbell, enclosing Del Monte's report, Washington, January 14, 1843, Dept. of State, Special Missions, I, pp. 190–94, marked "Private and Confidential," National Archives. *See also*

Cocking to Palmerston, Caracas, October 1, 1846, *Boletín de los Archivos Nacionales*, Habana, 1909, vol. III, No. V, pp. 3–9.

26. Hernández, *op. cit.*, pp. 287–88; J. C. Calhoun to Webster, November 4 and 6, 1842, Dept. of State, Consular Despatches, Havana, XVIII, National Archives.

27. Hernández, *op. cit.*, pp. 288–89.

28. *Ibid.*, p. 289.

2º. *Ibid.*, p. 290.

30. *Ibid.*, p. 291.

31. J. C. Calhoun to Webster, November 4 and 6, Dept. of State, Consular Despatches, Havana, XVIII, National Archives.

32. Guerra, *Manual, op. cit.*, p. 407.

33. Smith, *op. cit.*, pp. 101–02.

34. Extract of a letter dated Paris, France, March 20, 1844, in "Correspondence Addressed to John C. Calhoun, 1837–1849," edited by Clarence S. Boucher and Robert P. Brooks, in *Annual Report of the American Historical Association for the Year 1929*, Washington, 1930, pp. 216–17.

35. William L. Mathieson, *Great Britain and the Slave Trade, 1839–1865*, London, 1929, pp. 66–67, 141.

36. Zaragoza, *op. cit.*, vol. I, pp. 346–68.

37. *Ibid.*, pp. 377–80.

38. *Ibid.*, pp. 385–88.

chapter 12   LA ESCALERA

1. Hernández, *op. cit.*, pp. 52–53.

2. Aimes, *op. cit.*, p. 146.

3. Quoted in Cepero, *op. cit.*, p. 88.

4. Morales, *op. cit.*, vol. I, p. 355.

5. Aguirre, *op. cit.*, p. 97.

6. Campbell to Calhoun, June 9, 1844, Consular Despatches, Havana, XIX, National Archives.

7. Smith, *op. cit.*, p. 105.

8. Portuondo, *op. cit.*, p. 105.

9. Hernández, *op. cit.*, p. 294; *Slavery in Cuba: A Report of the Proceedings of the Meeting, Held at Cooper Institute, New York City, December 13, 1872*, New York, 1872, p. 17. (Columbia Univ. Library)

10. Guerra, *Manual, op. cit.*, pp. 415–20.

11. *Ibid.*; Emeterio S. Santovenia, in *Historia de la Nación Cubana, op. cit.*, vol. IV, pp. 172–73.

12. Hernández, *op. cit.*, pp. 294–96.

13. Morales, *op. cit.*; F. González del Valle, "José de la Luz y Caballero en la conspiración de 1844," *Memorias de la Academia de la Historia de Cuba*, La Habana, 1925; José Manuel Ximeno, "Un pobre histrión," (Plácido), *Primer Congreso Nacional de Historia*, II, La Habana, 1943.

14. Aimes, *op. cit.*, pp. 144–45.

15. Cocking to Palmerston, Caracas, Oct. 1, 1846, *op. cit.*, pp. 3–9.

16. Johnson to Buchanan, Dec. 6, 1845, Consular Letters: Matanzas, IV, National Archives.
17. Aimes, *op. cit.*, p. 161.
18. Cepero, *op. cit.*, p. 38.
19. Smith, *op. cit.*, pp. 125–26.
20. Jose Ferrer de Couto, *Los Negros en sus Diversos Estados y Condiciones,* New York, 1864, p. 105.
21. Smith, *op. cit.*, p. 107.
22. *Ibid.*, pp. 106–07.
23. Saco, *Historia, op. cit.*, vol. III, pp. 195–201.
24. Ramón de la Sagra, *Estudios Coloniales con Aplicación a la Isla de Cuba,* Madrid, 1845, p. 8.
25. José Antonio Saco, *Colección de Papeles Científicos, Históricos, Políticos y de Otros Ramos Sobre la Isla de Cuba,* Paris, 1859, vol. III, pp. 85–115.
26. Smith, *op. cit.*, pp. 133–34.
27. James Morton Callahan, *Cuba and International Relations,* Baltimore, 1899, p. 184.
28. Smith, *op. cit.*, pp. 109–11.
29. *Ibid.*
30. *Ibid.*, pp. 113–15.
31. Urbano Feijóo Sotomayor, *Isla de Cuba, Inmagración de trabajadores españoles,* Madrid, 1855, pp. 44–47.
32. Elías Entralgo, in *Historia de la Nación Cubana, op. cit.*, vol. III, pp. 328–29.
33. *Ibid.*, p. 344; Portell Vilá, *op. cit.*, vol. I, p. 476.
34. Webster to Campbell, Washington, January 14, 1843, Dept. of State, Special Missions, I, pp. 190–94, National Archives. Marked "Private and Confidential."
35. Campbell to Webster, Jan. 11, Feb. 9, 1843, Consular Letters, Havana, XIX, National Archives.
36. Charles Francis Adams, editor, *op. cit.* vol. XI, pp. 351–54.
37. Harrison to Forsyth, Aug. 27, 1838, Jan. 9, 1839; Harrison to Webster, March 21, 22, April 24, May 20, 1841; Harrison to Sec'y of State, June 14, 1843, Consular Letters, Kingston, V-VIII, National Archives.
38. Campbell to Upshur, Nov. 9, 12, 1843, Consular Despatches: Havana, XIX, National Archives; Jerónimo Becker, *Historia de las relaciones exteriores de España durante el siglo XIX: Apuntes para una Historia Diplomática,* Madrid, 1924, vol. II, pp. 59–66.
39. Becker, *op. cit.*, pp. 65–66; Basil Rauch, *American Interests in Cuba: 1848–1855,* New York, 1948, pp. 41–42.
40. Washington Irving to Upshur, March 2, 1844, Dept. of State, Despatches from Spain, XXXIV, National Archives.
41. Rauch, *op. cit.*, p. 44.
42. Calhoun to Upshur, August 27, 1843, Dept. of State, Miscellaneous Letters, National Archives, Marked "Confidential."
43. Calhoun to Pakenheim, Washington, April 18, 1844, Dept. of State, Notes to British Legations, VII, National Archives.

INDEX

Aberdeen, Lord, 207, 209, 221, 227
Abolition, of slavery, 85, 90–91, 184–85
Abolition, of slave trade, 95–98, 101–03
Adams, John Quincy, 135, 137, 141, 142, 143, 144–48, 149, 151, 152–61, 162–69, 225
Africa, 42
African slave trade, 47, 65–66, 71, 73, 85, 95–98, 101–03, 107, 108, 172–75, 176–78, 181–82, 186–87, 219–21
Age of Gold, The, 19
Agüero y Velazco, Francisco de, 121–22
Aguirre, Sergio, 93n., 94, 215
Aldama, Miguel, 214–15
Amaru, Tupac, 93
American Revolution, 43–44, 56–57, 58
Annexation, of Cuba to the United States, 74, 124–25, 126–30, 139–43, 147–48, 205, 207, 228
Annexationism, 74, 205, 207, 228
Annexationists, in Cuba, 127–28, 139–42; in United States, 74, 124–25, 126–30, 139–43, 147–48, 205, 207, 228
Anti-slavery, 201–11, 216, 217, 226. *See also* Turnbull, David.
Aponte, José Antonio, 91–93
Arango, José Augustín, 153
Arango, José de, 127–28
Arango y Parreño, Francisco de, 59, 61, 64–65, 66, 75, 77, 83, 86–87, 90, 95, 96, 102, 105n., 174, 197
Argüelles, Don Agustín, 85, 177
Autonomy, 76, 172

Balboa, Silvestre, 52
Barbrado, Juan, 93
Bayamo smugglers, 40
Benton, Thomas H., 162–63n.
Biddle, James, 140–41, 142

Biddle, Nicholas, 134
Blakeley, Josiah, 69
Bolívar, Simón, 80, 88, 105n., 110, 112, 134, 152, 153, 161, 167
Bonaparte, Joseph, 79, 81, 126n.
Bonaparte, Napoleon, 62, 69, 79, 86, 126
"Boriqua, Republic of," 105–06, 150–51
Bravo, González, 226
Brazil, 83
British and Foreign Anti-Slavery Society, 192
British West Indies, abolition of slavery in, 184–85
Bryant, William Cullen, 119n.
Bulwer, Sir Henry Lytton, 219

Caballero, José Agustín, 59, 61, 109
Cabrera, Pérez, 217
"Cadena Eléctrica," 111
Caguax (Indian chief), 25
Cajigal, Juan Manuel, 100
Calhoun, John C., 141, 142, 143, 227, 228
Campbell, Robert B., 215, 224–25, 226
Canning, George, 146, 147, 158, 168n.
Caonabó (Indian chief), 20
Caribs, 17, 21
Casas, Bartolomé de las, 16, 21, 26–27, 29
Casas, Luis de las, 60, 63, 66
Castillo, Bernal Díaz de, 19
Castillo, Núñez del, 127–28
Castlereagh, Lord, 96
Castro, Dr. Fidel, 192n.
Castro, Rafael, 201
Castro, Vicente, 201
Census, of 1791–92, 65; of 1817, 95n., 99; of 1850, 212n.
Chacón, Clemente, 93